THE PROCESS OF PRESENTATIONAL SPEAKING

THE PROCESS OF PRESENTATIONAL SPEAKING

SECOND EDITION

William S. Howell
Ernest G. Bormann
University of Minnesota

HARPER & ROW, PUBLISHERS, New York
Cambridge, Philadelphia, San Francisco, Washington,
London, Mexico City, São Paulo, Singapore, Sydney

Sponsoring Editor: Louise Waller/Marianne Russell
Project Editor: Ellen MacElree
Cover Design: 20/20 Services Inc.
Text Art: Fineline Illustrations, Inc.
Production: Paula Roppolo
Compositor: ComCom Division of Haddon Craftsmen, Inc.
Cover Printer: New England Book Components
Printer and Binder: R. R. Donnelley & Sons Company

THE PROCESS OF PRESENTATIONAL SPEAKING, Second Edition

Library of Congress Cataloging-in-Publication Data

Howell, William Smiley.
  The process of presentational speaking.

  Rev. ed. of: Presentational speaking for business
and the professions.   1971.
    1. Communication in management.   2. Meetings.
3. Oral communication.   4. Public speaking.
I. Bormann, Ernest G.   II. Howell, William Smiley.
Presentational speaking for business and the professions.
III. Title.
HF5718.H7   1988   658.4'52   87-8673
ISBN 0-06-042929-1

87 88 89 90 9 8 7 6 5 4 3 2 1

Contents

Preface

Presentational Speaking for Business and the Professions, the first edition of this book, was a pioneering effort that showed presentational speaking in modern organizations assuming an importance that required study as a specialized form of communication. This second edition, entitled *The Process of Presentational Speaking,* is formulated to meet the needs of today's managers, executives, and professionals and is well adapted to the needs of students preparing themselves for such positions. It focuses clearly on concepts and procedures that are immediately useful in preparing and developing presentational speeches. *The Process of Presentational Speaking* can be used in courses dealing with presentation and also in organizational communication, business and professional speaking, and business communication courses that are designed to be more than "public speaking" courses.

This book begins with an analysis of the nature of presentational speaking and provides perspectives and models of the process of presentation. Because listening is important to both presenter and audience, a chapter on listening is included early.

This material is followed by information about how to develop persuasive power in the presentation, how to achieve a reasoned response, how to maximize personal credibility, and how to manage technical, audiovisual, and media elements in a presentation. An appendix containing six detailed case studies shows each of the patterns of organization of presentational speaking in action.

The authors have for many years served various business and professional organizations as consultants in communication. The applications in this book, which grew out of current practices within the professional and managerial community, interpreted in the context of modern communication theory, have been repeatedly tested in courses, workshops, and on the job.

The authors wish to thank their reviewers, especially William Jordan, North Carolina State University; Mark Comadena, Illinois State University; Jeff Bass, Baylor University; Lois Einhorn, State University of NY at Binghamton; and Judy Jones, University of California at Santa Barbara.

William S. Howell
Ernest G. Bormann

THE PROCESS OF
PRESENTATIONAL
SPEAKING

chapter *1*

Presentational Speaking in Action

For two years John Jamison has supervised the development of a new product, an off-the-beaten-track breakfast cereal which John is convinced can be promoted and sold profitably by his company. Now the time has come to take the next step toward that goal. Manufacturing processes and techniques are reasonably well worked out and tested. Cost estimates of production are firm. A market test of the new cereal involving saturation advertising and marketing in two large cities, St. Louis and Minneapolis, has been readied.

To proceed, John Jamison must have the approval of the Board of Control of his company, a group of seven representatives of top management. He has been allotted twenty minutes for his presentation and has two weeks to prepare. His mission on P-Day: to persuade the board to approve manufacture of the new product and authorize the expenditure of $740,000 to ascertain its sales potential.

John considers his mission impossible because of the amount of information he feels obliged to transmit to the board and the absurdly brief time limitation of twenty minutes. A quick calculation shows him that if he tells the board what they really should know concerning the new product, about eight hours of lecture with visual aids will be required. To say that John is frustrated as he tilts back in his chair and contemplates the immediate future would be the understatement of the year.

With a nagging sensation of time running out, John has exhausted his conventional options and is seeking frantically for *some* offbeat long shot, a last refuge, a final desperate expedient. He remembers a memo from the

Training Division of a month or two ago that offered individual consultation to managers preparing presentations. Luckily, the one-page memo found its way into the bulging, dusty "Training" file instead of landing in the wastebasket. In a few minutes John has Paula Osterhus, an instructor in speech communication, on the phone, and Paula has agreed to join John at lunch in the company cafeteria.

Luncheon conversation between Paula and John takes several surprising turns, from John's point of view. He finds that his predicament of eight hours of material to present and twenty minutes to do it in is not exceptional; in fact, it is the norm. He learns that success in coping with this problem has come, not from a masterly condensation of information into well-organized essentials, but from meeting the expectations of individual members of the decision-making group. For the first time he is made sensitive to the "pitfall of projection," the tendency we all have to design a presentation that would satisfy *us*, disregarding the preferences and prejudices of the people we will talk to. And he is led to appreciate that his first step in preparing his presentation is to analyze the motivations of the people who are to receive it. When he knows the priority of interests each board member has in any new product, he is ready to select from his mass of information what will be most persuasive to that person. Paula recommends this strategy of selection, rather than comprehensive briefing, as the organizing principle and for one reason: in the past it has produced better results than any other procedure.

But John's biggest surprise during the luncheon with Paula Osterhus is the revelation that most of the necessary persuasion could and should be done *before* the actual presentation. Naively, John had assumed that his twenty-minute talk had to accomplish everything, informing listeners about this proposal, getting them interested in it, and inducing them to approve not only the expenditure of $740,000, but also a major modification of his company's product line. Paula gently reminds John that intelligent people need some time to think about important decisions like this one. Questions need to be answered, effects on the ongoing operation of the business must be reviewed, and opinions of other involved people must be considered. If possible, the presenter should talk with the audience members in person, answering their questions directly and ascertaining their feelings about the project. Such preliminary interaction, according to Paula, is the best insurance against unpleasant surprises at the time of the presentation.

Back in his office John thinks, "Yikes! I'm back to square one. But I'm glad to be there, with a chance to avoid blowing a great opportunity." How should he conduct the pre-presentation persuasion? He decides to send each of the seven Board of Control members a brief summary of his proposal, with the date, time, and place of his formal presentation. In the last line of his memo he thanks them for their consideration of his proposal and mentions that in the next few days he will talk with them about it.

John has observed the board in action for several years. He recalls that proceedings within the board have been dominated by the three senior members. The other four less experienced members he sees as lieutenants of the big three. Because of this dynamic and because his time is limited, John decides to phone the four junior members but to secure appointments and visit the seniors in their offices. He will preserve the egos of the less influential persons by being very interested in their reactions over the telephone, but his major time and effort in this preliminary persuasion will be directed to the power, exemplified by the big three.

In order to adapt to the dominant interests of the big three both in preliminary persuasion and in the formal presentation, John needs to know what their rewards and satisfactions are in the corporation. This process of discovering "where they are coming from" Paula Osterhus refers to as motive analysis.

John begins motive analysis with Joe Perkins, president of the company and the moderator at board meetings. Joe is "top status" man on the board in every way. He has the highest rank, the longest service with the company (he was one of the founders), and is older than the others. Joe Perkins' training for his present responsibilities was "in plant," on the job, totally. As the company grew and expanded into new product lines, Joe was solving associated problems of production. His particular talent was improvement of production techniques. Everyone knew that Joe could figure out how to produce any product more efficiently, for less cost. Now in his mid-60s, Joe has settled comfortably into thinking about the business operation in terms of the criterion that has served him so well throughout his career, "How can we keep costs down?" When previous new products had been presented to the board, John could remember how Joe kept harping at his one recurrent theme, costs. "O.K." he would say, "show me how soon we can pass the crossover point!" the "crossover" being that point in time when a new product starts showing a profit.

Next, John turns his thoughts to Homer Lydgate, head of the company's marketing operation. Homer is in his late 40s, a hot-shot up-and-coming executive who had become an influential member of the inner group through several breakthroughs in advertising and distribution. Homer was pirated from a rival milling company some six years before. His advertising caught the fancy of millions, and the decision to create a new salary bracket for Homer and start him near the top has paid rich dividends. Under his direction, company merchandising evolved from the dullest in the industry to perhaps its most novel and exciting. Naturally, Homer perceives each new product in terms of its advertising potential. Novelty is his hang-up. Sound but run-of-the-mill proposals have little attraction for him.

The third member of the influential trio is Marsha Everding, known throughout the company as the theory-happy character on the top-management team. As company comptroller, she manages the financial operation with high competence. She enjoys keeping up with new developments in data processing and computer technology. Her ideal is to run the company according to the most modern financial, engineering, and management theories, for only then, Marsha is convinced, can her company compete successfully.

One of Marsha Everding's favorite theories is that the company with the most complete product line, but one that is free of internal duplication, has a real competitive advantage that will build substantial profits over the long pull. Consequently, she fusses continuously about modifying manufacturing in the direction of making each product distinctive and, in the aggregate, covering the range of the market comprehensively. When a new product is being evaluated she has two questions: Does it overlap anything we are now producing? Is there a gap in our present line that this product can fill? If the person presenting the innovation answers the first question negatively and the second in the affirmative, to the satisfaction of Marsha Everding's informed and inquiring mind, then Marsha's initial apparent obstructionism usually changes to hearty support.

After the motive analysis, John feels confident about his personal interviews with the big three. He feels ready to discuss the vested interests of these key persons and believes he can demonstrate that his new product meets the needs of each. Now he turns to the planning of the actual presentation.

Certainly, the purpose of John's presentation is to advance a single proposal. Osterhus has suggested three possible organizational patterns to accomplish this end. (All three are developed in greater detail in Chapter 4). One of the three seems tailor-made for this situation, the "state-the-case-and-prove-it" pattern. This involves an introduction, the statement of the recommendation, the reasons for adopting it (each with support), and a summary conclusion that repeats the recommendation.

Now the presentation begins to take shape. Part 1 is a two-minute, rather technical, description of the new cereal he has developed. This information will be covered in his earlier memo, but John knows that, although each board member will have received and read his memo, people perceive things differently and remember details inaccurately. He will take the sting out of repetition by liberal use of "as you will remember," "as you already know," "you will recall that," and similar phrases. When he finishes his introduction, all board members will be in possession of the same information, to which he can refer.

Parts 2, 3, and 4 are of approximately equal length, none to exceed five minutes. Part 2 deals with the cost picture, with particular emphasis on evidence that the crossover point should occur in less than average time. Part 3 develops the novel advertising possibilities of this unique and extraordinary cereal. Part 4 of the presentation shows that the company, with the addition of the new cereal to its already extensive product line, can meet every known market better than can any single competitor. The time remaining, perhaps three or four minutes of the allotted twenty, John will leave for questions and comments, for he has learned the hard way that not every doubt can be anticipated, and unanswered questions block favorable response. The question period then becomes the last step in his five-part plan.

Implementation of the strategy is relatively easy. From his eight hours or so of material John can select impressive evidence to drive home his three-pronged attack; one prong aimed at each of the big three. He enlists the help of the audiovisual section of his company to prepare eight or ten simple, colorful visuals to be used with the overhead projector. He rehearses before a sympathetic and knowledgeable associate who comments frankly and suggests changes. When the production has "jelled," with all visuals and major content items in approximately final form, he rehearses some more, always before the videotape camera. His notes are discarded, and his timing is practiced until he knows that with only an occasional glance at the clock at certain checkpoints he can finish "on the button."

John does not memorize his talk, because he understands that only a professional actor can make memorized lines sound fresh and spontaneous. To be sensitive to his listeners, and particularly to the influential three, he must react to them continuously. So he practices in an informal, direct, and conversational style. Many words and phrases that seem to be effective are retained as the talk gains in ease and smoothness. But no paragraph is ever literally reproduced in a subsequent rehearsal. To communicate effectively in the small-group situation, John knows that he must preserve the extemporaneous character of his speaking.

When the appointed hour comes for the man to whom we have given the pseudonym of John Jamison, he is relaxed and ready. He feels that he has equipped himself to meet the needs of the occasion and, more pertinently, to supply the facts of the case that will be most vital to his audience. In the actual instance, approval of the proposal comes quickly.

During the days of preparation for market testing of the new cereal, John often reflects on this presentational speaking episode and on what he has learned from the experience. One question in his mind remains unanswered; "If you can do the persuading before the presentation, why have the presentation?" He calls Paula Osterhus and schedules a luncheon meeting to get the answer.

Paula finds John's puzzlement understandable but amusing. "John," says Paula, "Your concept of the presentation assumes that its purpose is to bring about change. Actually, the formal presentation of a proposal in itself is a 'ritual of confirmation.' Why is it important? All the involved people present witness their collective decision. Their agreement becomes a matter of record. The presenter is congratulated, everybody gears up for the new order, change has been validated, and perhaps more importantly, a final closure to the change process has occurred. The organization can proceed to other matters. As in the case of deliberations in a legislative body, nothing exists until the final confirmation takes place."

At this point John becomes aware that his concept of the act of

presentation has undergone profound change. Before this episode, presenting consisted of a brief period of talking to an audience. Now it is the *process*
of presenting, including everything from the introduction of an idea or
recommendation to the formality, the ritual of confirmation. He now understands why so many presentations fail. Presenters think (as he had formerly)
that the final speech is the whole process. As a result, they omit the vital
pre-presentation preparation needed for people to respond thoughtfully.
This omission insures their failure.

"Now that you are on top of that one, John," says Paula. "Let me
throw you a curve. Some of the most successful presentation speakers I
know say that you must never make a presentation of a proposal until you
are certain it will be approved. What do you think about that?"

John says, "Wow! What a switch from the old notions about presentational speaking! I don't know, but it makes sense as an ideal. The catch is,
is it an attainable objective? Even if it isn't always possible, it may still
illustrate the 'functional utility of an unattainable ideal.' Thanks for planting this notion in my head. I'll certainly check it out. Being even 90 percent
sure of a positive verdict would certainly relax the presenter, and help him
do a better job."

OBJECTIVES OF THIS BOOK

Many books deal with business communication, communication in organizations, interpersonal communication, and persuasion, but few, if any, are
devoted exclusively to designing, building, and delivering powerful presentations.

The authors have learned from experience with corporate, governmental, military, religious, and educational organizations that presentations
deserve a book that treats them as a unique and special way to accomplish
objectives.

We have witnessed or heard about innumerable instances in which a
meritorious proposal died because it was poorly presented. Even when
presentations serve more or less adequately their function in the "ritual of
confirmation," they often leave the participants with an uncomfortable
feeling because of the poor quality of the speech. We believe that presentations in working organizations may on the average be for higher stakes than
other forms of communication. Presentations precipitate results, positive or
negative, more promptly and directly than do other sorts of messages.

A presentation is a climactic event. Usually, much time and a great
deal of effort have brought about a situation important to the careers of
people who are involved, as well as to the future of the organization in
which it happens. When the great day comes, important people gather for
a final critical review of the contemplated change. This is their last opportunity to assess the question before a final decision is made. Obviously, it is
supremely important that the material being presented be organized and
delivered coherently, efficiently, persuasively, and interestingly.

The knowledge about communication essential to effective presentations is not intrinsically complicated, but it is *contingent,* that is, no formula will suffice. There are principles, directions, and procedures of adaptation that can be learned but every instance of presenting is unique. Becoming a good presenter is a matter of learning to be flexible within firm guidelines. Teaching those guidelines and how to apply them to circumstances and audiences to do a particular job are the purposes of this book.

Although we recognize the contingent nature of presentational speaking, it is our purpose to write a "how to do it" book that is completely operational. If we were to use academic jargon, we could assert that our objective is to attain "ecological validity." Jargon, though generally to be avoided, does sometimes have the virtue of being accurate, even when it is hard to understand. Ecology is the study of how organisms adjust to their environment, and our goal is to provide people who make presentations with the knowledge they need to succeed *in their environment,* in their corporations, churches, families, clubs, sales situations, and so forth. Every suggestion, principle, technique, and procedure advanced in this book has been derived from the application of communication knowledge to the "real world."

We are grateful for our theoretical grounding in a variety of academic disciplines, for this helps us see and interpret behavior. A few abstract concepts are necessary to explain our position on controversial issues, so these are included, but if you think of theory as abstract material unrelated to practice you will find little of that in this book.

COMPETENCE IN MAKING PRESENTATIONS

The reader who learns and applies the information in this book should experience an increase in three abilities that are desirable in all human communication and essential to making powerful presentations. The three basic competencies for communication are adaptability, creativity, and flexibility.

Adaptability to people and circumstances is a skill of anticipation. The adaptable person knows that you cannot step in the same river even once. This individual expects to confront new problems, different people, and situations that are unique. She or he has learned from experience that there is no possibility that any event in the past will recur. The attitude of the adaptable person is "back to the drawing board." Each job to be done requires fresh analysis. No assumptions from the past are allowed to distort the picture. Instead of looking for familiar details, the presenter focuses on the new and the different. Study of military leaders who lose battles and entire wars often reveals that in their equipment, strategies, and tactics they were fighting the last war, not the war they were engaged in. Surprises are pleasing because these demonstrate the need for new procedures and the futility of repeating the past to cope with the present.

Creativity blends anticipation and response. After adaptation sets the stage, creativity enters and designs the script. In the context of a fresh analysis of present circumstances and people, the creative speaker plans the materials to be used and procedures for implementing them. The creative speaker shows some respect for traditional boundaries, but free wheeling prevails. In the words of Jay Beecroft, former Director of Education and Training of the 3M Corporation, "No progress is made by anyone who stays within his job description." The creative person is horrified by blind repetition, no matter how successful a procedure may have been in the past. Creativity is the essential ingredient in a Research and Development Department. It is the ability to discover new options and how to use them.

Flexibility is receptivity to change. Once an operation is underway, unexpected developments occur. Responses to the unexpected may range from the rigid to the flexible. If rigid, past procedures are disinterred and applied. Understandably, none quite fits the new unique circumstance. If flexible, the response is to generate a remedy in context, devising on the spot something to meet present demands. Being flexible is difficult for most of us owing to our affection for the status quo. But we can learn and practice rearranging, omitting, emphasizing and deemphasizing, adding to and subtracting from our plans and practices on the spot as we read the trends in unfolding events. When we are able to adjust to change while communication is in progress, spontaneously improving the message and enjoying the discarding of prepared ideas and plans, we can claim to be flexible.

Adaptability, creativity, and flexibility, though not the only talents required by the maker of presentations, are the ones in most need of attention. Throughout this book we will endeavor to maintain an adaptable, creative, and flexible perspective as we discuss principles and procedures, and dispense advice.

THE PRESENTATIONAL SPEAKER AS CHANGE AGENT

This book begins with the John Jamison case in order to encourage the reader to think about presenting as a process. John's assignment was to advance a single, definite proposal. Other kinds of presentations, as indicated in the case studies in the Appendix, exist to serve other purposes. Now we can examine an overall purpose, one that applies to all task-oriented presentations.

We consider the presentational speaker to be primarily—first, last, and always—a change agent. How can we say that presentations are always intended to facilitate change when very often the job to be done is to communicate information? It is a deceptive notion that there are two kinds of presentations: (1) to inform and (2) to persuade. This dichotomy suggests that the informer does not bring about change and the persuader does not inform. Nothing could be further from the truth.

The introduction of pertinent new information causes a receiver to view situations differently, to reinterpret or adjust opinions and beliefs. The change that results may or may not be due to persuasion. If the person supplying the information *intended* the interpretation made by the receiver, then the interaction is persuasive, since persuasion is defined as communication intended to influence choice.

Here is a clearly nonpersuasive example. A presentational speaker may be addressing a new problem in an organization. Perhaps a competitor has marketed a product that performs as well as the company's most popular item and costs less. The presenter supplies the relevant facts to middle and upper managers. Details of the rival product, analysis of needs met by these devices, a survey of present customers and potential new markets, possible modifications in product design, manufacturing, advertising, and distribution, are major elements in the message. The presenter attempts to give all managers information that will help them cope with the present problem. The speaker's objective is to facilitate disciplined creativity, to produce productive innovation. The presentational speaker in this instance becomes a nonpersuasive agent of change. Remember, the persuasive speaker *intends* a specific response.

As this example shows, when change in opinion, belief, or action originates in the receiver and is not a response intended by the presenter, no persuasion occurs. The listener may have undergone significant changes as a result of learning something that seems relevant. The presenter often is surprised by the listeners' interpretation of the information which turns out to be, indeed, creative and productive but also much different from what the speaker thought those interpretations might be.

The process of communication involved in being a nonpersuasive agent of change resembles classroom education where an instructor presents information that allows students to cope more competently with events in their lives. The teacher does not instruct the students in how to apply the subject matter to specific situations after the class is over. All the same, important changes occur in the students because of their learning from the classroom experience. The teacher is an agent of change who does not usually see the specific results of the instructional communication.

We have demonstrated that informing can bring about change without persuasion. Now let us look at persuasion and its relationship to the process of informing.

The notion that persuaders do not inform is easily demolished by noting that evidence (information) is a major tool of persuasion. Facts of the case are used to advance particular propositions, to intentionally influence choice.

The strategic revelation of key information is perhaps the major technique of persuasion in the Anglo-American system of jurisprudence. Western societies and governments are based on the assumption that competing persuasions enable the comparison of contrasting patterns of information. This is one way we resolve conflicts and reach "valid" conclusions. Here, obviously, informing cannot be separated from persuading.

Whether the primary purpose of a presentation is to expand options, reduce the number of options, or limit recommended options to one, change can be seen to be the universal objective.

All presentations can be located on a continuum of purposes, from the goal of maximizing options, to establishing direction (limiting to several options), to limiting options to the one recommended persuasive proposition.

Purposes of Presentations

Maximize options	Establish direction	Limit options to one

The first step in planning a presentation is to decide on its location on the above continuum. The objective of maximizing options is to give the listeners a creative set and encourage them to consider a broad range of attitudes, opinions, and actions. If the speaker's purpose is to establish direction, then the presentation can list the materials and propositions to be excluded, and possibilities can be narrowed to specific and concrete options. If the presenter's purpose is to advance one recommendation, the speaker should word that proposition carefully and adapt every item of content to purpose and audience. Techniques and procedures of presentation differ with purposes. Throughout this book these distinctions will be noted, explained, and illustrated.

At the risk of being repetitious, we reiterate that, before gathering information or outlining a presentation, the presenter should make a firm decision as to which of the three possible purposes will be served. Laying the proper groundwork insures the presenter against wasted motion and makes it easy to achieve a sharply focused message. Beginning with a clear purpose based on our continuum of options diagrammed above is one of the secrets of building powerful presentations.

CONTEXT: THE AUDIENCE-PURPOSE-SPEAKER JOINT VENTURE RELATIONSHIP

With a clear purpose in mind, the presenter is ready to enlist the cooperation of his or her audience; without definite purpose, the participants have no basis for collaborative action. The term we prefer to describe optimum interaction of audience and speaker is *joint venture.* In contrast to the productive involvement of joint ventures is "sender-receiver" communication, where the speaker does all the work and the audience members listen passively. Active, involved audiences process information thoughtfully, that is, they examine what they are receiving and react to it, contributing their own knowledge, opinions, and feelings. Audience members who listen passively tend to pay only peripheral attention. Passive listeners attend momentarily and involuntarily to items they find interesting in the presentation, but they tend to daydream and fall into reveries when the material does not force their attention. Involved audiences comprehend more and remember more about the presentation than do passive audiences.

Presentational speakers should place creating a joint venture with their audiences at the top of their priority list. But achieving this audience-speaker collaboration is easier said than done. Let us look at some of the problems that confront the speaker who would operate in a joint venture mode.

The goal of presentational speaking is invariably change; the presentational speaker is an innovator. A universal characteristic of people is resistance to change. The status quo seems preferable to rearranging the world because of our inertia, which is another way of saying that we are naturally lazy. Those who would initiate significant changes can expect to encounter resistance; hence, innovators must be prepared to shoulder a burden of proof. This means they have a double job to do. They must satisfy the critical judgment of their listeners to the point where they will concede the soundness of their proposal. Then they must get the listeners involved, personally, with the project to the point where inertia yields to positive response. The pitfall for innovators is doing half a job. They produce signs of interest and stop there, not realizing that only agreement *plus* wholehearted involvement can precipitate change.

Above all else, the communication that occurs in successful presentational speaking is *interactional*. The X-factor that most often tips the balance in the critical presentation is not the quality of the information involved; rather it is the quality of the interaction between speaker and listeners. Typically, a trend sets in as communication continues. Either the audience and speaker grow closer together, or they drift apart. When senders engage the interest of receivers to the point that the receivers are "caught up" in the message and are thinking their way through the presentation within the senders, even forgetting that it *is* a presentation, the speakers have a kind of interaction that guarantees involvement. In the case of John Jamison we noted that he carefully avoided memorization, not only because he wanted to remain flexible and ready to adapt to developing interaction, but also because it is difficult to achieve joint reflective thinking with a message that is predetermined, word for word.

Before we leave our examination of the audience-purpose-speaker relationship, we should note some positive factors in the presentational-speaking situation. Expectations are tuned to an occasion that may produce a vital decision, so participants are prepared to pay close attention. The factors of significance and high stakes restrict the range of persuasive methods that are suitable. Typically, pressure-persuasion is inappropriate. A "hard sell" is ineffective, because emotional responses are sternly controlled. There are few impulse decisions. The decision-making group checks on each other's thinking. As a result, "facts of the case" persuasion tends to dominate interactive presentational speaking.

PROBLEMS IN PRESENTATIONAL SPEAKING

At present, we fear that presentation contributes little to the effectiveness of American task-oriented organizations. The state of the art is that presentational speaking lacks standards, is sporadic, and is little understood, with the result that presentations are badly prepared and poorly performed. The facts of life surrounding presentational speaking are little known. People labor mightily for details like visual aids, but as often as not these are superfluous rather than essential. Truly, the blind are leading the blind along quite different paths in the world of presentational speaking in modern corporate America. Perhaps this generalized judgment is a superficial but accurate answer to the perplexing question, why aren't presentations better than they are?

We feel the need, however, to be specific in detailing major omissions and errors of commission that contribute to the sorry state of modern presentations. These are popular "goofs," and most of our readers have been exposed to all of them. All are easily avoidable. Most of these blunders occur in the final presentation itself. This is understandable, for most of the presenters committing these errors believe that the formal delivery of the message is the be-all and end-all of making a presentation.

It would be easy to compile a lengthy list. But grumbling about inadequacies leads to self-indulgence, and so we limit ourselves to ten items, unproductive practices which by the frequency of their occurrence, have earned them the distinction of being on the ten worst blunders list.

AVOIDABLE DISASTERS

1. *Failure to prepare people prior to the presentation.* Neglecting to give the audience as much information as possible ahead of time "pulls the rug" out from under many a presentation. Minds need to be alerted to coming events, controversial issues require mulling over, answerable questions should be taken care of and cleared out of the way. Many presenters make no effort to talk with key audience members before the presentation. The motto found on some executives' desks "No Surprises" demands that planning activities go far beyond assembling a formal message. Obstacles that are not identified and prepared for spell future trouble.

2. *Abstract, ill-defined purpose.* Letting a presentation happen before its time usually indicates that someone with authority is disturbed and feels something should be done but does not know exactly what. So a presentation is scheduled to "get things moving." The result is a mish-mash of half-baked ideas. These form no coherent pattern; there is no logical sequence, no progress toward a concrete, clear-cut goal. Without a clear,

sharp, and definite purpose to motivate the presentation, the result is a confusing waste of time.

3. *Lack of organization.* Many presenters destroy the effectiveness of good material, sound reasons, and valid supporting evidence by random arrangement. They fail to appreciate the necessity of one point leading to the next, building steadily to a conclusion. Transitions linking parts of the message together, pointing out what has been done, how it relates to what is coming, and where the overall progression will lead are not supplied. Such presenters say they do not want to be "too obvious." It is very difficult for a working presentation to be "too obvious." The audience badly needs to be told and told frequently what the talk is all about, where it has been, where it is going, and why all this is important.

4. *A bad scene.* Inexperienced presenters assume that the environment of and the gadgets necessary to the presentation will be "A-OK," while experienced presenters know this seldom happens. When a carefully prepared presentation is spoiled by a noisy air conditioner, a microphone that works only occasionally, a 35 mm slide projector that is delivered to the wrong building, a bulb in the overhead projector that burns out early in the talk, with no replacement available, a flip chart without any magic markers or crayons to write on it, only one explanation makes sense: the presenter did not do his or her job. Murphy's well-known law applies; everything that can go wrong will. Competent presenters anticipate, check, and assure that all mechanical gadgets will work when the time comes for the speech. No excuses!

5. *Relying on memory or manuscript.* The notion that important utterances should be delivered from memory or read from manuscript significantly reduces the effectiveness of presentations. We all know that our competence in informal conversation depends on our flexibility, our ability to adapt to the unexpected. We throw away that most valuable asset when we choose to speak from manuscript or memory. Picture the problem of a manuscript reader who sees shaking heads and puzzled expressions, or who sees the audience going to sleep. Doing something about such emergencies is a top priority, but the "set in concrete" message makes it difficult or impossible to do so. When the fate of a presentation hangs on the presenter's spontaneous management of an emergency, as it often does, reliance on memory or manuscript guarantees failure.

6. *Amateurish delivery.* Probably the most amateurish pattern of delivery is one we can characterize as "lifeless." The speaker stands, motionless, behind the podium. She or he illustrates the opposite of "dynamic," speaks in a monotone at a constant rate, avoids eye contact, projects a weak low-energy voice, stares at notes or manuscript, makes few facial expressions and fewer gestures. Such speakers provide no vocal emphasis to help the listeners; they say everything as though all of it were of equal importance. Lifeless delivery can undercut a well-designed, potentially successful message.

Bad delivery makes the audience member a passive receiver. That virtually assures the speaker will fail to establish the joint venture interaction which should be the goal; good delivery helps create a joint venture. Good delivery for the presentational occasion is informal, with the speaker moving about, as close to the audience as possible, physically vigorous, with maximum eye contact, and responsive to audience reactions. In short, the good presentational speaker behaves as she or he would in being an interesting, dynamic conversationalist.

7. *Misuse of visual aids.* Visual aids are booby traps for the presentational speaker. There are so many opportunities to use them unproductively that our list of errors is in no way complete. Underusing gadgets, not using aids when they are needed, or overusing them, running from slide projector to overhead, to flip chart, to videotape, to blackboard—all have the result that the listeners better remember the frantic manipulation of gadgets than the subject of the presentation.

The projection of points and charts too small to be read is another common problem. A malicious person might enjoy seeing a presenter with an audience of 500 approach within a few feet of the screen so that he or she can read the tiny printed message. Television screens for videotape playback are usually too small. (With the current confusion and incompatibility of various tape formats, speeds, and sizes, the videotape machine is, in general, a Pandora's Box.) Providing too much material on a single frame is also a nearly universal problem, as is not giving the audience enough time to read and understand the material.

The use of 35 mm slides poses special problems. The presentational speaker who decides to use 35 mm slides usually will use more than necessary, for they are so colorful, professional looking, and easy to load in the slide magazine. When it is necessary to show a slide a second time, however, that retrieval process becomes awkward. Presentational speakers often place the screens for overhead projection behind them, when they should be across from them in the corner so that the audience members can see and the speaker does not have to get out of the way. Slides demand remote control or operator-assisted changing as well as darkening of the room, which requires another person at the light switch. Otherwise, the audience will be left in the dark in more ways than one. Whether one person is managing the entire presentation or whether there is a production crew, the fitting together of all of these elements is seldom smooth and professional.

A host of minor problems stem from misusing visual aids. Writing on flip charts is often illegible and too small. Extensive printed materials are often distributed at the beginning of a presentation, tempting the audience members to read instead of paying attention to the speaker. Whenever possible, handout materials should be delayed to the end of the presentation.

8. *Sabotage by the microphone.* The microphone bolted to the podium is an anchor holding the speaker fast to that position in the room. Either it destroys mobility or the speaker's voice fades in and out as he or she approaches and recedes from it.

Some presenters strike a blow for freedom by arranging to have a long connecting cord and then hold the microphone in their hand. While their mobility is restored and they can move closer to the audience, the cord tends to get in the way and gesturing becomes a one-handed activity. Still, with all its problems, the hand-held microphone is an improvement over the microphone on a stand or attached to a piece of furniture.

The long cord attached to a lapel or lavalier microphone is a further improvement, although becoming entangled in the cord is an ever-present possibility. The lapel microphone attached to a tiny FM transmitter (the so-called wireless microphone) offers the least distraction to the presenter. The hazard here is you may forget to turn off the transmitter in your pocket or attached to your belt when the presentation is over. If you forget to turn off the microphone, you may find your private comments booming over the loudspeaker.

Whatever microphone system one is using is liable to malfunction. Tapping, testing, and otherwise fiddling with the microphone tend to give the beginning of the presentation an amateurish flavor. "Can you hear me now?" is a plaintive question echoing from podiums all over the land. The microphone that cuts in and out, squeals, or distorts the voice is a further hazard. The professional does everything possible by careful planning and by pretesting to assure an efficient and working sound system for the presentation.

Microphones are, at best, a nuisance.

9. *Terminal dullness.* Americans separate work and play more than do most other peoples in the world. This may account for our notion that serious communication ought not to be fun. For this and other reasons, making a presentation interesting and exciting seems to be the lowest priority criterion to be met. Apparently, in a task-oriented situation we feel that people should pay close attention, regardless.

But people, being human on or off the job, listen well to things that excite and interest them and listen poorly to items that fail to catch their fancy. So, the speech that presents a good case for a recommendation but bores the audience fails. The presenter is mystified. How can this be? Look at all that solid stuff in the presentation!

The rejection of logically meritorious but boring messages leads us to refer to this condition as "terminal dullness." The lesson is clear, a good speaker adapts the message to the audience so that it catches, arouses, and maintains the listeners' attention.

10. *Timing.* Time in our technological society is all important. We run on schedule. We judge others and ourselves by how well we perform within the blocks of time we set for specific tasks. Since management of time is a dominant value in our culture, it is in one sense surprising and in another not so puzzling that timing is a major problem in the delivery of presentations. Given our preoccupation with time, it is surprising that failure to finish on time is a prevalent error in presentations. On the other

hand, given our preoccupation with time, it is not surprising that failure to finish on time is viewed as a cardinal sin by both the speaker and the audience.

People who make presentations generally have too little material to fill the allotted time or too much to finish in the time allotted. Typically, when notified that three minutes remain, presenters discover that they are only halfway through a twenty-minute talk. They then begin to talk faster and faster, omitting key items, and when the time is up they stop in midsentence, leaving both speaker and audience members disappointed.

The tragic circumstance of poor timing recurs because a fundamental feature of the human condition is not known or, if known, is ignored. That feature is: *The human animal is incapable of estimating the passage of time while it is talking.* Most people are so charmed by what they are saying that they forget to keep track of the time.

The trait of forgetting time while talking suggests its own solution. The speaker must be informed of the passage of time during the presentation so that adjustments can be made. A digital watch or a clock on the wall will do the trick, but only if the speaker uses the information these provide. Speakers who become so interested in what they are saying that they forget to look at the clock probably need to have a confederate in the audience who gives them time signals. A competent presenter should be able to finish within plus or minus thirty seconds of the appointed time if informed of the passage of time.

PLAN OF THIS BOOK

Because we consider creating a joint venture with the audience one of the high priorities in presentational speaking, we examine ways of accomplishing this in Chapter 2. The chapter describes the communication models that explain and guide speaking and provides an account of the context for the presentation in which these communication processes function in joint ventures.

Not only must the presenter be a good listener, but she or he should also understand listening for comprehension, critical listening, and creative listening, topics treated in Chapter 3.

Chapter 4 presents basic considerations in putting together the speech of presentation. It includes six "patterns," actually formulas, to follow in designing presentations to fit different situations.

Chapter 5 assumes that persuasion is a key element in the process of presentation; hence, it is devoted to persuasive techniques and ethical guidelines for their use.

Sound thinking is the essential element in all good presentations. In Chapter 6 we examine evidence and reasoning as these occur in the presentation process.

The presenter's credibility is an important variable discussed in Chapter 7.

Chapter 8, Audio and Visual Aids to the Presentation, supplies information about audiovisual aids and gives examples and suggestions that will help the presenter use these resources productively.

Finally, the Appendix presents case studies illustrating the application of each of the patterns of presentation. The Appendix supplies solid, how-to information on applying the material in the text to actual real-life situations.

At the end of each chapter, the reader will find questions for discussion and review, references for research studies, and suggested readings for further study of the concepts in that chapter. We urge that these aids to learning be used routinely. These provide both repetition and application of materials in the chapters, increasing understanding and facilitating retention.

SUMMARY

The John Jamison case illustrates in detail the nature of the process of presentation. The process is much more than a single speech. It includes all communication from the time the central purpose is formulated through to the final spoken interaction between speaker and audience. Analyzing the audience and preparing its members for the presentation are of prime importance.

The central objective of the book is to help readers become more competent in making presentations, especially to increase their skills in adaptability, creativity, and flexibility.

A presenter is an agent of change. The purposes of presentations range from maximizing options, to establishing direction, to limiting options to one, this last being the advocating of a single, definite proposal. The good presentation requires a precise purpose which the presenter develops very early in the process of presentational speaking.

The preferred relationship of participants in a presentational communication episode is one of a "joint venture" rather than "sender-receiver." Generating and maintaining a joint venture require that the speaker create an active rather than a passive audience, understand the nature of being a change agent, develop an interactional communication process, and be able to predict with some reliability the responses of others.

Ten prevalent causes for the failure of presentations are: failure to prepare people, abstract and ill-defined purposes, lack of organization, poor preparation of the setting, relying on memory or manuscript, amateurish delivery, misuse of visual aids, microphone problems, terminal dullness, and poor timing.

The remainder of this book provides materials and advice that will help the presenter avoid disasters of presentations. But skirting potholes is an elementary driving skill. Thoughtful application of concepts in succeeding chapters takes one beyond such defensive maneuvers. It may enable the practitioner to achieve distinction as a maker of sensitive, artistic, and predictably effective presentations.

QUESTIONS FOR DISCUSSION AND REVIEW

1. Why is it important that the presenter talk with members of the audience in advance of the presentation?
2. What is the nature of a motive analysis of the audience that is useful to the presenter?
3. If actual persuasion is done before the presentation, why is the presentation itself necessary?
4. What is included in the process of presentation?
5. What are the three dimensions of competence in making presentations?
6. What makes the presentation "a climactic event?"
7. What are the roles of "ecological validity," "contingency," and "flexibility" in presentational speaking?
8. What are the characteristics of a productive joint venture relationship between presenter and audience?
9. How can a presenter be a change agent when the purpose of the presentation is to maximize options?
10. How many of the "avoidable disasters in presentations" have you experienced? Analyze the ones you remember.

REFERENCES AND SUGGESTED READINGS

For some early references to the rise of presentational speaking, see:

Gould, D. R. "Philosophy on Oral Presentations." Convention Paper, Speech Communication Association, 1967.

Woods, David. "Presentations: A Semantic Illusion." Convention Paper, Speech Communication Association, 1967.

For more recent treatment of the importance of presentational speaking, see:

Goldhaber, Gerald. *Organizational Communication.* 4th ed. Dubuque, Iowa: William C. Brown, 1986.

Goodall, H. Lloyd, and Christopher L. Waagen. *The Persuasive Presentation.* New York: Harper and Row, 1986.

For clarification on the distinction between speeches of presentation and presentational speaking, see:

Capp, Glenn R., G. Richard Capp, Jr., and Carol C. Capp. *Basic Oral Communication.* 4th ed. Englewood Cliffs, N.J.: Prentice-Hall, 1986, pp. 168–175.

For more on the persuasive purposes of presentations, see:

Brembeck, Winston, and William S. Howell. *Persuasion: A Means of Social Influence.* 2d ed. Englewood Cliffs, N.J.: Prentice-Hall, 1976.

For a comparison of joint venture interaction and unidirectional communication, see:

Howell, William S. *The Empathic Communicator.* Prospect Heights, Ill.: Waveland Press, 1986, Chapter 2, "Sending-Receiving Versus Joint Venture Communication."

chapter *2*

Creating a Joint Venture with Your Audience

THE NATURE OF A COMMUNICATIVE JOINT VENTURE

Although it is sometimes useful to think of your talking as communicating to yourself (your internal monologue can be considered intrapersonal communication), much of our talking is a social affair. We talk at, with, or to others. Ideally, when we communicate socially we participate with each other in a joint venture.

Joint ventures are human social activities in which several people participate to shape joint action according to some agreed-upon model and standards. Joint ventures include such human activities as group game playing, musical performance, dancing, and communicating. In order to create a joint venture, all participants must agree to play the game or the music, dance, or communicate according to the rules, conventions, norms, and ideals of the activity.

Communication events should be joint ventures in which all parties understand the rules, conventions, norms, and ideal models of the event and make a social contract with one another to abide by the rules and strive to achieve the ideal model. In a sense, people may say to one another "shall we communicate?" in much the same way that they might ask, "shall we dance?" Unless all the participants agree to try for a joint venture, there is little hope of approximating the ideal form of such communication.

The dancers might decide to waltz or to do the Virginia reel; the players might decide to play American football or soccer; the communicators might decide to take part in a consciousness-raising group, a political

19

campaign, or a presentational speech. If some of the players think the game is American football while others think it is soccer, chaos is likely to result. If some of the communicators think the communication event is a decision-making group centered on presentational speeches, while others think it is a ritual designed to reaffirm the organizational culture, again confusion is the likely result. Furthermore, like the dancers or game players, the communicators must know they are taking part in a particular kind of communication. And to understand the particular form of communication they must know the perspective that governs participation.

Communication perspectives provide participants with the necessary information, understanding, and skills to take part in joint ventures. Perspectives include communication models that provide a description of the recurrent event in terms of an ideal example of good communication. Perspectives also include criteria drawn from the model to enable participants to critically evaluate communication. Finally, perspectives aid the development of advice on how to participate in the joint venture more effectively.

Communication events are conventional, artistic, and often more or less staged joint ventures. The difference between a law of nature and a conventional rule is the difference between necessity and choice. It is no good for people to say they will create a joint venture in nonverbal communication in which light waves will bend around corners. Rules, however, are joint agreements that participants may or may not choose to follow. Thus, although a rule in the game of basketball asserts that players must not kick the ball, some players may kick the ball nonetheless. The rule in a communication joint venture may be that listeners to the presentational speaker must strive to understand the message, but some listeners may choose to let their minds wander or to drop off to sleep.

Artistic joint ventures are formed to some extent by what the participants find pleasurable and beautiful as well as practical and useful. Thus, to an uninitiated observer the style of a dance may be quite arbitrary and seem unattractive. You may see films of some dances from the 1920s and find them laughable, or you may attend a modern dance troupe's recital and be confused or disgusted by the way the members dance while a connoisseur might find the dancing beautiful. In the same way, people who understand a communication perspective will be able to judge and appreciate the stylistic excellence of the speakers and listeners. After attending a presentation, they will be able to say that the speaker was especially good in the use of visual aids or that a member of the audience was an excellent listener.

All joint ventures, to a greater or lesser degree, are staged. Often they require a special place for their performance such as a stage, a dance studio, a playing field, an auditorium, or a meeting room. They may also require special equipment or special clothing. Joint ventures may be so completely staged that they approach the scripted and rehearsed nature of a theatrical play, film, or television drama. Ritualized yearly presentations of divisional budgets for the Board of Directors of a large business may exhibit such elaborate staging. Some presentational joint enterprises may result from minimal staging and be so unscripted that they contain much room for improvisation. For such enterprises the unfolding of any particular episode cannot be anticipated.

With practice over the years, certain norms and customs will emerge relating to joint ventures. These norms and customs, though not strictly required for the joint venture, add to its artistry and enjoyment. For example, the joint venture of intercollegiate football in the United States has evolved a custom of having male and female cheerleaders, marching bands, and public address announcements. Strictly speaking, the game can be played without such customary additions, but without them many of those who love intercollegiate football will feel something important is missing. Likewise, a company might adopt the custom of serving refreshments to the participants in the few minutes prior to a presentation.

THE COGNITIVE PERSPECTIVE FOR PRESENTATIONAL SPEAKING

An important part of any communication perspective is a model of the ideal way to communicate. The communication model provides a pattern or example that is a clear illustration of how to take part in a good joint enterprise. The model implies or specifies the conventional rules required to take part in the joint enterprise (to play the game). These rules take two forms, constitutive and regulatory.

Constitutive rules are those that serve to make up and form the joint enterprise. They specify what the purposes of the effort are and what constitutes success or failure. The participants agree to follow and not violate the constitutive rules in order to approximate an ideal joint venture. If the model of the dance is one in which participants move in the same space without touching, it implies the constitutive rule that participants should agree not to touch while dancing. If the ideal model is one in which one or several presenters give carefully prepared and uninterrupted speeches while other participants listen carefully and creatively, it implies a number of constitutive rules. If everyone were to speak at once or if the presenter were to appear and sit in the audience and when prompted by a question answer, "I really don't have anything special to say," we would be justified in saying, "We don't know what kind of communication event this was but it certainly wasn't a presentational speech."

Regulatory rules are those conventions that the participants agree to follow as the episodes unfold. Thus, if the constitutive rules specify that speakers are to have a limited amount of time to give their presentations but in practice people choose to speak overtime, the participants may agree on a regulatory rule penalizing those who go overtime or in some other way force strict compliance with the time limits.

The Source-Message-Channels-Receiver model of presentational speaking is an essential part of the rational perspective. To describe it, we will first discuss the model of person-to-machine communication and then present the rational model of person-to-person communication.

The Source-Message-Channels-Receiver Model of Person-to-Machine Communication.   Modern organizations are undergoing a rapid transformation in which person-to-machine communication and person-to-person communication by means of machines are becoming the order of the day. More and more businesses and industries are equipping their employees with work stations that have microcomputers or computer terminals. These machines allow people to network with one another, interact with mainframes and use the micros or the mainframes to do word processing, use spread sheets, manage data bases, and use other software programs as part of their daily round of communication. Thus, person-to-machine communication is assuming an important part of our daily information processing in its own right. In addition, one of the most important models of presentational speaking owes much to the ideals of people communicating with computers. We therefore begin our discussion of the Source-Message-Channels-Receiver (SMCR) communication model, as applied to making presentations, with an analysis of human-to-machine communication.

Let us assume that we want to carry on a conversation with a microcomputer. To begin with, the computer without its software is more helpless than a newborn infant, for the infant can cry and move and express some internal states. The first step is to teach the computer a language. We must next provide the computer with a set of rules about proper sentences and their grammatical forms and about the data we wish to discuss and where we would like to have them stored.

Once the microcomputer has a language and a program, it accepts the information which we encode by typing it into the machine by means of a keyboard, and it decodes the information into electrical charges that form patterns in its memory chips. Being careful to phrase our statements in precisely the right form, we can then tell the computer to process the information and show the results on a television screen or print them out on paper. The computer performs the computations we request and translates the results from electrical patterns into numbers or words.

The basic elements of the process are indicated in Figure 2.1. The first step is for the programmers to decide on some objective that can be achieved through the use of the computer. When the programmers have studied the machine and know its language capabilities and its logical capacity, they can plan their presentation to achieve their objective. To do so, they make a step-by-step analysis of the logic of their problem, and they work out a way for the computer to solve it. Next, they translate their plan into statements that the computer can understand, being careful that each statement is correct and that no crucial information is left out. When they take their basic message and put it into computer language, they are encoding their message. The programmers may select several channels to reach the computer with their encoded message. They may be able to use human

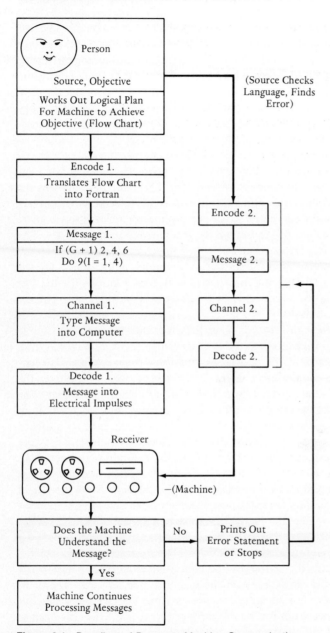

Figure 2.1   Paradigm of Person-to-Machine Communication

speech as a channel or magnetic tape or a floppy or hard disc. A very common channel for communication with a microcomputer is to type the message on a keyboard much as one types a letter.

Assume for the moment, however, that in the process of telling the microcomputer what to do the programmers make a grammatical error and omit a comma. The computer hums along until it comes to the bad grammar. It stops and prints out a message to the effect that there is an error of a certain type in a given sentence. The programmers check the message at the point indicated, puzzle about the problem, and, finding the error, insert the comma. They type the revised message into the computer again, this time in proper grammatical form, and the computer buzzes along, until it comes across a word or symbol that is not in its vocabulary. Again it stops and prints out an error statement. Again the programmers study the message, discover their error, and rephrase the direction.

Conceivably, somewhere during the joint venture the machine stops. The programmers hopefully await information about the statement that has confused the machine, but none is forthcoming. The computer only tells the programmer what has gone wrong if the error is one that the programmers foresaw and gave the computer directions on how to indicate the trouble. The current problem is one for which the machine has no vocabulary. The most trying time for the programmers trying to debug a new program often comes under these circumstances. The programmers must search for the error without a hint from the machine as to where it can be found. The programmers may try several times without success, but they must correct every error because only when the machine understands completely does it proceed with the joint venture. Thus, the programmers and the machine work together to achieve absolute understanding.

Several features of the process of humans communicating with machines are worth emphasizing. First, the machine does not initiate the communication. The flow of information is from human to machine. The machine talks back to the users primarily to clear up misunderstandings. Second, the machine always indicates when it is confused. It never pretends to understand. Third, the machine will not tolerate bad grammar, faulty analysis of its vocabulary, or demands for logical computations beyond its capacity. Fourth, when the computer is confused, it often feeds back messages to aid the programmers in clearing up the problem. With the rise of robotics and computers feedback has become one of the most important concepts in communication. Feedback consists of information about errors in the message that the computer provides the programmers, so that programmers can achieve a state of understanding on the part of the machine. Fifth, the users are the *source* of the communication; they develop the objective, frame the messages, start the machine, and so forth. The computer is the *receiver*. The machine does not have an objective and would not process data if it were not for the initiative of the source. Once involved in the joint venture, the receiver does not remain inert, however. The computer goes to work to absorb and understand the messages. Thus, the interdependence of the process is clear. The programmer must abide by the common rules of the joint venture just as does the computer.

If we abstract the main elements of the model, we are left with the *source* (user) *encoding* a *message* and sending it through a *channel* or *channels* to the *receiver*. The main process features of the model include a complex, reciprocal, interdependent, give-and-take typical of joint ventures. Both source and receiver must cooperate to achieve the objective. A crucial element in the joint venture is a corrective loop that includes a sensing mechanism to monitor failure and a sending device to indicate error and guide the source in debugging the messages. The corrective loop is called *feedback,* which is indicated in Figure 2.1 as "Prints Out Error Statement or Stops."

 The Source-Message-Channels-Receiver Model of Person-to-Person Communication. The SMCR model of person-to-person communication is essentially an adaptation of the person-to-machine model that takes human nature into account. Like the microcomputer, people as receivers of messages must have sentences in suitable form and expressed in words within their vocabularies before they can understand them.

Like the microcomputer, people as receivers of messages can feed back error statements and indicate difficulty in understanding messages in order to help sources increase high-fidelity communication. Indeed, humans are potentially more efficient at furnishing feedback than machines. Humans can provide a much wider and more descriptive range of error statements spontaneously than can computers. However, in practice human beings are often less efficient than machines because, unlike the computer, which will not continue the joint venture until it understands every bit of the message, people will tolerate and attempt to decode elliptical references, ambiguous statements, poetic flights, and sentences that violate the forms of good grammar. People will often think they understand or will pretend to understand a message when they do not. Hence, a person will not always provide feedback in the form of asking for more explanation or clarification at a point where the computer inevitably would.

In the final analysis, the major difference between humans talking to machines and humans talking to one another concerns objectives. What frequently happens to complicate our model of person-to-person communication is that after an individual makes the initial attempt to assume the role of source with another person as a receiver, a contest ensues over whose objective will be achieved and who will control the situation. As a result, the joint venture relationship required to achieve understanding is not established. Instead, a confusing communication episode is created, not unlike a group of game players milling around, each trying to play a different game.

The joint venture that results from people trying to achieve the ideals of this person-to-person perspective is heavily rational. The perspective emphasizes the ideals of information processing: rational decision-making, clear transmission of information, and calm unemotional communication. Norbert Weiner, a pioneer in developing the perspective, caught the essence of the model when he said, "Communication is a joint game against confusion."

Figure 2.2 presents the model of rational perspective of human-to-human communication. The message source with an objective in mind encodes a message into suitable language, keeping in mind the receivers' motives, interests, vocabularies, knowledge, habits, physical capacities, and so on. Next, the source selects a channel or channels and transmits the message to the potential receivers. The potential receivers agree to partici- pate in the joint enterprise and try to achieve the ideals of the model. They decode the message, and the interaction continues much as for the model of person-to-computer communication. Achievement of a high level of the meeting of the minds is, then, a function of the participants' knowledge of the rules, customs, and artistry involved, as well as their communicative skill.

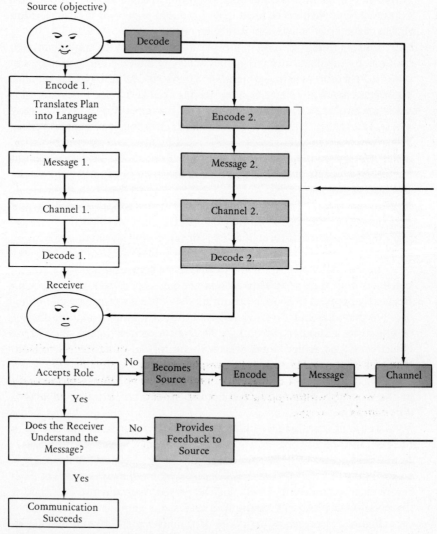

Figure 2.2 Paradigm of Person-to-Person Communication

A desirable debugging operation in person-to-person communication occurs when the receiver accepts that role but fails to understand the message. If the receiver provides feedback so that the source perceives the nature of the difficulty, then the information fed back enables the source to generate a supplementary message (shown in the encode column of Figure 2.2) to clear up the misunderstanding.

The presentational speaker may initiate a communication event in order to achieve an objective. The other participants accept the roles of receiver, feed back cues to facilitate understanding, and then, in effect, say, "Now let some of us talk for a while." The presentational speaker then accepts the role of receiver, and so they proceed shifting from the role of source to that of receiver and back. Always, however, they participate in a cooperative, interdependent way, providing feedback and achieving understanding in each basic unit of communication. The oft-deplored lack of good listening is frequently not a matter of lack of skill so much as it is an unwillingness of one or more of the partners in the joint enterprise to play the role of receiver. (This is not to say that good listening skills are to be neglected. Chapter 3 discusses the techniques of good listening and their importance to successful communication.) The point here is that until participants agree to work together to achieve the ideals of the joint enterprise, they cannot do so. Of course, if they are uninformed about the nature of the joint enterprise or inept in their communication skills, they cannot do well even when they are willing.

THE HOLISTIC PERSPECTIVE OF PERSON-TO-PERSON COMMUNICATION

The rational model has much to commend it, and it is an important factor in presentational speaking. You need to understand its ideals, goals, rules, and how they are to be implemented. It stresses analytic and logical thinking and tends to deemphasize intuition, emotion, and suggestion.

Recent research into the human brain has given us an important perspective that extends our understanding of the communication joint enterprise. These studies have demonstrated the out-of-awareness collaboration of left and right cerebral hemispheres made possible by the corpus callosum. This previously neglected method of responding with the brain system instead of with one hemisphere or the other is now termed *holistic information processing.*

In holistic information processing, the right brain contributes imagination and creativity, while the left brain adds rationality, editing, and refining and puts concepts into words and numbers. Rapid generation of sound innovation is explained by the verification of our ability to go beyond the purely rational, adding the holistic option to previously recognized intuitive and consciously logical abilities.

The holistic model portrays an ideal communication event in which the participants form a joint enterprise to achieve an end, make a decision, solve a problem, or create new ideas or products. The context of the communication event is an essential ingredient in the joint venture. The formal and informal organizational structures play an important contextual role in the ideal model. Participants will pay attention to and intuit the influence of formal position, status, and responsibility on relationships and the communicative interaction. The informal communication and structures create and sustain much of the organizing behavior, including the culture of the participants. For internal presentations, the informal structures and organizational subcultures are most important; for presentations given from representatives of one organization to audiences drawn from other organizations, the informal structures and cultures of both are important. When speaking to a specific audience, the small-group dynamics and the group culture become a strong component of the context. Participants in communication events need to sense the influence of formal and informal organizational structures, cultural norms, and small-group processes on their attempts to create communication joint ventures.

The emphasis on context within the holistic perspective also leads to a stress on the nonverbal elements of the joint venture. The nonverbal features—the way participants in the communication gesture, use vocal intonations, and position themselves in relation to one another—all become important in the holistic perspective. According to the ideal model, participants should process a vast amount of nonverbal cues, often out of awareness, and come to sense or feel the personal relationships that exist or are being established among the participants in the joint venture. The participants begin to intuitively make judgments about one another in terms of trust, intelligence, knowledge, ethics, and so forth.

The communication event itself has a free-wheeling and often nonjudgmental atmosphere. The emphasis may be on brainstorming and divergent thinking. Participants feel free to play with ideas and language, to use metaphors and figures of speech, and to fantasize. Options are explored and crazy ideas tolerated. A good meeting is characterized by the participants mulling over ideas, putting them aside, returning to the question again, more mulling over, and then an illuminating moment of group creative problem-solving when the participants achieve their goal. In the free-wheeling give-and-take of the joint enterprise, the participants suddenly have an "ah hah" experience in which a decision, the solution to a problem, or a new and attractive idea suddenly emerges into their awareness to the accompaniment of feelings of excitement and interest.

USING RATIONAL AND HOLISTIC PERSPECTIVES

On the surface, the rational and holistic perspectives may seem antithetical. A superficial reading of brain research might lead one to assume that the left and right sides of the brain are working at cross purposes. As we have noted, however, the two halves of the brain are connected, and the central system works most efficiently when it is totally involved. To be sure, for some tasks and some kinds of problem-solving one side or the other of the brain may predominate. Similarly, one or the other perspective may be dominant in a particular presentation. Chapter 4 discusses how presentations can be designed to stress one or another of the perspectives or to balance the two.

Still, in its highest flights of creativity and insightful problem-solving, the human brain acts as a totality. Thus, the moment of conceiving a new idea or a new project is often the province of holistic intuition and emotional excitement. But this is rapidly followed by a period of analytic and conscious study and preparation to see if the exciting new idea is as promising as it first seemed. This preparatory period often indicates problems and pitfalls, and the conscious part of the brain may turn the question over to the right brain to let the matter incubate and percolate. During this incubation phase, the conscious mind may be vaguely aware of the mulling over process, and ideas may appear to the consciousness as a kind of purposive daydream. There follows a moment of insight or illumination in which the solution comes to mind clearly and forcibly and again with feelings of excitement and delight. The analytic portion of the brain then takes over to check and validate the new solution or idea.

In the act of creation itself, when a writer is at work on a novel he or she may be in a sort of bemused reverie while the intuitive holistic part of the central nervous system projects characters, plot, and dialogue on a mental screen. The author may recall the writing later, saying that the characters seemingly took over the story so that all that was necessary was to record their actions and comments. Authors often remember with amazement that their creativity was responsible for the writing, and so they endow their creativity with almost mystical qualities.

While the writer seems to be under the total control of the intuitive, out-of-awareness portion of the brain, the rational, analytical portion is always there to monitor the creative flow. If the plot were to begin to go off the deep end or the overall form and shape of the novel threatened to become ungainly, the conscious, analytical, trained portion of the brain would call a halt and rein in the intuitive creative portion that was in danger of going out of control.

As noted above, the people who create a joint venture of presentational speaking may decide to choose the predominant rational model as the guide to their interaction and at other times may select the predominant holistic ideal. Even within the same presentational speaking event, the participants will want to stress the rational model at times and the holistic at other times. In the remainder of the book, we note where an emphasis on one or another of the perspectives is indicated for the presentational speaker.

THE IMPORTANCE OF CONTEXT IN CREATING JOINT VENTURES

The holistic model of presentational speaking stresses the importance of the context of the communication event in the development of a successful joint venture. The context includes the formal and informal communication channels and structures, the organizational and societal cultures, and the small-group communication processes.

Every presentation takes place in an environment that significantly influences the development, delivery, and interpretation of the message. Among the most important elements in this environment are the organizations that provide speaker, audience, and occasion.

In our discussion our use of the term *organization* is interchangeable with *institution* in the sense that an institution is an organization, establishment, foundation, society devoted to the promotion of a particular object. Organizations include business and industrial firms, hospitals, charitable institutions, local, state, and federal governmental agencies, as well as legal, educational, administrative, and legislative bodies, both public and private. We will not include crowds, mobs, audiences, public meetings, or other collections of people that have no officers, formal positions, bylaws, articles of incorporation, constitutions, or other rules of procedure established either in writing or by custom.

While ecclesiastical bodies differ from military establishments and while a manufacturing corporation contrasts in some respects with an educational institution, all organizations have much in common. Our purpose here will be to examine those common features of organizations that shape and restrict the presentation.

FORMAL ASPECTS OF ORGANIZATIONS

Some communication within the organization is official and follows the formal channels, while other messages are informal and unofficial. The presentation is a major technique for *official* communication and therefore flows through *formal* channels. One seldom prepares a presentation for the grapevine. The formal characteristics of corporate structure, therefore, play a vital part in the shaping of presentational speeches. By formal we mean those structures that are indicated by tables of organization, job descriptions, position titles, lines of authority, and formal channels of communication.

Typically, the formal structure indicates the difference in value to the organization of a given job by a status ladder. The basic organizational metaphors include climbing or descending, upper levels or lower levels, upper, middle, and lower management, moving up or dropping down, achieving the peak or pinnacle or slipping into the depths.

Notice that we are discussing the *form* of the organization without reference to individual differences in the people who comprise it. We make no ethical judgments at this point about the question of whether some people *ought* to be considered better than others or if the pyramid and ladder metaphors are wise or useful in structuring human relationships. The fact of the matter is that for organizations task specialization inevitably leads to such evaluations.

The formal organizational structure, therefore, includes channels through which messages are to go to achieve the necessary coordination of effort. The formal channels are of particular importance for presentations designed as internal communication since they are official messages designed to flow through channels. People seldom prepare a presentation for an informal luncheon meeting, a talk about organizational matters on the golf course, over coffee in the cafeteria, or at a bar. However, one does not skip levels of structure or bypass or ignore positions that are part of the formal structure when giving a presentation.

As large numbers of specialized task functions are coordinated to meet the requirements of building a bridge, meeting a mass market, teaching thousands of students, ministering to hundreds of patients, or providing a postal service for several hundred million people, the organization must be able to identify successful and unsuccessful performance. The usual answer to the problem of finding job breakdowns and correcting them or of finding and rewarding unusually good work is to make the person holding a key position responsible for the success or failure of the work within the span of her or his command.

With responsibility, the person has sanctions to punish and the ability to reward people within the jurisdiction. We will refer to the right to punish and reward as *authority*. Authority, as we use the term in the present context, refers to an organizational assignment of the right to impose sanctions, offer rewards, make decisions, and commit organizational resources (money, personnel, etc.) to certain projects. "Only the supervisor has the authority to hire and fire," illustrates authority in the organizational sense.

One can study the functions of every organization and make a graphic representation of the various specialized positions, their relationships in terms of higher or lower status, and the channels of communication among them. We will refer to such a visual representation as the table of organization.

Figure 2.3 presents a table of organization. Positions A, B, C, D, . . . J are managerial. The other unlabeled positions are of specialists of various sorts providing work and services to be integrated into the total effort. Some of the specialists, for example, those whose work is integrated by supervisor B, are of higher status in the organization than others (indeed, of higher status than some managers at the level of positions F and G).

Let us say that managers must make some important decisions about a very large project that requires the resources of the total organization. They must bring the work of the units managed by positions B, C, and D

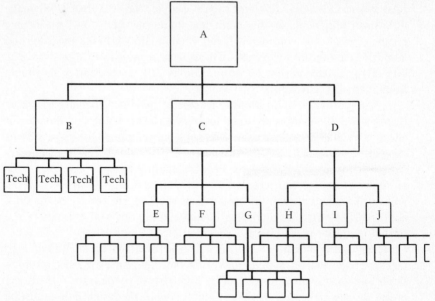

Figure 2.3   Table of Organization

into coordination. Position A is able to use formal channels to send messages to B, C, and D, and they in turn may send messages back to A and
to one another. Should the decision-making of the four individuals in positions A, B, C, and D require communication with the person in position
E, the formal channels require that the messages from A for E be first sent
to C and then on to E. Clearly, the transmission of messages through formal
channels under these circumstances can become extremely cumbersome.

The official meeting provides a way for individuals of varying status
whose positions are not ordinarily connected by formal channels of communication to communicate directly. People in positions A, B, C, and D may
meet with the person in position E and thus establish direct interpersonal
communication. The meeting supplements the formal communication systems effectively. Often, when the persons in position E must present vital
information to upper management in a meeting, they will use a presentation.

Position Status Related to the Source of the Message

Members of the organization who have little opportunity to communicate
with persons within other divisions seldom know at firsthand the people to
whom they sometimes give presentations. (Again, the informal communication channels such as the grapevine may provide rumors or gossip about a
given person.) John Jamison was fortunate in that he could develop his
presentation with some insight into the interests, abilities, and motivations
of the three key members of the Board of Control in his company. Had

Jamison been asked to make a presentation on the new product to upper management at the Beaumont, Texas, plant where the product was to be manufactured, he could not have made so thorough an analysis of the audience, and he would have had to rely on cues from their formal positions. Of course, Jamison should adapt to the cues which the audience in a branch plant provides him during the speech.

Furthermore, the source of a message influences the perception of the message. That is, the same presentation made by a person in position C in Figure 2.3 to people in positions E, F, and G will probably have a different effect than if given to members in positions H, I, and J. The same message delivered to the same audiences by the person in position A will have a different impact than if C delivered it. The prestige and credibility of the source of a message is a factor in the persuasiveness of the communication.

When the presentation represents a given unit within the organization rather than the personal position of the individual who makes it, the choice of the proper source for the presentation becomes an important part of the persuasive strategy. People planning the presentation should ask questions such as, would it be wise for the manufacturing manager in position C in Figure 2.3 to give the presentation (although it was largely worked out by the assembly manager in position E), or would it be better to have the person in position E do it?

The decision as to which person in what position should deliver the presentation ought to result from careful evaluation of the audience and the purposes of the message. The first basic principle relating to source status and the presentation is: *all other things being equal, the higher the organizational status of the speaker the higher her or his credibility and the greater the effect on the audience.*

The first corollary of the above principle is: *all other things being equal, the organizational status of a message source has a greater influence on internal organizational communication than on external communication.*

Position Status Related to the Receiver of the Message

Equally important to the persuasive impact derived from the status of the source is the effect of the formal position of the members of the audience on *their* perception and interpretation of a presentation.

The first basic principle relating to receiver status and the presentation is: *the presentation will have greatest impact if its preparation, context, and delivery recognize the formal status, authority, and responsibility of the listeners.*

One can hardly overestimate the importance of according each member of the audience the status, authority, and responsibility provided by position in the formal organizational structure. People seldom like to be treated as though they have less status and prestige than they think they have. If a speaker treats someone as being of less status than an organizational position implies, the typical response is a bristling "Do you know who I am?" Interestingly enough, if one behaves toward others as though their position has more status than is the case, they also become irritated. A lieutenant treated as a colonel, becomes uncomfortable. Perhaps, the lieutenant detects the irony, intentional or not. Lacking sound evidence to the contrary, a speaker ought to accord each member of the audience the respect due the prestige and status of the person's position.

Even the decision as to which members of the organization are to attend the presentation is important to its ultimate success. If people feel left out because they have not been invited to the meeting, if they feel that their position was not recognized as having the status and authority they feel it has, that very fact may cause them to oppose the change recommended by the speaker.

If the receiver of the presentation is of higher organizational status than the speaker, it affects the preparation, language, and delivery of the speech. When one speaks to a superior, these tendencies can be noted in the care with which messages are prepared (the higher the status of the audience, the greater the tendency to make careful preparation), the candor with which one speaks (the higher the status of the audience, the greater the tendency to make more guarded pronouncements and to phrase commitments carefully), and the formality of the delivery (the higher the status of the audience, the greater the tendency to adopt a more formal style of delivery). The status differential is important to presentations within and without the organization. John Jamison talking to his Board of Control had to adjust to the status differential. Likewise, a salesperson making a presentation to the president of another corporation needs to be sensitive to reactions stemming from his or her listener's high status.

Position Status and Barriers to Understanding

Low-status persons making presentations to high-status individuals tend to emphasize the positive and send on only the "good news," filtering out information that the speaker feels will be disturbing to the audience. When the listener has *fate control* over the speaker, the tendency to tell only good news is strongest.

Fate control is illustrated by the supervisor-subordinate relationship. A subordinate talking to the "boss," is usually conscious of the fact that the boss controls salary, working conditions, job security, and promotions. The dangers of succumbing to the "good news" barrier are clear. If the subordinate does not pass on the pertinent bad news, relatively minor difficulties may be suppressed until they become major crises.

When the speaker has higher formal status than the receiver, another set of barriers to communication appears. A speaker addressing listeners of lesser status tends to assume that the audience will interpret the message as intended. The high-status speaker tends to concentrate on speech content and neglect the audience. Generally, one finds it easier to be concerned about adjusting to the peculiarities of our superiors than to remember to be considerate of the habits and interest of those who work in positions over which we have fate control.

A speaker with higher formal status than the listeners can predict that the audience will carefully search a presentation for hidden meanings and that they often will draw unwarranted inferences from slightly ambiguous remarks about matters of particular interest to them. For example, if Milt Brewer, sales manager of Minnesota Mills, makes a presentation to his sales force to introduce a new method of evaluating selling practices, he may intend only to explain procedures. Jeannette Swenson, however, who is disgruntled with her territory, may infer that Milt is planning a sweeping reorganization of the division. Swenson may anticipate a different and better assignment. Should Milt make the evaluation but not change the territories, Jeannette may accuse him of having made promises he did not keep. Generally, therefore, when Milt makes a presentation to people over whom he has fate control, he should be careful to protect against his listeners making wish-fulfilling speculations or interpretations from his message.

Communication among peers is usually the most comfortable. Peers seldom have clear and direct fate control over one another and thus are not as threatening. One can predict a less formal, more candid, and freer climate for the give-and-take following a presentation. Nevertheless, peers who meet and work together frequently develop differing amounts of respect and esteem for one another, and an informal pecking order often emerges. The resulting informal structure will exhibit the same specialization of function and the same arrangements of status as do formal positions. This is true even though it may be unique to the people forming the group. If informal groups spring up among peers, the status differential that arises will affect communication in a way analogous to that affecting the formal status arrangements.

Position Authority Related to the Source

When the members of a division of an organization plan a presentation, they must examine the authority as well as the credibility of the source when picking a person to make the presentation.

At this point, we must carefully distinguish official organizational communication from the presentations of individuals. Often, the presentation is meant to be, and is clearly perceived to be, a presentation of the thinking and policy of an organizational unit or of the entire institution. Such official presentations contain the composite wisdom (or folly) of the group, and the person delivering the presentation is not speaking for herself or himself but for the entire group. On other occasions, however, a person may prepare a presentation that represents a personal approach to the question under discussion. The listeners all understand that the speaker is solely responsible for the content of the speech, with personal responsibility for it, and this in no way commits the organization to ideas within it. Official presentations by sources with the authority to take action are often drafted with great care, and the language is searched for legal, technical, and public relations implications. Under such circumstances, presentations may be partially or totally scripted. Often, too, while the presentation is made by the individual in the position of authority, a group of supporting resource people will attend the meeting and be prepared to deal with specific and technical questions relating to parts of the presentation. Official presentations by authoritative (in the organizational sense) people are designed to legitimatize and finalize the contents of the message.

Position Authority Related to the Receiver

The authority of the people who will hear the presentation is a factor in its preparation and development. John Jamison was making his presentation to a group that had the ability to accept and implement his recommendation or to reject it. When listeners have this amount of authority, the persuasive elements of presentational speaking are most critical. The speaker having fate control over listeners might succumb to the temptation simply to order them to accept a recommendation. Succumbing to such temptation is very unwise for any manager. It is true that giving orders is much easier and requires less discipline and understanding than developing persuasive presentations; hence, the threat of punishment is often used to force compliance. But the manager who resorts to "ordering" cooperation sacrifices the resources within the group. The employees' resentment at being deceived, apparently being consulted when actually they were dictated to, will prevent them from contributing their critical thinking and good ideas in the future.

The authority of the receiver of the message is a factor in presentations made by representatives of one organization to another. In today's corporate society, a frequent setting for interorganizational presentations is a conference involving representatives from two large enterprises. For example, Systems Dynamatic, Incorporated, may have embarked on a three-year development program aimed at ultimate sale of something to the Defense Department of the federal government. The project is speculative until the company can demonstrate a workable prototype. At that point, the investment of time and effort by Systems Dynamatic may be translated into profit or loss by the outcome of a series of sales meetings in which a team of people from Systems Dynamatic confer with a group representing the Defense Department. The salespersons make presentations explaining the software and hardware of the system and its capabilities. They may demonstrate the prototype, discuss potential delivery dates, costs, and so on. The authority (or lack of it) of the Defense Department group to commit the government to a contract is critical in shaping the content and conduct of the entire exchange.

INFORMAL ASPECTS OF ORGANIZATIONS

Our discussion to this point has considered the influence of the formal characteristics of organizations on the development of and responses to presentations. If people were, indeed, interchangeable as the standardized parts of mass-produced products like automobiles or washing machines, our discussion would be complete. However, individuals do differ in ways that affect their organizational behavior. The new manager does not do things in the same way as the predecessor, although the new manager inherits the authority and prestige associated with the status of that position. The way authority is exercised and subordinates come to like or dislike, respect or discount, the new person may well differ from their response to the former manager. The formal hierarchy of status, authority, and responsibility is reinforced, discounted, and changed by the informal relationships that develop among people as they work together in the various task-oriented small groups that compose the organization.

In the course of working together, some people demonstrate unusual competence in their specialties, so a person becomes not only a design engineer as predicted by the formal structure, job description, and so on, but others come to perceive the individual as an extremely responsible, hard-working, and gifted design engineer. Others may exhibit unusual skills at working together with groups; they are able to initiate group projects, build cohesiveness and *esprit de corps,* mobilize group resources, and guide the group to successful completion of its tasks. As people demonstrate these various abilities, others in the organization come to rely on them to perform their specialties, particularly in times of stress or crises, *regardless of the formal structure of the organization.* Thus, an individual may come to perform tasks that the table of organization would assign to someone else.

Power. When "sizing up" the audience before a presentation, therefore, one should always examine both the formal and informal working arrangements of the people within the organization. In order to keep the two features separate for the purpose of analysis, we will use the concept of power for the informal counterpart of the formal concept of authority. *Power* refers to the ability to make and implement decisions and changes. Power may be a function of the effective exercise of authority. Thus, the person in authority may make and implement the decisions and changes for which a position is responsible. On occasion, however, power may be exercised by a person without commensurate organizational authority. This circumstance generally results from an ability to command the necessary material resources and personal support of the members of the organization. Power differentials commonly emerge when people with varying amounts of authority interact closely in task-oriented small groups within the organization. The informal roles that emerge through

interpersonal interaction may thus give an individual power dispropor-
tionate to assigned authority.

The earning of *esteem,* which is the counterpart of prestige, proceeds
in much the same fashion as the accumulation of personal power. As people
get to know one another by working together over a period of time, some
demonstrate more commendable talents, personal characteristics, and accomplishments than others. The formal position of a person will to some
extent limit the range of task behaviors that the individual can exhibit, but
even so, persons can always earn greater or lesser amounts of esteem from
their colleagues no matter what position they hold.

THE INFORMAL AND FORMAL STRUCTURE OF ORGANIZATIONS

In a sense, the informal departures from formal structures of the organization represent a blurring of the lines of control, of the communication
channels, and of the specializations established to increase the efficiency of
the institution. From a theoretical point of view, the organization would be
much more efficient if the formal map matched the actual operations. When
power and authority coincide, when prestige and esteem approximate each
other, then those unfamiliar with the internal dynamics of the organization
will be able to cooperate in joint efforts, with less tension and wasted
motion. Learning the ins and outs, including skeletons in closets, feuds, and
attachments, requires time, effort, and tact. The energy devoted to such
study in preparation for making a presentation could be invested in other
activities if the organizational map fits the territory.

The student of presentational speaking, therefore, ought to begin with
a thorough analysis of the formal context of the communication as outlined
above. On occasion, one may have time for no more than that. Whenever
possible, the next step is to examine the informal matters of power and
esteem related to the personalities involved. For example, when John Jamison began his analysis of his audience person by person, he recalled the
dynamics of group interaction on the board and the fact that the board was
dominated by three powerful and prestigious members. He, therefore,
aimed his presentation specifically at the big three. Because he was an
insider, he knew that, although all members of the board had equal status
as board members, some (like Joe Perkins, the president of the company)
had higher organizational status and others (like Homer Lydgate) had
earned power and prestige beyond their years and formal status.

Even more specifically, Jamison knew some of the hobbies, interests,
and preoccupations of each individual in the big three. He could plan to
accommodate his presentation to the individual directly. Fully exploring
the adaptation of a message to a given individual takes us from the realm
of larger context to direct person-to-person speech.

THE CULTURAL CONTEXT

Organizations reflect the cultural context of a given time and place. The organization of the Methodist Church in the early nineteenth century in the United States was a reflection of the westward migration, the frontier living conditions, the optimism of the times, and the zealous desire of the leaders of Methodism to save the great heartland of the Ohio and Mississippi valleys for Christianity. The organization of the Ford Motor Company in the early part of the twentieth century in the United States both shaped and was shaped by the industrialization and affluence of post-World War I America.

As organizational forms developed in one culture (for example, North American business organizations) are transferred to others (for example, joint ventures of Minnesota Mining and Manufacturing Company and Sumi Tomo in Japan), the structures modify and are modified by the culture. Thus, we say that Japan is becoming Westernized even as we observe that American business practices must be changed in order to succeed in the Japanese culture.

What is happening around an organization, its cultural environment, reaches into the organizational structure to influence the nature and flow of communication. A person planning a presentation ought not limit the analysis to the situation within a given organization and assume it to be isolated from the larger community.

ADAPTING THE PRESENTATION TO THE SMALL GROUP

The person who is to give a presentation to a small task-oriented group should analyze the audience as a group in addition to making an analysis of individuals. The speaker ought not expect the group to absorb, discuss, and act on more than they can in the time available. The speaker must take into account such questions as: Is the decision-making group in the beginning stages of its work? Is it in the midst of a conflict phase, hammering out basic positions and lining up in opposition to or in support of solutions? Is it in the confirming stage, having made the decision and now meeting only to rubber-stamp that decision? One's objective for a presentation to a group that is beginning meetings on an important problem might well be different from the objective when the presentation comes at the height of the controversy and still different if the meeting needs a presentation to set up the confirmation of decision. (For a case study of a group starting consideration of a new problem see Case Study #4 "Inductive Exploration of Possibilities" in Appendix.)

In addition to analyzing the audience for a presentation to a small task-oriented group in terms of the realities of group process, a person making plans for a presentational speech should examine the characteristics of the listeners, as they are influenced by circumstances in which the group operates. Although not all meetings fall neatly into one of the two major categories of business and professional small-group meetings, the basic principles necessary for audience analysis are revealed by the committee meeting for only one session and by the work group meeting for a number of sessions with essentially the same membership.

THE ONE-TIME MEETING

In a one-time meeting, the participants have not met before in a group meeting and are not likely to meet again, at least not for the purpose under discussion. Some of the members may have participated in other meetings and some may know one another socially or at work, but the particular complement of people attending the meeting is unique.

Since the composition of the one-time meeting is unique, it is a zero-history group. The fact that a group has no history means that the members have no past experience on which to base expectations of present and future actions. A zero-history group has no feeling of cohesiveness, no culture, no norms to guide the trivial details of communication and social interaction. A zero-history group has no purpose, no direction for the future, no idea of what sort of group it is or where it is going. In short, both the social field and the task objectives are unstructured and ambiguous.

The one-time meeting is not only without history but also without a future. Some meetings start with a zero-history group, but the members anticipate that the group will continue for a considerable length of time and hold many more meetings. The committee studying the restructuring of the university may be told at its first meeting that the goal is to complete its work and make its report in eighteen months. Although the first session of the university committee resembles a one-time meeting in that the group has no history, the committee does have a considerable future, something that is important to the dynamics of the first session.

The zero-history group with a future is under considerable pressure to test potential leaders and influentials, to develop norms and other features of group culture carefully, to take nothing at face value, and to check reputation, formal status, and assigned structures before accepting them. Much is at stake; hence, the members search and evaluate the social realities of the group with more rigor in the first session of an ongoing group than they do in the one-time meeting.

Because less is at stake, the communication network, the roles, the norms, and other features of group process in the one-time meeting tend to be accepted uncritically and the use of stereotyping devices is common. Many presentations are received by one-time meetings. Selected persons often meet primarily to hear the presentation and take action on it, in a typical one-time meeting.

One of the most important tendencies in the one-time meeting is to accept leadership. Whether the person calling the meeting is a self-appointed moderator, or some organizational unit has assigned a person to lead the meeting, the members are likely to accept and appreciate guidance from that individual. The group needs quick help in getting underway. Members realize they have little time and tend to accept arbitrarily stipulated goals and procedures with little challenge.

Participants in one-time meetings tend to use formal organizational status or professional credentials as ways of assigning leadership and influence. Thus, if seven people in the meeting are all from the same company, the discovery that one of them is production manager, the highest status of anyone at the session, will cause the others to look to that person for guidance. If a group of citizens from various segments of the community gather together and discover one of the members is a famous lawyer, another a surgeon, and a third a public official, that information will help the others structure a hierarchy of influence and importance.

Once the discussion is underway, those members who do not hold positions of professional stature or who are not known by reputation tend to be quickly stereotyped on the basis of early contributions and behavior. Each individual strives to get some impression of every other and relies on superficial cues. Thus, a person who does not speak for fifteen or twenty minutes may be stereotyped as quiet, shy, apathetic, or uninterested in the meeting and thus figuratively dismissed. Another, who speaks in a loud authoritative voice and expresses strong opinions and makes flat judgments, may be stereotyped as rigid or "bossy" or "pushy."

The person preparing a presentation for a small task-oriented group formed for one session should understand the dynamics of the situation. The drive to hierarchical structure is widespread in our culture, and the superficial cues provided by organizational status, talking or not talking, come to have much more influence in the one-time meeting than elsewhere. Thus, analyzing the audience for the presentation in terms of what organizational and community positions will be represented is important.

Many presentations are made to small groups that have met one or more times before and that expect to meet one or more times in the future. Under circumstances of some permanence (even if the group expects to complete its work within four or five sessions and a period of several weeks), the inherent pressures to develop a sense of cohesion, to establish roles and order them into a hierarchy of ability, likability, and dominance, in short, to develop a unique group culture, are released. The pressures for group structure and allegiance are intensified if the members perceive their group as permanent and important. The more long term the group's prospects, the more important the group to the participants, the greater the initial tensions, and the longer the testing period.

ANALYZING THE SMALL GROUP AS AN AUDIENCE FOR A PRESENTATION

In preparing his presentation for the Board of Control, John Jamison not only examined the individuals on the board but also asked himself about the nature of the group and its structure. Jamison estimated the impact of the corporate organization on the dynamics of the small group, noting that Perkins was president and had top organizational status. He analyzed the board as an ongoing task-oriented unit. He examined the dynamics of the group's evolution and decided that the board was in a period of role stability and had developed predictable decision-making norms. He knew that the decision-making process was dominated by three important influentials, Joe Perkins, Homer Lydgate, and Marsha Everding. Jamison could then assume that his audience would conform to the behavior of the three influentials. His next task was to study the three key influentials by making an intensive motive analysis of each.

In preparing for any presentational speech, analyses from the points of view of organizational context, small-group theory, and the dynamics of face-to-face communication will set the stage for sound motive analysis of individuals. As was the case with John Jamison's presentation, there are usually a few influentials who can be counted on to lead and reflect the motivations of an audience.

The speaker preparing for a one-time meeting can rely on a quick and superficial analysis of the people to be present. He knows that organizational and community status and reputation will be major factors because the members of the meeting will be forced to make hasty judgments. These are the ingredients that must necessarily structure their perceptions of the meeting.

The real art of group audience analysis can be practiced with an ongoing group that has some history. The speaker can learn much about the development of the group from information about how long the group has been in operation. If the group has had only several meetings, the speaker should search for evidence that the process of role emergence is continuing. If several people are still in contention for leadership, they may approach the speaker before the presentation and indicate that an important difference of opinion exists in the group or that the speaker ought not pay too much attention to the other contender because that person has proved troublesome and destructive in the past. If the group frequently changes its mind and sends out conflicting reports, if members talk about their difficulties with the group in social situations or at coffee breaks, the indications are that the group is in a period of role instability. If the group has clearly developed cliques that are antagonistic to one another, the speaker has further evidence of what happened during the early shakedown cruise. A person delivering a presentation to a group in an early period of role-testing and contention must expect that the question-and-answer period will prove a difficult one. Members may get off on procedural matters or may digress into fields far removed from the topic of the presentation, and the speaker's attempts to practice good human relations with one questioner may result in an attack from another.

Somewhat the same pattern of evidence coming from a group that has been in operation for several months or years will indicate a group undergoing a reshuffling of roles. The speaker would be well advised to search for a change in personnel, of circumstance, or in ability or interest on the part of a high-status member to account for the instability. The history of the group will continue to influence its dynamics, however, and people in influential roles will continue to be important. One ought also to search for those with less seniority who are trying for more influential roles and are likely to achieve them and adapt to these comers in much the same way that one would to the established influential members.

SUMMARY

Joint ventures are human social activities in which several people participate to shape joint action according to some agreed-upon model and standards. Basic to communication joint ventures are the perspectives that provide the agreed-upon standards, including an ideal model of communication.

The model of the cognitive perspective for presentational speaking includes the *source,* the *encoding* process, the *channel,* the *message, decoding,* and the *receiver.* The rational process of communication includes a complex, reciprocal, interdependent give-and-take. The process exhibits a step-by-step approach to a clear objective, which both source and receiver must cooperate to achieve, and a corrective loop called *feedback.* Feedback includes a sensing mechanism to monitor failure and a sending device to indicate error and guide the source to develop new messages to achieve understanding.

The model for the holistic perspective portrays an ideal communication event in which the context is an essential ingredient and the event itself is free wheeling and nonjudgmental, with an emphasis on brainstorming and divergent thinking.

Organizations are formally structured conglomerates of people devoted to the achievement of a common goal that provide an important part of the context in the holistic communication model. The formal organizational structure affects important elements of communication such as the status and responsibilities of speakers and listeners. As people work together within an organizational context, they often achieve informal working arrangements that depart from the formal structure. Within the restrictions imposed by the formal structure and the geography of the physical environment people get to know one another, become friends or enemies, earn esteem and power, and so forth.

The speaker preparing a presentation for a small-group meeting should analyze the impact of related organizations on the structuring of the group and distinguish between one-time meetings and sessions of continuing work groups. In order to adapt successfully to the listeners, the presentational speaker should also analyze the group processes, including cohesiveness, roles, and culture impacting on the audience. Much has been learned about the theory and practice of listening. In Chapter 3 we apply this knowledge to presentational speaking.

QUESTIONS FOR DISCUSSION AND REVIEW

1. What are communication perspectives, and how may participants in a joint communication venture use them in presentational speaking?
2. How may participants in a communication joint venture use an ideal communication model?
3. How do constitutive and regulatory rules differ, and how may both be used in an ideal communication model?
4. What are the elements of the SMCR ideal model of person-to-person communication, and how do they relate to presentational speaking?
5. What are the elements of the ideal model of holistic person-to-person communication, and how do they relate to presentational speaking?
6. What is the relationship of ideas about nonverbal communication to the SMCR and the holistic models of communication?
7. In what ways can context be important in creating a presentational speaking joint venture?
8. How do the formal and informal aspects of organizations compare and contrast?
9. How is position status related to the source and the receiver of messages in terms of presentational speaking?
10. How do small-group communication dynamics relate to audience analysis for presentational speaking?

REFERENCES AND SUGGESTED READINGS

For more information on joint ventures and communication perspectives and how ideal models of communication differ from social scientific models, see:

Bormann, Ernest G. *Communication Theory.* New York: Holt, Rinehart and Winston, 1980.

For an early formulation of the SMCR model, see:

Berlo, David K. *The Process of Communication.* New York: Holt, Rinehart and Winston, 1960.

For more on the holistic perspective on communication, see:

Howell, William S. *The Empathic Communicator.* Prospect Heights, Ill.: Waveland Press, 1986.

For a discussion of the formal and informal aspects of organizational communication, see:

Bormann, Ernest G., Ralph G. Nichols, William S. Howell, and George L. Shapiro. *Interpersonal Communication in the Modern Organization.* 2d ed. Englewood Cliffs, N.J.: Prentice-Hall, 1982.

For a brief analysis of small-group communication, see:

Bormann, Ernest G., and Nancy C. Bormann. *Effective Small Group Communication.* Minneapolis: Burgess Publishing, 1980.

chapter 3

Listening in the Process of Presentation

To this point in this book, we have emphasized the process of communication from the point of view of the speaker. To restore a balance and reassert the interdependent nature of face-to-face communication, in this chapter we examine the receiver's role in the process. The dynamic interplay required for successful communication is facilitated when the audience understands its role. In addition, people playing the role of listeners should possess the skills required to comprehend and to evaluate presentations and the ability to creatively add deeper meanings to the messages they share with the speaker. The theory and practice of responding constructively to the presentation are the concerns of this chapter.

LISTENING COMPREHENSION

Perhaps the most basic response to a presentation is comprehension of the message. This implies considerably more than simply hearing what is said, for hearing is not identical to listening. Hearing means you are aware of a sound, while listening interprets sounds. Listening adds *perception* to hearing, a process of attaching meaning to the signs and symbols one hears.

Fortunately, the study of listening has substantially advanced our understanding of the process in recent years. We can now describe the behaviors associated with effective listening. Persons who would improve their listening comprehension can systematically practice these techniques and establish habitual patterns of response that enable them to learn more from a spoken message and remember it longer.

45

How to Improve Your Listening Comprehension

1. *Practice listening to difficult material.* One of the causes of poor listening may be labeled the "recreation syndrome." We do a tremendous amount of "fun and games" listening throughout our lives. We select from the casual and inconsequential materials in our environment what gives us pleasure, what interests and amuses us. Our never-ending search for entertainment builds firm habits of attending to what is instantly comprehended without effort and resisting or avoiding entirely material requiring forced attention and thought. The result is a tendency to engage in entertainment-type listening to serious, task-oriented communication. When the presentational speaker explains the steps in a complicated process, we may "tune out" and wait for something more interesting to come along. When speakers ask us to remember some statistical information because they intend to use it later in their talk, we resent expending the necessary effort. At this point, we may rationalize and tell ourselves that it is the speakers' job to make listening easy, and if they do not do that for their audience, they deserve not to be remembered.

The fact is that much necessary and important listening is difficult. The person who stops comprehending at the first sign of perplexity or confusion will miss much that needs knowing and will suffer the penalties of not being informed. Like most skills and abilities, the skills of comprehending heard materials are acquired rather than inherited. They are developed only through use. Systematic practice in listening to challenging lectures, discussions, public service programs on radio and television at regular and frequent intervals, modifies the "recreation syndrome" and establishes habits of persistence and tenacity in wresting meaning from spoken verbal stimuli.

A frontal attack on the improvement of listening ability can be made with the help of commercially programmed and recorded exercise materials. These can be used individually or in small groups and, with associated pretests and post-tests, supply learners with evidence of the nature and extent of their improvement. Courses in listening are now offered by most educational institutions and in many business and professional organizations. Taking such a course gives one a sound base for later self-improvement, since specific learning techniques are taught and practiced under supervision.

Courses and commercial materials are helpful but not essential to the improvement of listening skills. Simply listening to difficult material regularly and endeavoring to extract from it central ideas and significant supporting evidence will benefit the listener a surprising amount. The guiding principle to implement general self-practice in listening is *be selective.* Selectivity must be in terms of an objective, and for most materials listeners should ask themselves "What do we want to remember to meet our needs and interests?" With this question as a criterion, they identify what seems central and necessary and carefully discard most of the other facts and concepts. Such selective listening forms habits useful in separating the wheat from the chaff in a presentation.

2. *Empathize with the speaker.* When a listener feels involved with a speaker, that is, has an ongoing empathic relationship with the person, comprehending what the speaker says becomes effortless and efficient. What can listeners do to facilitate the development of their empathy with the speaker? Mainly, they can play the role of ideal auditor. The listener can mentally note, "I am going to be on the speaker's side. I will ignore mannerisms that might distract me. I will figure out how the speaker would like me to react, and respond that way. In effect, I will function as an assistant." With this attitude the listener can sense what the speaker is feeling and thinking, and empathy can grow.

In the speaker-listener dyad, we can identify two main components that produce empathic interaction. One is natural, the automatic tendency of one human being to participate in whatever goes on inside the other. The second element is voluntary and purposeful. *Trying* to be empathic increases empathy. When listeners are consciously attempting to sense the feelings in the speaker, when they are studying nonverbal behavior and tones of voice and relating these to the content of the message, their perceptions are other-than-self-centered. Because they can perceive more cues to speaker response when they are concentrating on the speaker, they collect more empathy-producing data and become more empathic.

3. *Work hard at listening.* Techniques 1 and 2 above suggest that voluntary concentration in listening accomplishes wonders. This leads to our third recommendation, since voluntary concentration implies work. But why should listening be hard work? Because the nature of human attention is such that task-oriented listening violates its patterns severely.

Human attention is sporadic. It comes in short bursts rather than persisting steadily. Typically, we listen to a speaker for fifteen to forty seconds, and then turn off for a while to think about something else. We stay with the speaker for a longer or shorter period, depending on how much what is being said interests us, then turn off again to pursue our other mental activities. Often, the periods of attention to the speaker become shorter and shorter, and the periods during which we are occupied by other thoughts become longer and longer.

To break the pattern of sporadic attention requires "work" behavior. Listeners must discipline themselves by resisting attractive mental excursions and applying their energies to the task of listening. Such voluntary attention usually becomes nonvoluntary, for forcing attention to a speaker normally leads to becoming interested in what is being said. Certainly, the only way such an intrinsic interest can come about is to compel attention through an act of will until perceptions generate favorable responses.

Three common-sense admonitions help "worked at" listening to be productive. The first points a finger at a barrier to communication everywhere, "Don't fake attention." All of us have learned to fool speakers by looking as though we are eager listeners, while we are actually woolgathering. Fake listening subverts any effort to work at unscrambling a difficult message.

The second advice is, "Overcome the bad news barrier." When a speaker states a fact that is contrary to our belief or distasteful to us, we often use the defense mechanism of ceasing to listen. To handle difficult material we must remove the barrier to hearing what we do not like, and learn to welcome differences. Many people have trained themselves to be more attentive to material they disagree with than to concepts conforming to their prejudices.

Finally, in working to generate an interest that does not come naturally, do not settle for a neutral and passive willingness to receive what you hear. Try to "pump up" a genuine interest, one with enthusiasm. While the "power of positive thinking" can be overestimated, listeners who tell themselves that they are interested in and excited by the presentation often increase their comprehension. A positive attitude is needed to neutralize our natural skepticism, which keeps informing most of us that if an idea is new to us and contrary to our thinking, it can have little merit!

4. *Review and preview as you listen.* A hazard for the listener to overcome is the differential between thought speed and speech speed. The presentational speaker talks at a rate of 125 to 175 words per minute, while audience members can think 600 to 800 words per minute. Sporadic attention is encouraged by this differential. One problem confronting the well-intentioned listener is, "How can I keep busy?"

The first answer is, keep busy by thinking about the speaker's topic, not about other things. Selective listening, identifying central concepts and their support, is one excellent exercise. The game of anticipation is a constructive maneuver. Where is the speaker going next, and how will the talk develop from this point on? Once listeners have guessed what is coming, they are sure to listen carefully to check on their prediction. If they have guessed correctly, they are reinforced in their listening, and if they have predicted poorly, they will listen better to improve their batting average with their next prediction. Also, the listener can always utilize time while the speaker is repeating a point or adding an unnecessary illustration to review what has gone before. Recapitulation is a powerful aid to the memory, and recapping the parts of a presentation gives an improved grasp of the entire structure, as a unit.

The belief that spoken material is assimilated when received without the listener "chewing it over" and working at it seems to be universal. Research on the process of good listening contradicts this notion. Continuous review and preview contribute significantly to retention and understanding.

5. *Suspend judgment.* We tend to be compulsive about decision-making. Confronted by a problem, we want to seize a solution and have it "over and done with." In listening, our compulsiveness often urges us to make up our minds early about the speaker's proposition. We await some significant statement or bit of factual information to help us make up our minds. If we find it and thereby prejudge the issue, we can relax and fake attention for the remainder of the speech. If we behave in this fashion, we are guilty of making an "inductive leap," jumping to a conclusion without the necessary evidence, a nasty hazard to the business of task-oriented listening.

In order to avoid hasty and unwarranted decisions, a listener must "hear the speaker out," by consciously resisting the temptation to make tentative decisions along the way. Rather than listening for a decisive item, we suggest that the listeners arrange two columns, mentally or on paper, one of "pros" and one of "cons." At the end of the presentation, the columns will be complete and the pros and cons can be "added up" and compared. In this procedure, clusters of variables can be kept in order and related. Without some such device, important items will be overlooked and the more dramatic points, those in sharp conflict or in marked harmony with the views of the listener, will exert an excessive influence on the outcome.

6. *Keep calm.* All listeners have tender areas easily irritated by hostile notions. If people permit themselves to respond emotionally to some content item in a speech, interesting distortions occur that unbalance their decision-making mechanism. Chapter 4 treats the effects of an emotional condition on problem-solving ability, noting that the three concomitants of emotion (shock, diffusion, and transference) all function nonrationally. We can only conclude that if listeners become upset in any way, their ability to solve problems deteriorates and their decisions made in an emotional state are less wise than those formulated when they are calm.

Sometimes, keeping calm is no easy matter. One tested technique is to separate in one's mind the person and the concepts the speaker is discussing. When a speaker says something that irritates a listener, the impulse of the receiver is to become angry at the speaker for saying it. This is entirely unproductive because it not only produces emotion, but it also takes the listeners' minds away from the topic. If listeners refuse to be diverted by their tendency toward such aggressive retaliation and instead analyze the offensive item and how it fits into the case made by the speaker, they are much less likely to be emotionally disturbed.

The speaker's choice of words is often the factor that causes upsets in listeners. A defense against this irritant is the listener's ability to identify and classify what might be termed the "language of alienation." Each individual has a long list of words that that person responds to by overreacting. Here are some words and phrases that have been shown to upset the nervous systems of certain Americans: *dictator, Communistic, graduated income tax, national debt, Mary Jane, nigger, mother-in-law, abortion, data processing, computerization, mother-fucker, sex education,* and so on. The compilation could be nearly endless. Probably you felt at least one twinge as you read through the list. We should identify the words to which we have become sensitized and, when one comes along, say to ourselves, "Oops, let's not get excited. The word is not the thing, and it would be foolish to become upset over a grouping of letters from the alphabet. Rather, what point was the speaker trying to make?"

A final suggestion for maintaining self-possession is to resist identifying with a controversial position. Particularly when one is a member of the audience to a presentation, it is appropriate to assume an objective attitude. Deliberately detach yourself from your vested interests in the ongoing argument and become a disinterested observer, a collector, and an interpreter of points made and support offered. Playing the observer role keeps your prejudices in check to some degree and increases your tendency to be reflective rather than impulsive in reacting to a message.

Perhaps you can maintain your personal stability by simply telling yourself, "Keep calm." However you do it, you will be a better and more useful listener to a presentation if you succeed in resisting the temptation to become upset.

7. *Overcome unfavorable listening conditions.* A skilled listener will not tolerate an unfavorable listening condition that can be corrected. If a person has difficulty seeing and hearing from a present location, a wise listener will move to a better seat. If the speaker is not talking loudly enough to be heard by all, our good listener will inform the speaker of that fact, not just once, but persistently until the deficiency is remedied. Should the public address system be malfunctioning or a visual aid be out of adjustment, the good listener will assume responsibility for bringing about proper functioning of those devices. Good listeners will not tolerate disturbances within the audience. If other listeners are carrying on a private conversation, they will "shh" them and do whatever is necessary to terminate the distraction.

Learning to aggressively attack unfavorable listening conditions is difficult for most of us. We have accustomed ourselves to passively accept not only boring speakers, but also circumstances that make comprehensive listening categorically impossible. The dull speaker may be something we can do nothing to improve, but the conditions of listening can be controlled. We can only conclude that the knowledgeable listeners who identify something in the environment that is restricting comprehension for themselves and/or other listeners should overcome their passive auditor habits, and perhaps a natural shyness as well, and act boldly to remove the obstacle as soon as possible.

8. *Minimize note taking and other doodling.* Analysis of notes taken during speeches and of the use of those notes later might well lead us to the conclusion that note taking is a form of doodling. While some note taking may be necessary, most of it serves no useful purpose. Hence, we argue that note taking should be minimized in the interest of improving listening comprehension.

Serious note takers follow various unproductive systems. A favorite is the standard outline form, with heads, subheads, and sub-subheads, and for every "1" there must be a "2," for every "A," a "B." A difficulty is caused by the fact that most speakers do not follow standard outline forms. Consequently, note takers try to outline something that is not there. They rearrange the content into a basically different speech and in so doing, miss much of what is said.

Another popular pattern for note taking is to list main points to be remembered on one page and important facts on another. When a main point is also an important fact, the classification dilemma is likely to divert the listener for some time. Then, too, facts separated from the points thus supported tend to lose meaning, and usually criteria for selecting the "important" facts are unclear and indefinite. If note takers attempt to relate facts to main points by a number system, they soon confront a complicated, crisscrossing, interlocking network that is sufficiently perplexing to discourage any later reference to those notes.

The pitfall common to all note taking is the compulsion to write more than is needed. Recording connectives, articles, most adjectives and adverbs, memorable phrases, and side comments is superfluous and amounts to verbal doodling. For the rare occasions when the taking of notes is essential, we recommend the following guidelines:

Be rigorously economical. Ask yourself, what will I almost certainly use later and will as certainly forget if I do not write it down?

Strip away all unnecessary verbiage. Avoid complete sentences and paragraphs. Simply list skeletonized items of content with no attempt to number or letter them or to show superior-subordinate relationships.

Within two hours after a presentation, review your notes and extract what you wish to keep in a coherent memo to yourself or to someone else. Throw away the remainder of the notes, for with the passage of time on-the-spot notes become less and less meaningful, and reading old, cold notes is both frustrating and deceptive.

More important, learn to gradually substitute the active listening techniques of review and preview for note taking. A trained and disciplined memory far outclasses any shorthand system of written symbols that must be later decoded and interpreted.

9. *Use the key active listening techniques.* When circumstances permit you as listener to participate in a dialogue with the speaker, use the key active listening techniques of *encouraging, restating, reflecting,* and *summarizing.*

The possibility of responding verbally to the speaker is often present in presentations, and it can be exploited to improve listening comprehension dramatically. The four active listening techniques do not require the listener to have prior knowledge of the topic; yet through them the listener contributes interaction that converts a basically one-way talk into an effective dialogue. Figure 3.1 explains and exemplifies these techniques.

The source of the key active listening techniques is nondirective coun-

Type of Statement	Purpose	To Achieve Purpose	Examples
A. Encouraging	1. To convey interest.	Don't agree or disagree with a person. Use noncommittal words with positive tone of voice.	1. "I see. . . ." 2. "Uh-huh. . . ." 3. "That's interesting. . . ."
B. Restating	1. To show that you are listening and understanding. 2. To let the other person know you grasp the *facts*.	Restate the other person's basic ideas, emphasizing the facts.	1. "If I understand, your idea is . . . ." 2. "In other words, this is the situation. . . ."
C. Reflecting	1. To show that you are listening and understanding. 2. To let the other person know you understand *how he or she feels*.	Reflect the other person's basic feelings.	1. "You feel that . . ." 2. "You were pretty disturbed by this . . ."
D. Summarizing	1. To pull important ideas, facts, etc., together. 2. To establish basis for further discussion. 3. To review progress.	Restate, reflect, and summarize ideas and feelings.	1. "These seem to be the key ideas you have expressed. . . ." 2. "If I understand you, you feel this way about the situation. . . ."

Figure 3.1   Key Active Listening Techniques

seling. The counselor participates by making statements like the examples cited that both stimulate and sharpen communication without influencing its content. Similarly, the listener to a presentation can achieve clarification and generally increase understanding of the speaker's message by making these four types of statements at appropriate times. Like the nondirective counselor, the good listener does not introduce substantive materials but can contribute significantly to improving the process of communication.

CRITICAL LISTENING

Listening to learn requires perception, understanding, and retention. To move toward decision from understood and remembered materials requires a further operation: *evaluation*. Critical listening is the process of adding systematic and valid evaluation to information already comprehended.

Much has been said in this book that can be used to achieve critical listening. Chapter 6 supplies standards for evaluating statistical support, nonstatistical materials, and information about reasoning as it is used to advance propositions in a presentation. The first and most basic technique of critical listening is to apply the criteria from other chapters to the message being received. We will briefly summarize the major questions to be answered in evaluating these three important aspects of the presentation and encourage the reader to refer to the appropriate chapter for explication of any concept that is not completely clear.

Listening Evaluation of Statistical Support. The first test of points based on numerical information is twofold: Is there sufficient information, and is it clear and unambiguous? Clarity is achieved only when every item of data has an obvious purpose.

Is the relationship between support and the statement to be supported necessary and important? Often, statistical facts are "mixed up" with statements to be proved to provide the illusion of support, without an actual close relationship between the two.

Next, the critical listener scrutinizes the overall patterns of statistical evidence. Do the statistics omit relevant areas of information? Is the most meaningful index of typicality used? What indices of variability are utilized, and is the choice appropriate? Does the overall use of statistics add to understanding of the problem?

A closer analysis of the speaker's statistical methodology raises these questions: Are the statistics descriptive or inferential? If inferential, are they representative? What were the sampling procedures? Is a confidence level computed, and is it satisfactory?

Statistically supported statements almost always yield comparisons and predictions, which suggest that these questions be answered: Are units in the statistics constant and comparable? Are they of the same magnitude or corrected? Are trends clearly presented quantitatively in tables and graphs? Do tables and graphs distort the data in any way?

While the above capsule summary of tests of statistical support is severely condensed, it provides guidelines for the critical listener. If a numerically based presentation is judged to be satisfactory on all the mentioned criteria, it will have some merit.

Listening Evaluation of Nonstatistical Support. Critical listening is facilitated if the receiver distinguishes between *evidence* and *clarification.* Evidence furnishes grounds for belief, or *proof.* Clarification contributes to understanding. These are different functions, though they are often combined. The distinction between them is important because different standards are applied to the ingredients of proof than to materials intended to increase understanding.

Proof is developed primarily through use of statistical evidence, real case studies, and testimony. Statistical support has been discussed, so we will turn to tests of case studies and testimony of witnesses used as proof.

Is the case study cited genuine? Often details are left out, or added, to make a more effective example. Is it representative or the exception? Are sufficient details supplied, and is assurance provided that necessary observation has been complete and accurate? Where several cases are used, are there enough of them to validate the claim? Are the cases, considered collectively, fairly representative? Where statistical evidence is also used, do the case or cases supplement the statistics and are they in harmony?

Testimony is the observation and/or judgment of a witness, and its first criterion is that of relevance: Does the testimony bear *directly* on the point to be proved? Other tests are of the witnesses: Are they experts in the subject on which they testify? Did they have an opportunity to observe at firsthand the events they report? Are the witnesses respected by their peers? Are they known to be biased or to have related vested interests? When several witnesses are used, is their testimony in agreement or does it present contradictions?

Tests of clarification are less rigorous but perhaps just as important to the evaluation of a presentation. Hypothetical case studies are frequently useful: Are they reasonable in that available evidence indicates it would be possible for them to occur as described? Do they contribute significantly to the understanding of the problem? With analogies, literal and figurative, is there an identity of principle in the events related to each other by the analogy? Does the analogy make a truly pertinent point? Are narratives and anecdotes necessary? Is reiteration helpful? Do all the devices of clarification have a cumulative effect?

Evaluation of nonstatistical supporting material is accomplished in part by relating it to statistical supports. A final test is the extent to which they are integrated, the amount of weight each adds to the proof of the other by its supplementary function.

Listening Evaluation of Reasoning.   Much of our advice on evaluating statistical and nonstatistical supports involves criticism of the reasoning process. But the critical listener will find it rewarding to make a judgment of the overall quality of the thinking that was evidenced in the presentation. For this reason we isolate factors that are important to the constructive use of logical devices and relationships and suggest means of assessing them.

Can you as a listener readily perceive a comprehensive structure that relates all the parts of the speech in a systematic and sensible fashion? Does one point follow another in natural sequence, with a sense of progress and inevitability? Could you brief the talk as you listen, with relative ease?

Is the speaker's central purpose clear? Do all propositions contribute to that purpose directly? Is every proposition adequately supported? Are the propositions as concrete and specific as possible? Single? In report language? Worded positively? Not figurative or colloquial?

Viewing the speech as an attempt to solve a problem, does the speaker make clear that an accepted problem-solving system was followed? Does the speaker omit any essential steps? Are exceptions and opposing arguments noted? Is appropriate documentation supplied? Are concealment and other deceptions avoided?

Since reasoning is effective with a particular audience only if it is adjusted to their expectations and abilities, is the reasoning used by the speaker adapted to the knowledge, interests, and motives of the audience? And, since thoughtful materials are communicated more effectively when worded concretely rather than abstractly, is the factual and reasoned content of the presentation worded as concretely, specifically, and simply as possible?

To be effective as reasoned discourse, a speech must be delivered in a manner that encourages a deliberative, thoughtful response. A final criterion of reasonableness deals with speaker-audience interaction: Do the style and tone of the speaker make clear to the members of the audience that the intention is to think through a problem with them, step by step, and reach a solution through the exercise of their best judgment?

CREATIVE LISTENING

Our earlier discussion of speaker-audience interdependence suggests that in situations of empathic relationship and involvement the listener has opportunities to contribute to the ongoing communication by initiating changes in events. Members of the audience possess knowledge and abilities to interpret information that, added to the speaker's, can increase productivity of the presentation. We term participation of this sort by people in an audience *creative listening.*

Being creative in listening requires the making of personal decisions to attempt to change the course of the presentation in some way. Usually, this is accomplished by adding a bit of information or an idea, or by selecting a concept and interpreting or elaborating it, or by advancing new integrations of materials previously mentioned. But we must note a rare and occasionally appropriate act of creative listening: the decision to "turn off" the speaker.

There are instances when the good judgment of critical listeners tells them that the present speaker-audience interaction is impossible. Given the task, the speaker, this audience and situation, nothing significant *can* result. Once listeners have arrived at this decision, the sensible thing to do is sit quietly and direct their mental energies to some other problem. Too often we behave in a ritualistic fashion as though progress is being made and everything is going well when it is not. The creative listener can help most by refusing to cooperate in this group self-deception.

In potentially productive speaker-audience interactions a developing empathy and involvement set the stage for increasing listener participation. If this is to advance the thinking of the group and improve its attack on a common problem, it must be creative rather than redundant. In Chapter 4 we discuss the way a person can prepare a creative analysis for a presentation and the way creative thinking usually takes place in a purposive daydream. Often the images tumbling through the consciousness are fragmentary, and sometimes ridiculous or farfetched, but many times important insights come in a flash of illumination during such "mulling over" while driving a car or before dropping off to sleep at night.

On occasion, people talking with one another find themselves caught up in a chain of fantasizing similar to the creative moments that individuals experience. Someone suggests an idea that is picked up by another, and soon a number of the participants are excitedly adding to the dialogue. Under the pressure of the fantasy, the constraints that often operate in group discussion are released and people feel free to experiment with ideas, to play with concepts, and to be ridiculous. More and more members of the conference are drawn into active involvement in the communication, and the level of excitement and cohesion among the participants rises. Like the abstract picture or the ambiguous modern poem, the original message serves as a stimulus for the others to interpret or "read in" additional meanings or feelings of their own. If the speaker accepts the additions, gains from them, and encourages them, the speaker and listeners can help one another to greater insight and understanding.

The total creative involvement of the listener in the communication thus creates a situation in which the flow of meaning is no longer from source to receiver, as in the paradigm of a person talking to a machine, but rather both source and receiver add to a common reservoir of meaning until the result is greater than either could have produced alone. Thus, the final growth in learning and insight takes place in the source as well as in the receiver. In the highest level of communication, involvement interdependence, listeners respond to the original message by testing, adding, and modifying the meaning. If the listeners' contributions stimulate the speakers to see more in the idea than they originally had in mind and they resist the temptation to criticize the modification, their next suggestion may stimulate the listener to still further creative additions. Ideally, the speaker and listener, source and receiver, take turns shaping the original message, adding meanings until the final outcome of the communication is much more complex and exciting than the original meaning intended by the source when initiating the first message.

Basic to creative listening and involvement is an attitude termed "dialogistical." People with a dialogistical attitude coming into involvement interdependence create what modern communication theory calls a *dialogue*. The dialogistical attitude is one of not being defensive, of being subject-centered. Dialogistical persons are always independent, free agents. They are *open*, willing to reveal themselves and their convictions. They are equally willing to hear others, and convey to them an eagerness to learn their opinions. Their speaking shows trust in all other individuals and the group by its frankness and sincerity.

Dialogistical persons are disciplined, assuming responsibility for themselves and others. They give themselves freely and openly in dialogue but restrict themselves to guard against infringing on the freedom of others. They see to it that others are free to initiate as they will, and reinforce their attempts to be creative. They shape their own contributions in the context of the statements of others, being always careful that their openness generates complementary openness. They show that they not only welcome differences, but that they enjoy them.

The dialogistical person tends to approach each new idea with the attitude that it is worth considering, modifying, and adopting. How can the idea be used, or improved, or encouraged? When speakers have a dialogistical attitude, they do not immediately go on the defensive when a listener suggests a modification of their original ideas. When listeners have a dialogistical attitude, they do not immediately search for flaws in the ideas, but rather they search for strengths as well as weaknesses.

The dialogue we are describing shows a delicate balance of freedom and restraint. It is far from the chaos of "saying whatever you feel at the moment," yet impulsive response is necessary as is a playful attitude at times. The limitations come from group considerations. A person striving to create dialogue subordinates self-interest to the group's welfare. In dialogistical interactions we cannot be individuals going our separate ways but must be individuals working together.

The process of presentational speaking has become less formal and more "interactive" in recent years. The trend to dialogue will continue. Listeners will initiate idea modifications with greater frequency. The ideal of dialogue, admittedly unattainable, furnishes guidelines to insure productivity in the implementation of the new freedom. Resources of the group become available through disciplined creative listening, directed toward achievement of dialogue among the speaker and members of the audience.

John Jamison had barely finished his twenty-minute presentation to the Board of Control of Minnesota Mills when Homer Lydgate, who had become restless and eager as John built his presentation to the close, broke in. Lydgate excitedly accepted the idea of the new product but suggested a production modification to meet a developing consumer trend in flavoring. John felt a wave of anxiety, but recalling his coaching with Paula Osterhus he repressed his urge to respond with rebuttal arguments and instead concentrated on listening to what Lydgate was saying. Lydgate's excitement was contagious, and John began to see the potential in Homer's suggestion as he listened to new information about the latest developments in advertising and marketing. He also realized that the required modification in production plans would be slight. He picked up the idea and suggested the possibility of revisions without undue delay in production. John was delighted when Joe Perkins broke in bringing all of his production talent to the problem of modification. When even Marsha Everding grew excited and involved in the financing of the new modifications, the board meeting became an involved, task-oriented conference approaching the ideal of dialogue. The end result was not only approval of John's basic proposition, but also modifications and improvements that assured the success of the new venture.

Not all presentations move as smoothly through the stages fro planning to fruition as did John Jamison's speech at Minnesota Mills. Nor are all communication events as crucial and successful. Yet, in tracing the development of the case of the new product, we have seen the necessity, complexity, and satisfactions inherent in making presentations in business and the professions. The mixed or multimedia communication event is the basic way that important information and persuasion will be presented to the decision-makers of the future.

SUMMARY

Listening is a critical variable in the presentation. The most basic listening ability is to understand and remember the message. It is known as listening comprehension. "Listening to learn" can be improved by several procedures: (1) practice listening to difficult material, (2) empathize with the speaker, (3) work hard at listening, (4) review and preview as you listen, (5) suspend judgment, (6) keep calm, (7) overcome unfavorable listening conditions, (8) minimize note taking and other doodling, and (9) utilize four key active listening techniques.

Critical listening adds evaluation to understanding and remembering, and is a separate listening ability. To evaluate parts of a message the listener applies appropriate criteria. In particular, the receiver needs to know and apply the tests of statistical support, of nonstatistical supporting materials, and of the reasoning process used in the presentation.

A third listening skill that has recently been recognized is that of creative listening. This ability increases the contributions of the individual listener to group thinking and problem solution. The ideal pattern of speaker-listener and listener-listener interaction for creativity in listening is the communicative relationship known as *dialogue.* When listeners work to achieve dialogue, their opportunities to be constructively creative increase.

Having examined elements of creating a joint venture and effective listening we are now ready to consider designing the presentation, discussed in Chapter 4.

QUESTIONS FOR DISCUSSION AND REVIEW

1. What are the differences between listening and hearing?
2. What is the "recreation syndrome," and how does it interfere with listening comprehension?
3. Which of the nine techniques of improving listening comprehension seem to you to be the most important? Why?
4. Why is it important to keep calm and suspend judgment while listening to a presentation?
5. How can a person overcome unfavorable listening conditions while responding to a presentation?
6. What are the elements that enter into critical listening?

7. How might the critical listener distinguish between evidence and clarification?
8. How is creative listening influenced by the nature of speaker-listener inter-dependence?
9. What are the characteristics of the kind of communication we call "dialogue"? How does this relate to creative listening?
10. What are several ways in which an audience can respond constructively to a presentation?

REFERENCES AND SUGGESTED READINGS

For two early and helpful articles on listening, see:

Nichols, Ralph G. "Listening Is a 10-part Skill"

Rogers, Carl R., and Richard E. Farson. "Active Listening." In Richard C. Huseman, Carl M. Logue, and Dwight L. Freshley, eds. *Readings in Inter-personal and Organizational Communication.* 2d ed. Boston: Holbrook Press, 1973, pp. 534–557.

For more recent works on listening, see:

Floyd, James J. *Listening: A Practical Approach.* Glenview, Ill.: Scott, Foresman and Co., 1985.

Steil, Lyman K., Larry L. Barker, and Kittie W. Watson. *Effective Listening.* New York: Random House, 1983.

Wolff, F. *Perceptive Listening.* New York: Holt, Rinehart and Winston, 1983.

Wolvin, Andrew B., and Carolyn Gwynn. *Listening.* 2d ed. Dubuque, Iowa: William Brown, 1985.

chapter 4

Designing the Presentation

Although the process of presentation includes much preliminary work such as analyzing the audience and occasion, collecting information, and accomplishing as much pre-presentation informing and persuading as possible, the climactic event remains the speech itself. John Jamison knew that the way he presented his recommendation was critical, but no more so than was the presentation of himself. Final responses would be influenced by reactions to how he introduced his proposal and by the impact of his speech personality on the nervous systems of his listeners. His carefully designed and practiced effort resulted in his passing the test of presentation to the assembled Board of Control.

When presentational speakers design speeches, they should attempt to answer a single question: How can we arrange our materials to best achieve their potential effectiveness?

To help our readers answer that question, in this chapter we examine the earmarks of sound organization and the procedures for flexible preparation of the message. In order to apply this advice correctly, we next present six basic patterns for presentations. Each pattern is a sequence of steps designed to guide the arrangement of materials. The patterns cover the range of purposes of presentations discussed in Chapter 1. Since preparing and managing notes is an ever-present necessity in presentational speaking, we close the chapter with a section on the use of notes.

Examples of the patterns in action are essential to help the reader visualize details of their application. Because a valid example must be *in context,* that is, recognize unique circumstances and particular persons, each must be a somewhat long and complex unit. To keep the present chapter from being unwieldy, examples in the form of case studies are placed in the Appendix. The reader is encouraged to turn ahead to the case study of the pattern being read to see concrete implementations of the steps in determining that particular organizational plan and presentational design in context.

THE EARMARKS OF SOUND ORGANIZATION

Many of us have only a vague notion about what constitutes organized material. If a message can be outlined or is presented in outline form, we often judge that it is well organized. (Indeed, many business and professional people make a habit of developing messages in outline form. Somehow, they seem to assume mistakenly that a series of assertations, each properly numbered and indented, will carry more important information more quickly and clearly than an integrated series of clear topic sentences with explication and supporting information.) Actually, all that outlining indicates is that someone has listed and numbered some points, provided a list of alphabetized subpoints, and, perhaps, a further listing and numbering of sub-subheads. The process of systematically skeletonizing a series of sentences or phrases does not insure that a given sub-subhead fits logically as a supporting point for a subhead and that the subhead in turn fits logically under the main head. Nor does such outlining require that the sequence of ideas presented in the outline be the best for a particular topic, occasion, message source, or group of listeners. Sound organization, on the other hand, is characterized by unity, coherence, relevance, conciseness, and comprehensiveness.

Unity. A well-organized message has unity. One can evaluate the unity of presentation by first searching for and finding a central theme to which each element logically relates. Usually, the central theme is expressed or implied in terms of one clear statement. Frequently, the central statement is expressed explicitly in the message and highlighted by the speaker in a way that makes it obvious. All major subdivisions of the unified message are related to the central theme and often to some of the other subdivisions.

Coherence. A well-organized presentation is coherent. Coherence, in this sense of the term, refers to how the various parts of the message cluster together. Each part of a coherent presentation relates to every other part in a way that reveals some global design. The practical demands of structure are generally met by having each element closely related to the immediately adjacent element. Thus, when building a structure of bricks, each brick is cemented to its neighbors. The ultimate design of the building is clear only after the completion of all of the connections and when one can step back and see the finished structure. Similarly, each element of the presentation should be related to the preceding and succeeding parts to establish a coherent message.

Relevance.   A well-organized message contains only those ideas and information that are clearly and directly related to the central theme of the presentation. If the speaker feels that a seemingly unrelated element is important and relevant, that line of reasoning should be explained to the audience. One of the most common problems of the individual who organizes poorly is the inclusion of material that comes to mind whether or not it is related to the topic under consideration. People who prepare a speech have their mental processes stimulated by many different impressions. Many of us "free associate" ideas. One notion gives way to another, one mental image triggers other images, one anecdote, experience, or thought leads to another, quite often through idiosyncratic and illogical processes. We include these irrelevant materials because, at the moment, they interest us, but there is no reason to assume that such materials will seem logical, interesting, or useful to others.

Conciseness.   A well-organized presentation is concise in the sense that it is not repetitious. Each topic is dealt with in comprehensive fashion and then not handled again except for emphasis, as in summaries, transitions, or conclusions. A very common organizational fault is to deal with a topic, drop it, take up a second idea, perhaps a third, and then return to the first.

Comprehensiveness.   A well-organized message is comprehensive in that it deals with all of the important topics relating to the central theme. Of course, the comprehensiveness of speech communication is a function of the audience and the occasion. The comprehensiveness of John Jamison's presentation was restricted to what was possible with an audience composed of the Board of Control and the time limitation of twenty minutes. Comprehensiveness implies that the presentation is limited to territory that can be covered in the time allotted, given the understanding and interests of the audience. The Board of Control had a high level of interest in and knowledge about the topic; thus, John could cover more territory than he could if he were making a presentation to people unfamiliar with the business.

FLEXIBLE PREPARATION OF THE MESSAGE

Presentations that are unified, coherent, relevant, concise, and comprehensive result from a two-stage process of message preparation, analysis, and audience adaptation.

The Analysis Stage.   Once people receive an assignment to deliver a presentation, they should assemble all of the information they think important and begin to study it. Some of their thinking ought to be systematic and disciplined, and some ought to be more free wheeling and creative. The beginning ought to be systematic. Collecting the basic information relating to the topic sets the stage for a process we term "mulling over." The function of the mulling over is to make an analysis of the topic.

The process of analysis consists of close study of the materials to find important points, basic questions, and core issues. When people begin the study of a topic, many pieces of information may seem equally important, and even those ideas that appear significant may not relate clearly to other significant ideas. John Jamison may have a feeling that information about the crossover point for the new product is of vital importance, but early in his preparation he may not know precisely how and when he will use it.

Once a person has discovered the core issues in a body of material, the process of analysis continues on to reveal the central focus and, ultimately, the way each of the basic parts relates to the central theme and to one another. When the process reaches its conclusion, the end product is a logical brief that lays out the basic points in tightly ordered and reasoned fashion as they support the main topic.

When one makes an analysis of a complicated subject, the parts seldom fall easily and neatly into place. After the systematic collection of data and careful study, a person should make an attempt to arrange and structure the main points. The typical first result of such arrangement will be the kind of outline we referred to above; that is, an unsatisfactory listing of points of differing levels of abstractness in an order that could be shuffled without disturbing any logical progression. When a person reaches a dead end, the time has come for more "mulling around." At this point, creativity is to be encouraged.

Usually if time permits, and presentations often are carefully prepared so there is some time for preparation, the speaker is well advised to put the topic out of mind for a bit upon reaching the end of fruitful disciplined planning. Typically, the topic of the presentation will come to mind at those times when one's attention is not directly engaged. When a person is driving a car, walking, doing routine chores like mowing a lawn or cleaning a house, or shortly before dropping asleep at night, thoughts about important matters often tumble through the consciousness. The images are sometimes free associative and fragmentary and, on occasion, ridiculous, but many times during these periods of purposive daydreaming an important organizing principle will come to mind or a particularly apt illustration or anecdote to be used in the presentation will surface.

Many busy and productive people keep a notebook or note cards to jot down ideas that occur to them during such periods. Quite often they have these handy by their bedside, for example, if they are likely to get an idea before going to sleep. The best presentations often result from a particularly happy insight arrived at during one of the mulling around periods that reveals a basic pattern or structure for the whole topic of the presentations. In this book we refer to these experiences as "holistic" information processing.

Some psychologists refer to an insight of this sort as an "ah ha" experience because a light suddenly turns on and illuminates the entire problem. When one has an authentic "ah ha" experience, the feeling that accompanies it is one of excitement and pleasurable anticipation. A person wants to try out the idea and see if it will work and if it is, indeed, as elegant and gratifying as it seems. The testing or verification of the insight requires systematic disciplined thought.

After a person finishes a careful verification of the ideas developed during the creative phrase of analysis, the result will be an outline of the topic. Subpoints will be arranged in a logical progression, so that moving them about arbitrarily would do violence to the chain of reasoning which they represent, and all of them relate to the major theme. With the final verification, this first stage of the preparation comes to a close.

The Audience-Adaptation Stage. After a sound analysis of the topic, the speaker has a thorough understanding of the material. The job of preparation for a presentation is not yet finished, however, because good speakers do not simply present every audience with the analysis they found convincing, for what is necessary to convince them may be different from what is necessary to convince their listeners. Untrained persons often want to include everything that led to their understanding of the question and find time limitations frustrating. If a person wants to present the complete analysis that results from months of study and labor by a division of the organization, thirty minutes or an hour is too short, but the occasion does not usually require the complete analysis. The presentation is set up to give key people only that part of the analysis that they require to do the job. On the other hand, speakers may be so sophisticated in the job that even fragmentary items in the analysis are more meaningful to them, but for the listeners they must be spelled out, amplified, and made operational.

Presentational speaking is a subfield of the ancient art of rhetoric whose essence is to take information already in mind and artistically fashion it for a specific audience and occasion. For our concerns, therefore, the second phase of message preparation is crucial. In the second phase the speaker with a thorough understanding of the topic begins to analyze the audience to discover the best way to present all or part of the ideas to them.

Again the preparation in the second phase should be disciplined and systematic at times and at others should be more free wheeling. What is the formal organizational context for the presentation? What is the formal status, authority, and responsibility of the message source? What is the receiver's formal position? What do speakers know of the actual power and esteem of their listeners? What about listeners' individual idiosyncrasies, interests, attitudes, drives, and preoccupations? Jamison had already gone through the first stage, he knew what he wanted to say, and he thoroughly understood his case. What he needed was help with the second stage of preparation when he adapted and organized his material for the twenty minutes he had with the board.

We now turn to our recommended patterns, the six designs for speeches that help to answer the key question, "How can I arrange my materials to best achieve their potential effectiveness?"

SIX BASIC PATTERNS FOR PRESENTATIONS

Patterns of organization are strategies of arrangement that simplify the task of the presenter who confronts the problem of deciding on and implementing a format for the final speaker-audience interaction. You will recall the "Purposes of Presentations" continuum in Chapter 1 and the distinctions we made among three kinds of purposes: limiting options to one, establishing direction (with a limited number of options), and maximizing options. By considering the best ways of achieving these categories of purposes, we have derived six organizational patterns. Three patterns are suited to situations that attempt to limit options to one, two are appropriate when the purpose is to establish direction, and one fits nicely when the objective is to expand or maximize options. We provide examples of these patterns of action in the Appendix. There the reader will find a detailed outline, description of context, speaker's notes, and other details of presentation illustrating the application of each of the six patterns.

Selecting an Appropriate Pattern of Organization to Advance a Single Proposal.   "Advancing a single proposal" is another way of saying "limiting options to one." If the job the presenter undertakes is to persuade the audience that a recommendation (plan or proposal) should be adopted, accepted, or implemented, then one of the following three patterns will serve well as an organizing device.

State the case and prove it.   One of the earliest and most famous books on preparing material for oral presentation that has survived from antiquity is attributed to the famous Greek philosopher Aristotle. In that work, the *Rhetoric,* Aristotle suggested that speakers met the minimal organization requirement when they stated their case and proved it. The pattern is a straightforward development of a central thesis by supporting elements, each of which begins with a topic sentence (a contention) followed by supporting material. Typically, the pattern would consist of

1. Introduction.
2. Proposition (thesis).
3. Contention 1, plus support.
4. Contention 2, plus support (etc.).
5. Summary and reiteration of the proposition.

An oversimplified version of the state-your-case-and-prove-it pattern is "Tell them what you're going to tell them, tell them, and then tell them what you told them."

The particular utility of the state-your-case-and-prove-it pattern is found in handling familiar, much argued topics of controversy. When a person addresses a well-worn issue that the audience has heard discussed many times, there is little reason to explore it comprehensively and gradually develop it. Usually, one is well advised to state a position, and support it as clearly and systematically as possible.

The introduction of a presentation based on the state-your-case-and-prove-it pattern is nearly always an explanation of why it is necessary and appropriate to reopen discussion of an unresolved problem on this occasion. Probably recent events, or new knowledge, have modified a previously stable situation, and the old controversy needs to be reexamined in a new light. If successful, the introduction will leave the audience eager to learn the effects of the new situation on the old problem.

The central thesis is usually stated immediately after the brief introduction. If the central thesis is stated clearly and highlighted by the speaker's manner of delivery, the audience will remember it as the main idea of the speech and test every argument and bit of evidence to see if these do, indeed, support the proposition.

Contentions with proof for each follow the proposition. The speaker indicates that the contentions logically support the proposition by means of clear comments and transitions. The speech ends with a summary that is not simply a mechanical repetition of the contentions but that is an effective reminder of the highlights of the evidence and reasoning taken from the several contentions. Reiteration of the proposition terminates the speech, encouraging the audience to reflect once more on the adequacy of the proof that was presented. If the proof is conclusive, the reasonable auditor finds it difficult to resist the recommendation.

Impromptu 1.　A variation of state-your-case-and-prove-it has developed from the experiences of many speakers who were forced to make a presentation when preparation time was minimal. It can be used even on those occasions when, without warning, someone tells you the audience is expecting you to "say a few words" within the next ten or twenty minutes! We call this variation of stating your case and proving it the "impromptu 1" pattern, because it serves the cause of impromptu speaking—speaking with little specific preparation—so well.

Impromptu 1
1. *Begin* with an illustration.
2. Overview (number points).
3. Follow through (cover each point in turn).
4. Recap, with a *twist*.

The impromptu variation begins, *without explanation,* with an example. The speaker simply supplies an illustration, preferably one with human interest and visual imagery, that is intimately involved with the topic and the audience. The speaker does not say, "I am going to talk about . . ." or set the stage for the example in any way. The speaker just begins and tells it, and the resulting response is twofold: high interest, and curiosity as to what the purpose of the illustration may be.

The second step is the overview (state what you will talk about), consisting of listing and numbering the points to be covered by the presentation. For example, the speaker says, "Today I'm going to make three points, first . . . second . . . and third . . ." The points should be crisp and concise in their wording. The third step is to carry out the speaker's commitment to develop the points in the promised order.

When the numbered points have been covered, the speaker rounds out and ends the speech with the fourth part of the pattern, which is a recap, with a "twist." A recap is an extremely short reminder of each point talked about, in different language. The "twist" is a surprise ending that makes the speech sound finished by referring back to the opening example with a tie-in that shows the relevance of the introduction and unifies the speech.

The impression produced by (1) an opening example that is central to the presentation, (2) a crisp, numbered overview that is meticulously carried out, and (3) a "twist" ending that sensibly relates the conclusion to the beginning is that the speech is thoughtfully planned and well organized. Audiences tend to believe that if speakers can remember how they began at the end of the speech, they must have prepared it very carefully indeed!

In actuality, impromptu 1 turned out to be useful in other than impromptu situations, and it met the needs of varied presentations so well that the anticipated modifications of the pattern, 2, 3, and so on, were not developed. The authors are somewhat concerned because this pattern is so easy to learn and use, and it produces a speech that is so obviously well organized that many neophyte speakers are inclined to use no other arrangement. Hence, we caution the reader to avoid relying totally on impromptu 1. You will find it useful but no universal panacea. On many occasions another pattern would be more successful.

Psychological-progression pattern.   One of the most used and useful patterns of speech organization is the psychological-progression pattern, the third and final basic arrangement for limiting options to one. It brings together logical and nonlogical modes of thinking and feeling to evolve a solid persuasive presentation. The psychological-progression pattern was first discovered by evangelical preachers in the early part of the nineteenth century. In more recent times Charles H. Woolbert and Andrew T. Weaver applied the findings of contemporary psychology to the problems of public speaking and grouped all purposes of speaking into five categories: (1) attentiveness, (2) understanding, (3) deciding, (4) acting publicly, and (5) yielding fully. Alan H. Monroe adapted these ideas to public speaking in an attractive pattern that he called a "motivated sequence." His arrangement has served as a basic plan for a public speaker in a series of popular textbooks.

The psychological-progression pattern is an adaptation of the historically effective structure to the particular needs of the presentational speaker. It consists of five steps: (1) arouse, (2) dissatisfy, (3) gratify, (4) picture, and (5) move.

An attractive feature of the psychological-progression pattern is the ease with which it can be remembered. Five key words, each indicating clearly the purpose of that part of the speech, arranged in an order that follows so naturally that the steps are not ordinarily interchanged, result in the person, having once become acquainted with the sequence, finding it difficult to forget. Many people who give frequent speeches use the five divisions as a means of adapting to different audiences. In an automobile or on a plane they can rearrange familiar speech materials by asking themselves questions about the specific audience they will next confront. How will I *arouse* the audience's interest? How can I *dissatify* them by showing them the mess we are in? How can I show them that my recommendation will *gratify* the need? How can I get these people to *picture* the concrete results when my recommendation is implemented? How can I *move* them to act appropriately and expeditiously on my proposal?

Another virtue of the psychological-progression pattern is that a person can eliminate some of the early steps to fit the needs of an audience that is already interested in the topic or that is already aware of the mess that it is facing. Such an audience will be ready and waiting to hear the speaker's gratifying proposal. When planning a presentation using the psychological-progression pattern, a person should estimate the audience's willingness to bypass the first couple of steps, for it may become impatient if the speaker insists on discussing them when the audience is already in agreement.

By now the reader has probably noted that the psychological-progression outline has a rationale that differs profoundly from the rationale of the state-the-case-and-prove-it and impromptu 1 patterns. We have mentioned that the psychological-progression approach is both logical and nonlogical. The other two patterns rely heavily on the cognitive perspective of presentational speaking for their rationale. This does not mean that information supplied in a speech using psychological progression is not considered thoughtfully and "logically" by the listeners. Rather, a logical structure is reinforced by the holistic perspective as represented by emotional and suggestive elements much more in the psychological-progression pattern than in the other two outlines.

If a speaker using the psychological-progression pattern succeeds in getting an audience dissatisfied, and then relieves the listeners of that unhappy condition by gratifying them, the change is psychological rather than logical. Validity and truth are not the primary criteria for developing and evaluating a speech using psychological progression, although these are necessary to the reasoned core of the persuasion. A successful presentation using psychological progression triggers powerful impulsive responses that sweep the listeners along on a wave of feelings and desires. While state-the-case-and-prove-it and impromptu 1 patterns are designed to generate thoughtful symbol responses, the psychological-progression outline not only relies on the critical faculties of the listeners, but also adds appeals intended to produce suggestive, signal responses to the symbols in the presentation. When a presenter wishes to increase emotional tensions, build enthusiasm, and set the stage for immediate action, the psychological-progression pattern offers many advantages.

We hope that the reader at this point is curious about integrating reason and suggestion, signal and symbol responses, and managing emotions. These important and fundamental topics are treated in detail in Chapter 5.

Selecting an Appropriate Pattern of Organization to Establish a General Direction.   The presentations continuum in Chapter 1 provides a middle ground between the goals of advocating a single proposal and stimulating explorations of a maximum number of possibilities. We term this intermediate purpose "establishing a general direction." When a presenter wishes to discourage further work on some segments of a problem and encourage vigorous development of others, the job to be done is to establish a direction for the undertaking. If successful, the presentation results in the group concentrating their expenditure of energy in a manner that the presenter believes to be the most productive. By eliminating the less promising options, the presenter hopes that progress will be made toward a limited number of the best possibilities and, ultimately, toward consensus.

There are two ways a presenter can set about establishing directions. One is to use the method of induction in which all possible directions are surveyed and compared. As a result, those judged to be less fruitful are assigned low priorities. The other, the cease-and-desist pattern, makes no claim of being comprehensive as does the inductive exploration of possibilities. Cease and desist, as the name suggests, selects one aspect of the problem, condemns it as wasteful of time and resources, and recommends that work pointing in this direction be terminated. When it succeeds, the cease-and-desist pattern contributes to problem solution by "killing off" certain superficially attractive but unsound options.

Now we turn to more detailed explanations of the two organizational patterns suited to establishing a general direction.

Inductive exploration of possibilities.   The inductive pattern is particularly useful in two situations: (1) when the problem is complicated and hostility is anticipated, and (2) when the problem is complicated and the audience is relatively unfamiliar with the facts involved. The great strength of the inductive approach is that it provides an easy-to-follow order in a topic that might well be baffling and chaotic. The bases for the inductive pattern are the sequential steps in problem-solving, introduced by the philosopher-educator John Dewey at the beginning of the twentieth century. Dewey observed how the trained mind attacked a problem in the scientific laboratory. He noted the way an individual begins reflective thinking with a felt difficulty—an irritation or disturbance that sets the person to puzzling or acting to relieve the tension. He discussed the way a person casts about and tries to discover the reason for the felt difficulty. As the vague feeling of perplexity comes under rational analysis, the causes of the problem become clearer and the mind leaps forward to suggest possible solutions. Trial-and-error problem-solving is characterized by trying each solution as it pops into the mind. Reflective thinking, on the other hand, postpones the implementation of a solution until the representative answers have been weighed pro and con. Only after methodical reflection does the person select the best of the solutions to try.

Dewey's analysis provides the basis for a step-by-step consideration of a problem beginning with an introduction, definition of the problem, exploration of the problem, listing and examinations of representative solutions, and selection of the best solution.

Dewey's famous inductive method had its roots in the scientific laboratory, in situations where a single best solution was the necessary outcome. Our application of the inductive approach to presentational speaking uses only Dewey's first three steps:

1. Introduction.
2. Definition of the problem.
3. Exploration of the problem.

In a situation in which further exploration and the development of solutions remain to be done, proceeding to a final solution is obviously premature. Our pattern substitutes for the last two steps of the Dewey analysis the following points:

4. What directions can we identify in what we have done so far?
5. From this point on, how should we proceed?

The objective of the inductive exploration of possibilities in a presentation is to refine and make more efficient further individual and group work on a problem. Therefore, it is necessary to keep selected directions open for new solutions, ideas, and procedures.

This pattern designed from Dewey's analysis of reflective thinking leads listeners to be objective and thoughtful and disarms them of some of their prejudices as they are led along what appears to be a completely reasonable sequence. Hostility is difficult to maintain in the face of a completely open investigation of a problem, through the inductive procedure. The speaker says, now let us define the problem so we all agree on just what it is and what it is not. Then the presenter says, let us explore the problem just defined to discover what caused it, what its effects are, and what criteria must be met. The openness of the pattern leads even persons with prejudice to follow along thoughtfully, examining facts and interpreting them in each step. If the speaker is comprehensive and thorough, and the speaker reasons soundly, it will be difficult for competent thinkers in the audience to avoid joining in determining future directions.

In the second circumstance, when the audience is less than informed on facts of the case, the inductive development of the topic furnishes a natural framework to convey essential information. In short, the inductive approach is an excellent teaching device as well as an effective means of persuasion. In defining and exploring the problem, elementary facts can be tactfully mentioned by prefacing them with "As you know . . ." or "You will recall . . ." and so on.

One caution to speakers using the inductive pattern: because its posture is one of objective problem-solving, that is, applying the scientific method to human affairs, any emotive or "loaded" language is out of place. The ideal manner of speaking to implement the inductive approach is "report language," the matter-of-fact, direct, and "unloaded" use of words that minimizes emotional response. Even a single prejudicial term may seem so out of place and improper that it could imperil the outcome of the presentation.

Cease-and-desist pattern of organization.   The inductive exploration of possibilities is appropriate when the presenter intends a joint venture with the audience, where speaker and audience combine forces to decide priorities in future directions. When the presenter's objective is to reduce options by eliminating selected directions, the inductive approach is quite unsuitable. Rather than asking the audience to review possibilities and directions, the cease-and-desist speaker asks them to concentrate on one. The purpose of such a presentation is to convince the audience that the object of the attack, a phase of investigation and development already underway, is going in the wrong direction. We will be better off, the speaker tells the audience, to cease and desist in this effort and turn our interests and energies elsewhere.

Working organizations and individuals frequently waste money, time, and talents pursuing directions that have become unrewarding. Perhaps the respected American maxim "Never give up" is responsible in part for the willingness of intelligent persons to keep trying to get the flying machine airborne after it has passed the point of no return and the wheels are still on the runway. Why we should conceptualize abandoning an unproductive venture as failure is difficult to explain. Often it would be better if we said, "Oops, this certainly isn't working. I'm doing something positive and constructive in dropping the project and taking the loss!"

When a failing direction is dear to the heart of an upper level manager, the presenter who would use the cease-and-desist approach faces some delicate decision-making. The principle we have advocated of talking about a coming presentation with all concerned people applies here. The individual with warm affection for the suspect phase of the program should be consulted first. A gently reasonable review of the history, present circumstances, and future trends may persuade the partisan to join the presenter in sponsoring a closer examination of the direction in question. Of course, if the addiction to the faltering activity on the part of its supporters is unyielding, it may be impossible to secure collaboration. But in any event the foremost supporter of the target of the cease-and-desist effort should be thoroughly informed about the plans for the presentation.

The delicate decision-making occurs when the presenter estimates the amount of support that exists for the program under attack. If a heavy-handed, roll-over-the-opposition-by-majority-vote situation seems to be developing, a wise choice may be to work out a compromise of modification. If defenders of the defective element are numerous, firmly convinced, and powerful, the time for taking action against the wasteful program may not have arrived. The presenter may then opt for a postponement of the presentation until a more suitable time.

The point we are making here is that many forces other than facts of the case enter into deciding either to go ahead with the cease-and-desist presentation or to seek other means of changing the status quo. Vested interests, personal relationships, and previous commitments are examples of important elements that seldom yield to quantitative analysis and logical demonstration. Here the would-be presenter "senses the situation" and pays attention to the holistic information processing that is commonly termed "intuition." When out-of-awareness common sense tells the change agent that too many toes will be stepped on, and that the upset conditions following the attempt to stop the program will outweigh the benefits, proceeding with the presentation may well be unwise. Similarly, if a powerful hunch informs the agent that the audience, although superficially supportive of the program to be attacked, is ready to turn against it, proceeding with the cease-and-desist attempt may be an appropriate choice.

We have stressed "mulling over" as a vital part of the preparation process. "Mulling over" may produce insights of great value that are too often disregarded by persons who insist on tangible, concrete data for all substantive decisions. Feelings and emotions often prevail, and hence must be recognized and dealt with. Thoughtful rationality is helpful but insufficient for assessing these ingredients of decision-making and predicting their effects.

Cease-and-desist pattern

1. Introduction.
2. Quick enumeration of present procedures.
3. Selection of one procedure as least productive.

4. Reasons and evidence showing this option lacks potential.
5. Advantages of diverting resources elsewhere.
6. The cease-and-desist recommendation.

The introduction step should explain the purpose of the presentation —for example, to consider a possibility that might save time, money, resources, and increase efficiency.

The quick enumeration of procedures is precisely that, a survey of the directions the organization is presently taking. This step is brief and skeletal. Directions are identified, but not explained or illustrated.

Selection of one procedure as least productive informs the audience that the remainder of the presentation will be devoted to close examination of this option. Here the cease-and-desist pattern begins to resemble the state-the-case-and-prove-it approach. The presenter at this point is committed to argue against an ongoing operation and promises to prove that it is unworthy of support.

The fourth and fifth step do the work of the presentation, the preceding steps having set the stage. In Step 4 the speaker presents proof in the form of reasons and evidence showing this option lacks potential. Step 5, advantages of diverting resources elsewhere, is the positive, constructive complement to the negativity of Step 4. This step shows how resources made available by the termination of the unproductive procedure can be put to use to greater advantage in ongoing directions or in opening a new frontier. A carefully developed Step 5 enables the speaker to finish his or her presentation on a strong, positive, optimistic note.

The final step, the cease-and-desist recommendation, shows in as much detail as possible how the weak program can be phased out. It suggests adjustments in utilization of personnel and other resources to smooth the transition to the new order. It stresses the need for immediate action and invites questions, comments, and suggestions.

A successful cease-and-desist presentation resembles a surgical operation in which a foreign growth is excised to the benefit of the parent organism. It is a drastic and conclusive maneuver. Its incisiveness makes it risky. But when circumstances make it appropriate, it meets a need no other approach can satisfy as well.

Selecting an Appropriate Pattern of Organization to Expand Options. As we have seen, advancing a single proposal is a sharply focused, unidirectional operation, while establishing a general direction points the way in a less precise fashion. Expanding options is a contrasting objective. Here we are interested in stimulating people to think new thoughts, discover unexplored directions, and conceive innovative possibilities. Instead of limiting or channeling responses, exploration of new territories and formulation of fresh hypotheses are the desired outcomes. Of the six patterns for organizing presentations, this is the one dedicated to encouraging creativity, to spanning boundaries instead of creating or conforming to them.

To serve the unique purpose of expanding options, we recommend a single organizational pattern, creative program development.

Creative program development
1. Define the problem.
2. Explore the problem area.
3. Identify possible directions.
4. Apply brainstorming techniques.
5. Consolidate without restrictions.

Step 1, defining the problem, is somewhat tricky in a creative development approach because at this stage the precise nature of the problem is unclear. There is a felt difficulty, but the variables involved have not been listed and the relationships among them are poorly understood. The presentational speaker must make clear that the efforts to define the problem are tentative and subject to revision as interaction with the audience occurs. However, the presenter boldly attempts definition, going beyond the data into guesswork, always calling attention to the fact that these personal opinions may well be in error. If the experimental attitude is conveyed successfully, the audience's interest will be aroused and its involvement in the joint venture will increase.

The "explore the problem area" step actually continues efforts to define the problem but goes beyond definition to pin down constituent elements. What are the factors that combine to produce the felt difficulty? What variables must be dealt with? Which relevant circumstances can be changed and which cannot be modified? At the end of the problem exploration step, the presenter and the audience should share a fairly precise, tentative definition of the problem and a list of difficulties to be overcome.

Step 3, identify possible directions, is a preliminary priming of the pump to facilitate the brainstorming activity to follow. The presenter asks the audience to speculate about general procedures that might possibly be fruitful. No specific action proposals are appropriate here. Rather, the audience and the presenter talk about what sort of effort might yield results if implemented by the right activities. Step 3 is a survey technique, outlining fundamentally different ways of attacking the problem. A good guideline for the presenter in managing this step is, *keep it brief.*

Ideally, creativity takes over and becomes productive in Step 4. The presenter conducts a brainstorming session in which any idea, direction, or proposal related to the problem is admitted. The original brainstorming rules created by Alex T. Osborne should be followed:

1. Criticism is ruled out.
2. Free wheeling of ideas is welcomed.
3. Quantity of ideas rather than quality is emphasized.
4. Hitchhiking (adding onto) or modification of an idea is encouraged.

Contributions are recorded on a blackboard or on a flip chart by someone who writes quickly and legibly, or preferably by two recorders, handling alternate items. The brainstorming rules are generally known, but because they are so important we will explain them briefly. No criticism or comparison of items is permitted, since all evaluation is postponed to a later time. Welcoming free wheeling means that wild and far-fetched contributions are encouraged, since an apparently frivolous idea often leads to something practical and useful. Emphasizing quantity of ideas and disregarding quality suggest that the goal is as long a list of ideas as possible. The worth of a final solution seems to be related to the number of items from which it emerges. Encouraging hitchhiking means giving priority to a contribution that refines or extends a previous contribution.

Time allotted to the brainstorming activity should be no longer than twenty or thirty minutes. The complete list of recorded items should be duplicated and a copy sent promptly to each participant. Elaboration of options takes place in the following days and weeks. People remember the brainstorming, occasionally look at the transcribed items, and by mulling over these matters tend to develop new insights.

After the brainstorming session, the presenter concludes the presentation with a step we label "consolidate without restrictions." This cannot be prepared in advance, as happenings during the event are then unknown. It may be wise to mention high points of the audience-speaker interaction as the speaker perceives them. Certainly, the presenter should request that the participants read and think about the items they have developed in the brainstorming period. Afterthoughts are as important as the brainstormed items, so an easy, direct avenue to get these to the presenter should be provided.

Six unique patterns of organization serving three kinds of purposes have been presented. As mentioned earlier, illustrative examples of each can be found in the Appendix. We trust that the reader has noted how each pattern differs from the others and has come to appreciate the importance of careful diagnosis of a situation, definition of the precise purpose of a particular presentation, and selection of the appropriate pattern. Although it is possible to combine patterns, our observation is that a better organized performance results when a selected pattern is followed closely. We believe that the organization process is sufficiently important that we are justified in giving the presenter three bits of advice: (1) organize, (2) refine the organization, and (3) organize once more.

THE USE OF NOTES

In the case studies in the Appendix that illustrate the patterns of organization, we have included notes used by the speakers during the presentations. This may give the reader the impression that notes are a necessity and that all speakers should use them. Of course, this is not the case. We can generalize that all speakers tend to use more notes than they need and to stare at their notes instead of maintaining contact with their audience. People who are completely familiar with their subject need no notes. To some degree, notes break the contact speakers have with their listeners. To use them when they are not needed is to place oneself under an unnecessary handicap.

On some occasions notes may be necessary. When speakers wish to be absolutely accurate about statistical information, direct quotations from authorities, or factual detail, they may need to have the information before them. Some individuals feel much more confident and thus improve their delivery when they can have a brief outline of their presentation available should they need it.

Speakers who are using notes should not try to hide that fact from the audience. Listeners who discover that a speaker is trying to hide the notes often become diverted from the ideas in the presentation in their eagerness to catch the speaker's furtive references to the cards. The best procedure is to use notes openly and only when absolutely necessary. Speakers ought to guard against the tendency to glance at their notes whenever they lose their poise. Looking down to keep from looking at the audience can become a bad habit.

Speakers should also be careful not to twist, bend, or rumple their notes in a random aimless way, for audiences are often distracted by such movements.

The person who wishes to speak without notes does not memorize the details of the presentation but concentrates on getting the major points of the outline in mind. Speakers who remember the three main points can then turn to the first point and memorize the two subpoints under it, and so on. By getting the organizational pattern firmly in mind, persons making a presentation can largely do away with manuscript or detailed notes and free themselves for speaking directly to the listeners.

We should mention something about notes that many of our readers have figured out for themselves. Properly prepared visual aids may make notes unnecessary. In addition, when an overhead projector is used, notes can be written on the cardboard mounting of a transparency.

SUMMARY

Designing the presentation begins with understanding the context in which it occurs. This includes identifying the resources available and the circumstances that will aid or obstruct communication in the spoken presentation.

The earmarks of a sound organization are unity, coherence, relevance, conciseness, and comprehensiveness. Flexible preparation of the message occurs in two stages: analysis and audience adaptation.

Serving the three kinds of purposes of presentations—limiting options to one, establishing direction, and maximizing options—requires basically different strategies of organization. Six organizational patterns meet these needs: (1) state the case and prove it, (2) impromptu 1, (3) psychological progression, (4) inductive exploration of possibilities, (5) cease and desist, and (6) creative program development.

Preparation of notes is a final step in arranging materials for the speaker-audience interaction that is the presentational speech.

Because persuasion is all-important to many presentations Chapter 5 shows how to increase a presentation's persuasive effectiveness.

QUESTIONS FOR DISCUSSION AND REVIEW

1. How do the two central elements of presentation of recommendation and presentation of self relate to one another and to the presentational speech itself?
2. What is the key question to be answered in designing any presentational speech? How can answering the question help in preparing the presentation?
3. What are the two stages in flexible preparation of the message? How can each be accomplished flexibly?
4. How do analytic and holistic processes contribute to the analysis stage of preparation?
5. How does a properly worded proposition help in selecting material?
6. What are the differences among unity, coherence, relevance, conciseness, and comprehensiveness?
7. What are the three organizational patterns "to advance a single proposal"? How do they resemble and differ from one another?
8. When presenters wish to "establish a general direction," on what basis might they choose between the inductive exploration of possibilities and the cease-and-desist patterns of organizing materials?
9. What aspect of the creative program development pattern facilitates expanding options?
10. How should presenters use notes appropriately and productively while speaking?

REFERENCES AND SUGGESTED READINGS

For a review of reasoned supports in persuasive presentations, see:

Ross, Raymond S. *Speech Communication: Fundamentals and Practice.* 7th ed. Englewood Cliffs, N.J.: Prentice-Hall, 1986.

For help in increasing both interest and understanding of holistic information processing, see:

Ferguson, Marilyn. *The Aquarian Conspiracy: Personal and Social Transformations in the 1980s.* Los Angeles: J. P. Tarcher, Inc., 1980.

Orrstein, Robert E. *The Psychology of Consciousness.* San Francisco: W. H. Freeman, 1972.

For the sources of Dewey's analysis of problem-solving in terms of reflective thinking, see:

Dewey, John. *How We Think.* Boston: D. C. Heath, 1910.

For a description of the psychology of conversion, see:

Tracy, Joseph. *The Great Awakening: A History of the Revival of Religion in the Time of Edwards and Whitefield.* Boston: Tappan and Dennet, 1842.
For the early development of the psychological-progression pattern, see:
Monroe, Alan H. *Principles and Types of Speech.* 6th ed. Chicago: Scott, Foresman, 1964.
Woolbert, Charles H., and Andrew T. Weaver. *Better Speech.* New York: Harcourt, Brace, 1922.

chapter *5*

Increasing the Presentation's Persuasive Power

Before we set about to increase the presentation's persuasive power, we would do well to examine "persuasion" as a process. Precisely what is persuasion, and how does it relate to and affect other kinds of communication? Is persuasion a wholesome and socially beneficial activity, or is it a sneaky, subversive, unworthy means of influence?

Let us begin with a definition: *persuasion is communication intended to influence choice*. According to this definition persuasion is communication, but only one kind: that which is intended to induce someone to prefer one option over another. Thus, the intention to persuade makes the communication persuasive. Influencing choice, then, is the business of this particular category of communication, and the distinctive element about the outcome is that the person to be persuaded has choice. The listener can choose whether or not to be influenced. The fact that the act of being influenced is voluntary makes persuasion different from coercion, which relies on force or threat of force to influence people. Securing compliance by persuasion is a matter of winning willing cooperation, whereas accomplishing this end through coercion is, expressed metaphorically, arm twisting.

We Americans must believe that persuasion is socially beneficial because we choose our leaders and settle our differences by encouraging competing persuasions to vie for our willing cooperation. Moreover, the Anglo-American system of jurisprudence seeks justice through professional persuaders contending before a judge or jury. Persuasion is an integral part of our way of life.

Other kinds of communication found in presentations are *information* and *entertainment.* A good persuasive presentation informs (teaches unknown facts and circumstances) and entertains (is interesting and fun to listen to). Persuading, informing, and entertaining are not mutually exclusive, as is popularly believed. All are done competently in any successful presentation. How can we sort out these functions if they are mixed together, thoroughly and artistically? The answer is, by applying the concept of *predominant purpose.*

In Chapter 4 we discussed the three patterns of organization to advance a single proposal which have as their predominant purpose persuasion. The inductive exploration of possibilities pattern is meant predominantly to inform, the cease-and-desist pattern to persuade, and creative program development is mainly to inform. However, all presentations, regardless of their patterns of organization or predominant purposes, should be entertaining, informative, and persuasive. Selecting as a predominant purpose one of these three never excludes the other two; it simply assigns a secondary importance to them.

The persuasive power of a message is increased in three ways: (1) by supplying good reasons and sound evidence, (2) by securing impulsive unthinking responses, and (3) by arousing appropriate emotions.

RECURRING FALLACIES OF PRESENTATION

The persuasive power of a message is increased by supplying good reasons and sound evidence, as noted above, but it is also increased by bad reasoning and unsound evidence that are perceived as good. Fallacies, those units of unsound argument that may be mistakenly accepted as valid, can be used intentionally to deceive audiences, but more often presenters deceive themselves. They advance fallacies in the sincere belief that they are contributing critical thinking to the discussion. Three particular fallacies persist because of their persuasive power: the *post hoc,* the hasty generalization, and the either-or analysis. These occur so frequently and their effects are so devastating to thoughtful response that we will explain and comment on each in turn.

Post hoc **Fallacy.**   The complete Latin name for this classic fallacy explains its nature: *post hoc, ergo propter hoc;* after this, therefore because of this. Its deceptive effect is a result of the unwarranted assumption that because two events are related in time sequence, the first is the cause of the second. Since causes precede consequences, it is easy to believe that an earlier related happening brought about modification of present circumstances, that a causal "connection" indeed exists.

Republican administrations are associated with depressions and Democratic administrations with wars in the United States because of *post hoc* thinking. Republicans took office and a severe recession followed, leading to the instant conclusion that the new regime was responsible. Wars were begun or declared in Democratic administrations. Therefore, Democratic leadership causes wars. Other variables that functioned as partial causes, many of them in the nature of trends over long periods of years, are ignored.

Post hoc interpretations are attractive because of their simplicity. A somewhat dramatic incident is followed by a significant, atypical event. The human mind, perpetually in search of explanations, makes an inductive leap to account for the event by assuming that the prior incident was responsible. The fallacy is abetted by our loose use of the language of causal relation. We talk of single causes when multiple causes are necessarily operating, as: "What was the cause of World War II?" Similarly, we are careless in using words to predict effects: "If we automate that operation in the assembly line, the union will strike the plant." Our habitual thinking is undisciplined in accepting oversimplified explanations of phenomena and in taking for granted causal relationships for which there is little or no proof.

Post hoc thinking often results from a failure to note that both the apparent cause and effect may be effects of a more remote causation. A sensible challenge to the belief that smoking cigarettes causes cancer of the lungs is the hypothesis that the heavy smoker has a neurophysiological makeup that facilitates both smoking and cancer. Reorganization of an enterprise frequently involves a change in leadership. If, subsequently, the organizational machinery runs more smoothly, the almost universal interpretation will be that the new leader caused the improvement. In most cases among the many variables, organizational changes probably influence the shape of the new order more than do the actions of the person who is imported or promoted. Generally, the higher the status of the officeholder, the more the new leader is credited with influencing people and events. Sometimes it seems that the President of the United States is considered to be the cause of everything that happens during and immediately after his administration.

To avoid the *post hoc* fallacy, a speaker must distinguish cause and effect from another important logical operation, reasoning from concomitant variation. To make the point that two variables are associated in a concomitant variation is simply to show that they occur together, reliably. This is useful knowledge. Not long ago in medical research when a drug was found to relieve the symptoms of a disease, the drug was not released for use until cause-and-effect actions had been discovered. Tracing cause-and-effect connections through the human body often consumed years of labor. Now to a significant degree concomitant variation has replaced causation as a laboratory research method. If administration of a drug reliably accompanies relief of symptoms of a disease, after a check to make sure there are no serious, undesirable side effects the drug can be marketed and distress can be alleviated.

The critical listener is ever alert to the possibility that the speaker may confuse time sequence with a cause-and-effect relationship. The listener knows that sound cause-to-effect or effect-to-cause arguments are rare, because of multiple variables present in all human interactions. When a speaker uses the language of concomitant variation and resists the temptation to talk loosely about causes and results, the listener can be assured that the speaker appreciates the deceptiveness of *post hoc* thinking.

The Fallacy of Hasty Generalization.   A lay definition of the hasty generalization fallacy is "jumping to conclusions." While this is a figurative rather than an operational definition, it suggests very nicely the essence of hasty generalization: making a premature statement of definite and sweeping character that goes far beyond available supporting materials. The *post hoc* fallacy may be considered a special instance of hasty generalization, one in which the cause is assumed. Typically, however, *no* evidence of causation exists in *post hoc,* and hasty generalizations are made from some, but inadequate evidence.

We will list several types of hasty generalization, and our readers can discover other categories. A popular form generalizes about a class of phenomena from a single instance. "Adapt this plan of participative management? We tried it five years ago, but it didn't work." The implication, not often stated in so many words is, "If one attempt to implement participative management failed, all other such attempts are doomed to failure." Here, as is often the case with fallacious reasoning, stating the implied assumption reveals the absurdity of the argument.

Another much used and abused hasty generalization makes statements about groups of people or phenomena, asserting similarities without factual evidence. The sources of these statements are usually legend or folklore. Strangely, because the base of such a generalization is a well-known belief or stereotype, many accept it as soundly reasoned. Here are current examples: "Bosses are not interested in the welfare of their employees." "Members of a labor union will attempt to restrict production." "Companies with extensive data processing equipment are cold and impersonal places to work." "Colleges are Ivory Towers that fail to teach people how to make a living." "Salesmen have to be supervised or they won't do their work." "Policemen mistreat their prisoners." "Ministers cheat on their income tax." Hasty generalizations like these resemble mottos or maxims that people persist in believing in spite of their contradictory nature, as is the case with "A stitch in time saves nine" and "Haste makes waste."

When hasty generalizations about people and events occur in a presentation, they usually fill the role of a basic assumption. "Since this is known to be true" reasons the speaker, "it should guide our decision, and we should do thus and so." Attention is thus turned away from the generalization, and critical listeners must remind themselves to ask, "Is there any proof for that sweeping statement?"

A third kind of hasty generalization "loads the dice" by concluding from a collection of unrepresentative instances. You can make any kind of generalization about the interests, personalities, or abilities of college professors or executives that you wish to make—providing you control your sample. If we study five professors who are homosexual, artistic, and impractical, we can conclude logically that our sample is homosexual, artistic, and impractical, but we cannot logically say anything about "college professors" from our research. But people tend to draw conclusions about an entire population from samples as biased as this one. The distortion is made palatable by suppression of the clearly implied word "all"; instead of "all college professors are thus and so" we say "college professors are—." A confusing ambiguity is introduced, and the speaker, if challenged, can reply "I didn't say *all,*" a weasel way to avoid responsibility for the claim. Listeners will be aided in their search for suspect generalizations if they supply the word "all" when they feel it has been omitted.

Another fallacy of hasty generalization is the application of a sound normative conclusion to an individual instance. Practically all sound generalizations are statements of central tendency; that is, they imply the words "by and large" rather than "each and every." Consequently, they admit there are occasional exceptions, and any single case may be one of those exceptions. "Executives are more intelligent than their employees" is a sound generalization, but it would be fallacious to say, "Therefore, boss Simpson is smarter than electrician Voltsman." Attributing a trait of a group to a member is similarly unjustified. "Baggage handlers are brawny so Muscles O'Donovan must be brawny" is bad reasoning, for Muscles may be an exception, a ninety-pound weakling. Dealing with operations rather than people is still more tricky: "Chrome-plating parts in our machines has been more successful than nickel-plating, so we should chrome-plate this pipe" may be a hasty and invalid conclusion because of particular chemical agents in the vicinity that attack chrome.

Thoughtful speakers seldom, if ever, apply a normative generalization to an individual instance, and the critical listener will heavily discount any attempts to make such an application.

A speaker's use of generalizations is a major indicator of the quality of the reasoning. Conservative, precise, and meticulous generalizing is reliably associated with clear and logical thinking. We might class this relationship as an example of concomitant variation.

The Fallacy of "Either-Or" Analysis. Deeply rooted in our habitual thought patterns is the tendency to maximize differences. We strive for contrasts and push toward extremes. We like to make clean-cut and definite decisions. We tend to classify people and events in mutually exclusive categories. By so doing, we simplify the world so we can feel we understand it. If we emphasize similarities instead of differences, things and people seem very much like each other, and sorting them out for purposes of reacting to them becomes very complicated indeed.

Semanticists refer to our preference for extremes as "two-valued orientation." We like to classify our surroundings as black or white rather than in shades of gray, to phrase it metaphorically. We refer to a movie as "exciting" or "boring," seldom as "mildly interesting." Personalities we classify as "outgoing" or "introverted." Human abilities are similarly dichotomized: A musician is "talented" or "talentless," a design engineer is "imaginative" or "without imagination," and a student is either "bright" or "stupid." In reality, most musicians are probably talented to some degree, design engineers are reasonably imaginative, and the average student is part bright and part stupid.

When speakers in a presentation indulge in either-or analysis of a problem, they distort it severely because, to hear them tell it, the favorable features have no disadvantages and the unfavored aspects have nothing worthwhile in them. Thoughtful confrontation of pros and cons is ordinarily a balancing process with much to be said on all sides. All solutions have advantages and disadvantages. Only by the "shades of gray" kind of analysis can the small but important differences be isolated. The presenter who habitually analyzes the issues and evidence on a continuum rather than a dichotomy will be contributing to the realistic appraisal of the situation that the audience faces.

How is it that people are influenced by fallacious patterns of stimuli that resemble valid argument? Their responses cannot be reasoned, for they are reacting nonlogically. But they believe they are reacting thoughtfully and reasonably.

The power of a fallacy comes from the fact that it suggests reasoned discourse. The receiver who is deceived by it accepts the form of the argument without examining its substance. Such response is automatic rather than deliberate. Quick, unthinking responses direct much of our behavior. That process is *suggestion*.

SUGGESTION AND REASONING COMPARED

The human being is a suggestible animal. If told to believe or do something when there are no impulses or reasons to the contrary, a person believes or does it. Behavior resulting from suggestion occurs without deliberation, often with little recognition that any change has taken place. Controlling people by suggestion is basically a button-pushing procedure. Reponse to suggestion often approximates the automaticity of a conditioned reflex.

In the presentation, elements of suggestion supplement reasoned arguments. Properly controlled, suggestion clears the channels and paves the way for favorable reception of recommendations and supporting materials. Improperly used, suggestive elements contribute roadblocks to favorable response that neither source nor receiver may fully understand. Much of the artistry in the successful presentation consists of developing verbal and nonverbal suggestive support to enhance the impact of the "hard core of common sense" that is the reasoned content.

The extreme state of suggestibility is hypnosis. A person in a fairly deep hypnotic trance reacts to suggestions as does a machine to programmed instructions. The unhypnotized person thinks about most messages to some extent, but will probably be unthinking in reaction to certain stimuli.

The process of persuasion is diagrammed in Figure 5.1 in a way that shows both the differences between reasoning and suggestion and their interaction.

Response to either suggestive or reasoned appeal depends on the knowledge, interests, habits, and motives of each individual member of the audience. These shape the perception of the incoming message. If the receiver perceives the stimulus as something outside his or her knowledge, interests, habits, and motives, little or no response results. However, when a familiar item that relates to the welfare of the listener comes along, close attention is paid and incoming material is processed by the receiver. The message is not only perceived in detail but is also interpreted and remembered. These operations are prerequisite to attitudinal and behavioral changes, or to both.

If a person responds thoughtfully, the response is a *symbol* reaction, one that takes some time and is consciously mediated. If the person responds without thinking, automatically, the response is a *signal* reaction, one that is quick and largely subconscious. Both signal and symbol responses occur continuously during an act of communication. When they are harmonious, each reinforces the other, and when they are contradictory, favorable response to a message is inhibited.

The dotted arrows in Figure 5.1 leading to the responses "suggest" that often an intended suggestion produces a symbol response, and the intent to reason with a receiver may trigger a signal response. The ultimate decision about the nature of response to a message comes from observation of the receiver rather than from knowledge of the source's intent.

An example will make the functioning of suggestion concrete. Let us suppose someone is driving across western North Dakota on a hot August afternoon. She is tired and hungry and preoccupied with the problem of deciding whether to stop overnight at Minot or drive on to Williston. As she slows to conform to the speed limit of a village, a large sign before a

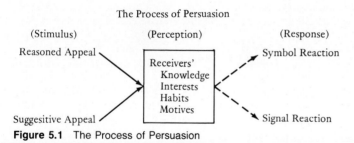

Figure 5.1   The Process of Persuasion

tiny restaurant enters her field of vision. It states simply, "EAT." She brakes her car and drives nearer to the curb. A small sign in the restaurant window says, "Air-Conditioned." She parks, enters the restaurant, has a hamburger and a cup of coffee.

Probably, her stopping for refreshment was not a conscious decision. The familiar signs "EAT" and "Air-Conditioned" triggered habitual, auto-mated response patterns. Because she was without impulses or reasons to the contrary, she "reflexed" suggestion to action. Meantime, her conscious mind was free to examine the pros and cons of stopping early for a good night's sleep or pushing on to cover more miles in the cool of early evening.

The example is of further interest because two kinds of suggestion are involved. The "EAT" sign is *direct suggestion,* telling you what to do. The "Air-Conditioned" sign is *indirect suggestion,* hinting that you will be cool and comfortable while following the directly suggested recommendation. The categories of direct and indirect suggestion are further explored and illustrated in this chapter.

To conclude our introduction to suggestion as a method of presenta-tion, we should observe that its advantages spring from bypassing the critical thinking mechanism of the receiver. Among the desirable conse-quences for a speaker of getting an uncritical response from the audience are these:

1. The method of suggestion gets past defenses. When evangelist Billy Graham tells a university audience that he knows the Psychology Department has come to study him, he causes that audience to "drop its guard" and be more receptive. When he tells the story of labor leader Walter Reuther speaking to the National Associa-tion of Manufacturers with brutal frankness and being rewarded with a standing ovation, his listeners become more inclined to listen to Dr. Graham's message without prejudice, reading frank-ness into his speech.
2. Suggestion skillfully used is efficient, colorful, memorable, and impressive. Instead of noting that the corporation's new venture is unprofitable and difficult to terminate, the speaker may say, "We are the flies that captured the flypaper." The Antiballistic Missile program that was proposed for the United States in the late 1960s was damaged by the suggestion in the statement, "The ABM will be our Maginot Line (the useless French defense line of World War II) in the sky."
3. Positions established by suggestion are difficult to attack. Sug-gested concepts are "nonlogic," and logical analysis is thus often irrelevant. Reasoned refutation of suggestion tends to be cumber-some and complicated. How would one be reasonable in answering this:

Obey that impulse! You may be robbing yourself of happiness and success by not following your hunches! Are you missing out on the richer life and greater achievement that *could* be yours—simply because you fail to act on your "inner flashes" before they cool off?

4. Good suggestion has a universal "human interest" appeal. A clever columnist wrote a piece about a spell of hot weather in Minneapolis, relying on the suggestive power of hyperbole, extreme exaggeration. The title of his column showed hyperbole: "Conversation Droops Too, When Tongue Hangs Out." Here are two paragraphs about some effects of a recent heat wave.

> Political oratory sank to a new low in the hot spell. Children's screeching rose an octave and had more penetrating power. Buses gave off more nauseous fumes. Lake levels dropped so far you could wade across Lake Calhoun. Ice cubes in drinks were actually warm.

> As you recall, a high pressure area came to town, stayed five minutes and then retreated. Humidity was so high that you could collect a glass of water by merely setting out the glass. Mosquitoes were so fagged that when they lit on your arm they just sat there without the ambition to probe.

Writer John K. Sherman suggested common experiences through his vivid pictures which caught and held interest. Although his absurdities were pure fantasy, his readers enjoyed them, thereby intensifying and elaborating recollections of the "hot spell."

These four advantages of using suggestion skillfully constitute an incomplete list. As we proceed with discussion of various forms of suggestion, the reader will see how the more exciting, titillating, shocking, and surprising factors that enliven a message and hold rapt attention are suggestive in nature. Breaking away from literal, earthbound reasonableness can help to transform a presentation from "clear" to "eloquent," from "understandable" to "fascinating."

NONVERBAL TECHNIQUES OF SUGGESTION

Researchers are at long last studying the little understood and grossly neglected factors of physical relationships and delivery of a message by a speaker. Training in interpersonal communication in the last decade has developed a "nonverbal dimension." How speakers look and sound, the location and arrangement of their audiences, lighting and ventilation, what comes before and after their presentations, visual aids and their use, all these and many other elements independent of the words they say contribute substantially to their success or failure. Now it is as necessary to study suggestion originating in nonverbal arrangements and behaviors as it is to learn the disciplined use of evidence and reasoning.

We will examine the nonverbal, suggestive constituents of the presentation by separating the details of arrangement from the delivery of the speech. We will call physical relationships and environmental conditions "proxemic" items and those associated with the behavior of the speaker "personal."

PROXEMIC ELEMENTS IN THE PRESENTATION

Proxemics refers to the way available space is utilized by living organisms. In presentational speaking, proxemic elements, then, include the characteristics of an immediate environment and the physical relationships of the people who inhabit it. Planning the proxemics of the presentation should be a central concern of those preparing for the event.

There is little appreciation of the amount of influence which general comfort, pleasantness, and appropriateness of surroundings have on a presentation. When one adds the dimension of *arrangement* of the people who interact in communication, with resulting ease or difficulty in seeing and hearing each other, a host of important variables are involved. Fortunately, people preparing for a presentation can easily control physical conditions and relationships. In most cases, speakers fail to manage these ingredients of the presentation properly only because of ignorance of their effects on the communication process.

An optimum environment for a presentation includes a tastefully decorated room, acoustically perfect, large enough for the intended audience, and no larger. Comfortable chairs should be easy to turn and rearrange, and table space for each person should be conveniently located. Room lighting should be shadowless and continuously controlled from bright to dim. Audiovisual equipment should be built in, with tape recording and playback, sound motion picture projection, videotape playback, overhead projector, flip chart, and blackboard immediately at hand. The room should be soundproofed to the extent that noises from outside can never be loud enough to cause distraction.

Only in an environment that approximates the above can a high quality of production for the presentation be achieved. "High quality" in production can be described by two adjectives: "smooth flowing" and "inconspicuous." A presentation flows smoothly only when there is no delay caused by any visual or audio or mechanical failure or ineptitude in any other part of the performance. Production is inconspicuous when it looks easy and natural. If the listeners ever find themselves thinking about *how* a point was made, or admiring an elaborate visual or the tricky timing required to integrate the flip chart and overhead projector, then production is deficient. Whenever production calls attention to itself, that attention is diverted from the subject of the presentation. Effective production focuses total attention on the content of the message.

Smooth-flowing, inconspicuous production is a powerful technique of suggestion. Many a proposal has succeeded because it was presented skillfully rather than because of its intrinsic merit. The quality of production is assigned to the content of the message through the psychological phenomenon known as *transfer*. Transfer is the mechanism through which much suggestion produces its effect. More will be said about it later.

An important proxemic consideration is the physical relationship between speaker and audience. It is the custom in American and in European cultures to locate the speaker apart from the audience, elevated, and placed behind a large speaker's stand, or podium. Does this contribute to effectiveness? Usually not. The amount of interaction between human beings is increased by proximity. Increased interaction means better communication. The notion that a speaker gains esteem by being set apart and elevated is unfounded and obsolete. Rather, esteem grows through being more easily seen and heard by the audience. Since a speaker communicates nonverbally with the whole body, little benefit can come from hiding most of it behind the podium. Furthermore, speakers have a universal impulse to grasp the speaker's stand and hang on, thereby eliminating the possibility of movement and gesture. In short, placing the speaker behind a podium on a platform suggests separation from the audience, implying a lack of common interests that is difficult to surmount.

Exceptions to the rule that a speaker should be as close to the audience as possible occur where transmission of the message is subordinate to other elements in the occasion. For example, the annual report made by the president and the executive committee to all employees may be as much dedicated to emphasizing the status and prestige of top management as it is to communicating information about the company. The imposing spectacle of well-dressed, distant, elevated executives may promote feelings of awe and respect. Since the information they impart is available in printed form, communication of content is not vital. In this and other ritualistic situations, including most meetings of stockholders, impressing the audience by physical separation of listeners and speakers may be advisable. However, there is little speaker-audience interaction in such environments and the possible development of rapport is thwarted.

A useful guide in handling the speaker-audience physical relationship is found in a simple formula: $R = 1/D$. R is the amount of overt, or observable, response in the audience. D is the distance between speaker and audience. So the formula tells us that the amount of overt response a speaker achieves from an audience is inversely proportional to the distance between the presenter and that audience, other factors being held constant. Since overt responses correlate well with the attention and interest necessary to success in a presentation, speakers are well advised to get on the same level as their listeners, be as close to them as possible, and talk directly to them, with maximum eye contact.

Common-sense observations support our formula metaphor of $R = 1/D$. When speakers are close by, they are more easily heard and seen, which means that their subtle nonverbal cues will be better understood. They can more easily control attention and overcome distractions. The speakers who are close to their listeners get better feedback. They see the nods and smiles and other expressions of agreement, as well as the frowns and grimaces that tell them something is wrong. Only by being near can they develop circular response, where they react to the audience and the audience reacts to them in a way that builds approval for them and thus maximum support for their recommendation.

PERSONAL, NONVERBAL TECHNIQUES OF SUGGESTION

Let us assume that a speaker has planned appropriately the proxemic factors in a coming presentation. How can personal conduct utilize suggestion to harmonize with and enhance his or her message? Proxemic considerations have placed the speaker close to the audience, with no barriers between them.

The image the speaker would like to create in the perception of listeners serves as a guide to speaking behavior. A message will be more favorably received if the individual delivering it is seen as a sincere, active, alert, informed, confident, warm, and friendly person. What speaking behaviors suggest these characteristics?

Vigorous, dynamic, informal, direct, and unaffected speaking help to generate such a perception. Good posture, much eye contact, lots of movement and gesture, and a strong voice with many changes in pitch, volume, and tempo suggest confidence and sincerity. A natural, easy, conversational manner and an obvious interest in the reactions of the audience convey to them the impression that the speaker is a warm and friendly person. Facial expression is a most flexible and useful tool of nonverbal communication. The speaker should carefully avoid the "deadpan" delivery affected by many speakers. Reaction to what is being said should "show in the face" freely and continuously.

VERBAL TECHNIQUES OF SUGGESTION

While the nonverbal elements discussed above clearly "bypass the critical faculties" of an audience, it is less obvious that language can stimulate the nervous system to unthinking response. However, such is the case, and we will set about seeing how this can be so.

You will recall that the two basic kinds of verbal suggestion are *direct* and *indirect*. Direct suggestion, like the restaurant sign "EAT," tells the receiver what to believe or what to do, in so many words. It is explicit. Indirect suggestion, like the sign "Air-Conditioned," is implicit. The proposition it suggests is concealed. It does not tell the receiver in so many words what it means. That the reader discovers.

Verbal Techniques of Direct Suggestion.   Direct or explicit suggestion occurs in presentation in three forms: positive, negative, and autosuggestion. Positive suggestion recommends a belief or course of action as directly and affirmatively as possible, as "Buy Buick," "Smoke Marlboros," and "Fly Northwest to Hawaii." Negative suggestion tells the receiver *not* to do something, and is identified by its negative wording, as "Thou shalt not steal" and "Don't put beans up your nose." Autosuggestion is a form of self-persuasion. The salesperson who looks in the mirror in the morning and shouts "Boy! Am I enthusiastic!" is using autosuggestion, as is the computer programmer who says, "I can get the bugs out of that program. I *know* I can!"

Positive suggestion, clearly and forcefully worded, has substantial persuasive impact. Just telling a person that something is so produces perceptible belief. When the receiver lacks reasons for disbelief, the effect is multiplied. In addition, a high-prestige source further increases the power of positive suggestion, as does a judicious amount of repetition. Belief is easier than doubt, and more comfortable. And all of us, to some degree, have been trained to do what we are told. Is it any wonder that positive suggestion is an effective means of persuasion?

Negative suggestion is less effective than positive suggestion. A major weakness results from its calling attention to an undesired belief or behavior. Human nature being what it is, many of us are tempted to try the forbidden fruit. The sign "DO NOT OPEN THIS DOOR" guarantees that someone *will* open it, and soon. The denied possibility is often made irresistible unintentionally, as when the mother tells her teenage daughter, "Don't kiss boys. It will feel so good you won't be able to stop!" Comparison of positive and negative suggestion forces us to conclude that a speaker is wise to rely on positive suggestion and avoid negative suggestion. Truly, suggestion is strongest at its "positive pole."

Autosuggestion is a highly respected source of motivation, and its effect is often designated as the "Power of Positive Thinking." The speaker making a presentation can use this "power" by leading members of the audience to envision their future roles. By suggesting to Fred that his job will be made easier, and to Joe that his assembly line will produce more at less cost, the speaker will be telling these men something they will wish to believe. Belief has been found to correlate with desire. Fred and Joe will repeat the attractive promises to themselves, and through autosuggestion will increase their faith in the recommended beliefs.

Verbal Techniques of Indirect Suggestion. Whenever communicators hint at a point but avoid saying it outright, they are using indirect suggestion. The mechanism of indirect suggestion is generally misunderstood in that many people believe an implication must be subtle in order to be indirect. To the contrary, an indirection can be of any degree of complexity, extremely obvious or very difficult to decode. An example of an effective use of obvious indirect suggestion is the instance of the manager who spilled a bottle of ink on the floor. Her note to the night janitor read:

Dear Janitor:
   I think ditto fluid will remove this stain.
   Thank you.

The methods of indirect verbal suggestion are so many and varied that one is tempted to conclude that it is impossible to enumerate them. Without attempting to be comprehensive, we will select four major categories useful in presentational persuasion, discuss them, and illustrate their application.

Simple implication.   The manager's note to the janitor is an example of simple implication. By being indirect, she was spared the necessity of making a possibly embarrassing request. In this situation, as in many other delicate human relationships, it often seems more diplomatic to avoid the bluntness of asking directly for what you want.

Simple implication, then, is somehow talking around a point in a way that would seem to assure that a receiver "reads into" a message the desired meaning. The "reading into" process reveals the built-in hazard of using any form of indirect suggestion: When you rely on other people to guess what you actually mean, you can be sure that wrong guesses will occur. To phrase it in scholarly language: "Response to indirect suggestion is more variable than to direct suggestion." To avoid distortion of the implied point, two precautions are indicated: (1) resist the temptation to be clever, and (2) suggest your point in several ways, thereby making it easy for your audience to conclude correctly.

Are there guides that help the speaker decide when to be direct and when to use implication? When an audience is hostile to your proposal, indirect suggestion is a way of avoiding the jolt of direct confrontation. A young speaker talking to a more mature and experienced audience is well advised to be indirect, while in the reversed situation a highly respected older person talking to a group of juniors may well be predominantly direct. Direct suggestion may be necessary when immediate action is the goal, while planting seeds for a long-range program is often better accomplished by fairly subtle indirection. It is possible and usually desirable to introduce an idea in such a manner that listeners perceive it as their own, through implication.

Countersuggestion.   Contrasuggestible people are those who can be relied on to do the opposite of what they are told. A few of the population are predictably contrasuggestible every day of their lives, but all of us have this perverse, contrary tendency to some degree. When the communicator uses what would appear to be direct positive or negative suggestion with the intent of precipitating an opposite response, we have an example of counter-suggestion.

The roofing salesman tells his prospect, "That beautiful roof for your house is a major investment. Don't you think you had better call your wife and talk it over with her?" If the salesman has correctly identified the contrasuggestible customer, the prospect will reply, "I don't need to check with anybody. Where do I sign?"

"Charlene, you probably better not take on this account. It means a lot of business and more people to supervise, and you're busy now." "We can get along without modern data processing. We'll just move a little slower and work longer hours." "Keep at it, Jack, the end isn't in sight but after another month, it may be." "Dear, I understand and I'm not complaining. I know you can't afford to buy me a mink stole." Other examples will come to the mind of the reader, illustrating the wide use of countersuggestion.

The danger in using countersuggestion is the "boomerang effect." Occasionally, the receiver accepts the suggestion literally, and the persuader has brought about the opposite of the intended result. Satire is countersuggestion, and it is a risky literary device because many people "take it straight" and thus act on a message that is completely contrary to the one the sender intended. For example, some *All in the Family* viewers took Archie Bunker literally, admired him, and missed the intended satire completely.

Before countersuggestion is used in a presentation, the people and situation involved must be thoroughly understood. Both circumstances and motives must point strongly in the direction opposite to the apparent recommendation. Then, if a wording can be contrived that would invite these listeners to react against it, countersuggestion may be judged sufficiently free of risk to try. When it works it is conclusive, for the people who were influenced have formulated their own position in the crucible of opposition, so they regard it affectionately and cling to it tenaciously.

Word manipulation. Choosing one's language provides unlimited opportunity to build suggestion into a message. Words are slanted, positively or negatively, causing persons to accept or reject the thing talked about. Consider the contrasting impact of referring to the Mayor's assistants as his "executive staff" or as his "henchmen." Changing "War Department" to "Department of Defense" is a typical, purposeful switching of labels. Attempting to control responses of receivers by linguistic variables used in conveying a message is the form of indirect suggestion we term "word manipulation."

The "henchmen" and "Department of Defense" examples illustrate, respectively, negative and positive name-calling. We illustrated hyperbole, intentional overstatement, and exaggeration earlier. Understatement, the technique of concluding much less than the situation justifies, is a powerful persuasive device. When an audience expects a sweeping conclusion and is given a restricted, conservative understatement, it rewards the speaker with greater trust.

Figurative language in the form of analogy, metaphor, and simile can be effective suggestion. Saying that "Fighting communism is like killing a snake. You cannot do it by chopping off its tail" supplies little logical analysis about U. S. policy in the Far East, but it may influence attitudes concerning involvement there. Simpler than analogy, metaphor and simile add visual imagery and interest. President Lyndon B. Johnson told U.S. troops in Vietnam that he wanted them "to nail the coonskin to the wall." When Neil Armstrong, the first man on the surface of the moon, stepped from his landing craft, he said, "It's a small step for a man, a giant leap for mankind." A mausoleum salesman happened on a tested statement that sold his product, "You don't rot. You just dry out, like a prune." Figurative language increases impact by converting a matter-of-fact statement into something colorful and memorable.

The illustrations given above demonstrate that word manipulations can be deceptive or enlightening, constructive or destructive to the welfare of the individual and the group. In a final word on this controversial topic, we would leave with the reader the conviction that ingenuity in language can contribute to both clarity and impact of communication. It is choosing the less effective alternative to ask, "Are we ready to change?" when you could say, "Do we have the gumption to break away from the shackles of custom?" Typically, the language used in organizational communication is lifeless. Bringing a ruddy glow to its cheeks is a worthy project in itself.

Humor.   All skilled speakers use humor as a device of suggestion, and for many it is a major method of communication. Yet the use of humor has received less study and has been less written about than any other rhetorical method. Perhaps the academic community considers the use of humor to be undignified. The effectiveness of the method is its claim to dignity.

Humor is, necessarily, pure suggestion. No critical deliberation lies behind the guffaw. But because everybody craves to be amused, a point made in a context of tasteful fun is viewed more receptively than one that is deadly serious. Over recent decades public speaking has steadily become less formal. Conversational style is suited to humor, with the consequence that jokes appear where before they were unknown, in sermons, commencement addresses, presidential inaugural speeches, and funeral eulogies. The humor content of public address is on the rise. It behooves those of us who would master the art of the presentation to become serious students of humor.

Humor can be used in the presentation to establish rapport, to control attention, and to improve retention.

A relevant criterion for selection of humor is, does it suit the source? Speakers must learn what kinds of stories and jokes are suited to their personality and style. For example, some speakers find it easy to get "belly laughs," while others excel in quiet, chuckle-producing humor. Furthermore, the stereotype of the speaker limits choice of stories and dictates language in telling them. The college professor or clergyman cannot use certain material acceptable to the American Legion commander or the sales trainer. The audience sees the speaker in his professional role, and while he may "stretch the stereotype" a little to indicate that he is a "regular guy," if he goes too far his listeners will be alienated and they will punish him for his indiscretion.

Humor is perhaps the best single method of establishing rapport for a very good reason. It is difficult to dislike the person who makes you laugh. In addition, the pattern of informal social interaction in our culture utilizes amusing related materials to open a conversation. After chuckling together, the participants turn to serious matters. Using humor to gain a fair and sympathetic hearing encourages a warm acceptance and conforms to the habits of relating to one another socially in Western cultures.

To phrase it figuratively, humor can provide pegs on which to hang the key points of a speech. The humor is recalled later, and perhaps to the surprise of the person remembering the funny story, there also is the concept he or she acquired along with its peg.

Using humor to carry speech content demands a delicate balance between being funny and being serious. The response of laughter is so rewarding to the speaker that the use of humor may be overdone. Amusing sidelights may obliterate the point to be emphasized. The speaker then becomes a crowd-pleaser, using humor as a crutch and assigning a low priority to the message. Listeners remember the jokes but cannot recall what was talked about.

Because people forget so much so easily, the most valuable speech material is that which tends to lodge in the mind. We are not sure what it is that people remember best, but in all probability, very close to the top of the list are real-life stories about what happened to people. If these have humor in them, so much the better, and most of them do. The great speakers spend their lives collecting just those experiences that illustrate the points they want to make. They know that if the story is a good one, and if it is an example of the related point, later both it and the point associated with it will be recalled and retold.

In addition to the "piggy-back phenomenon" described above, retention of materials in a presentation is aided by anything that influences positively the quality of attention paid to the speech. Since humor is a major means of raising attention levels, it also operates indirectly but significantly to increase the amount remembered.

FORMULAS OF PERSUASION

Suggestion to aid persuasion comes in many forms. Indirect formulas, the hidden short cuts to acceptance, are one category of considerable importance. These procedures are true indirect suggestion, for they operate effectively only when the recipients of the message do not know they are being used. If a receiver identifies a particular short-cut technique, it loses much of its effect. This dependence on concealment will become obvious as we discuss kinds of short cuts and give examples of their use.

Common Ground.   The mind of a listener is prepared for agreement when early in the presentation a speaker talks about beliefs shared by those present. Such "common ground" may include praise of past accomplishments, reiteration of goals and objectives, endorsement of leadership, dedication to progress and improvement, and so on. Each fact and value judgment on which audience and speaker agree becomes a building block in the foundation on which the speaker can rest a proposal. Because the use of common ground shows the speaker to be much like them, members of the audience become inclined to accept both person and ideas.

Language can constitute common ground. A speaker who uses the vocabulary, colloquial expressions, and verbal stereotypes of the audience, becomes one of them and without thinking about it, their guard against a recommendation is lowered.

An effective variant of the common-ground technique is the "together" device. People have an impulse to conform, to go along with the crowd. If the speaker can show that a recommendation is part of a trend, that the rush has started to "get on the bandwagon," the listeners will feel that they, too, should become a part of the movement. The "together" appeal works best as a subordinate theme. Ideally, "the trend" and "everybody is moving in this direction" concepts are casually mentioned from time to time but are never permitted to assume the role of a major reason for change.

The ways in which common ground can be utilized in a presentation are limited only by the ingenuity of the speaker. A list of all agreements that might be mentioned to reinforce habits of agreement should be prepared and items selected from the list.

Yes Response.   Closely related to the use of common ground is a technique of encouraging tendencies toward agreement through providing opportunity for affirmative responses. A person who answers "yes" to each one in a series of questions becomes more likely to say "yes" to the next question. A habit of either affirmative or negative responses is easily established, and the maker of the presentation should take care to encourage only yes responses by careful wording of statements and rhetorical questions.

With thought and planning, transition questions can be so worded as to insure predominantly positive answers. Here is a list of a half dozen such questions that might occur along the way as the presentation proceeds.

1. Are we acknowledged to be leaders in our field?
2. Have we introduced more well-accepted new products than any of our competitors over the years?

3. Is demand for our product increasing?
4. Does our top management support reasonable risk-taking?
5. Are there gaps in our product line?
6. Would it be desirable to make our product line more complete?

The link between the "yes response" technique and "common ground" appears in the above questions. Each "yes" opens another area of shared interest. Coordinating yes response and common ground devices in this manner is easy, and the effect is cumulative.

Transfer. The most varied of the short cuts to acceptance is transfer. Transfer is the effect of stimuli unrelated to the topic of the presentation on readiness to accept or reject a recommendation. The nonverbal suggestive elements of environment and production mentioned earlier operate through transfer. For example, distractions produce negative transfer, and a pleasant speaking manner transfers positively. Here we are concerned with verbal incidents that might influence audience response positively or negatively and that are separate from evidence and reasoning used to develop the topic.

Positive transfer occurs when speakers choose their illustrations from the interests of their audience. Using an analogy from tennis to a group of golfers would probably cause negative transfer. Positive transfer is associated with providing opportunity for audience questions and answering them carefully; negative transfer comes from cutting them off. Unnecessarily technical and complicated language builds hostility through negative transfer, while easy-to-understand, layperson's translations of technical terms generally transfer positively.

Contingent situations lead to positive or negative transfer. If an audience is slow in arriving, the speaker can proceed regardless, or delay beginning, probably by talking informally with the audience about related matters, until the audience is assembled. The latter choice transfers positively, because it shows the speaker's concern for the listeners.

What a speaker says about an audience transfers to the topic. If the speaker credits hearers with expertness and defers to them in their specialization, positive transfer takes place. When a speaker goes "beyond the fact" in awarding merit to listeners, we term this act "flattery." Unless it is outrageous, flattery tends to transfer positively, due to the ability we all have to enjoy hearing nice things said about ourselves.

The speaker's attitude toward self as reflected in words is a rich source of transfer. An assumption of authority of position and expertness that is not egoistic transfers favorably. But either pretension beyond position and achievement, or excessive humility (the "humble bit"), is apt to transfer negatively.

In discussing humor we stressed the importance of quality and relevance. Through transfer an improper or irrelevant story can reduce the impact of good evidence and reasoning, while these can be equally enhanced by pointed and pertinent humor.

Pronunciation, grammatical correctness, and language appropriate to the occasion have great negative or positive transfer potential. How much, if any, slang and profanity to use is a related and difficult problem. This decision is another contingency, made after considering the norms of current practice and the peculiarities of a particular situation.

To maximize positive transfer and reduce negative transfer to a minimum, a speaker must scrutinize whatever is planned and ask, "How could that possibly affect the reception of my message?" If a planned behavior has even a possibility of creating an adverse effect, it should be replaced with one of greater positive potential.

Multiple Options. A person preparing a proposal tends to be trapped in a rut. Typically, the speaker attempts to perfect a single possibility and channels all efforts to support this one goal. By doing this one becomes vulnerable. If there is some aspect of this recommendation that fails to win approval, the listeners have but one choice, to reject the whole package. The result is a "something or nothing" proposal when there might have been an option of "something or something else."

The "multiple options" approach consists of preparing two or more versions of a recommendation. These need not differ drastically, and, ideally, each should be acceptable to the maker of the presentation. The posture of the speaker becomes more comfortable. Options might be worded: "There are two or three ways of going about this. I'm not sure which is best. Let me tell you about the possibilities."

With multiple options the tendency of the audience is to concentrate on choosing among the possibilities or attempt to combine them rather than deciding to accept or reject the entire proposal. When the strategy is successful, speaker and audience work together as a team to decide what is, indeed, the best recommendation. Typically, the listeners become so involved that they find it difficult to reject the version they decide is best. After all, they selected it!

The multiple-options strategy is probably less well known than the other short cuts to acceptance. But it may well be the most powerful of them all. Our readers are advised when next they prepare a proposal to submit it in two or three versions and observe how many listeners assume without question that one of the proposals will prevail.

Team Play. To differing degrees, all people like to work with others, to be a part of joint effort, to collaborate on a worthy cause. People are social beings. When they have an opportunity to join a team and play an interesting game, they usually want to do it.

The speaker who uses the "team-play" approach assumes the role of enlisting helpers to join in building a better world. Many advantages accrue to this posture. The proposal becomes the center of interest rather than the maker of the proposal. Each listener begins to think in terms of contributing. A task-oriented interpersonal relationship develops among members of the audience, leading to a sharing of skills and ideas. A "gung ho, let's get on with it" attitude gains momentum. When the recommendation of the speaker becomes a project for the group, success is at hand.

Participative management is an application of the team-play device. Individuals play needed roles in group efforts. Work becomes a game, with rewards to both the collective and the individual participant. Both satisfactions and output increase. From the point of view of getting the job done, the basic advantage comes from the employees becoming more interested in the job they are doing, for its own sake. Their achievement-motivation increases, causing their energies to be focused on the task more effectively.

What happens in good participative management occurs when the team-play approach is skillfully applied in a presentation. Resources of the group focus on the recommended project, and the resulting momentum will do much to implement the proposal.

INTEGRATING REASON AND SUGGESTION

We have said that suggestion can supplement reason in a presentation. In order to grasp the full implications of the relationship between suggestion and reason, we must understand in some detail the way the brain reacts to incoming information.

First, the brain (central nervous system) can respond without processing the information. With pure suggestion the brain produces a knee-jerk, reflex response that is automatic. The cheerleader shouts to the rooters "Gimme an M; gimme an I; gimme an N; gimme an N." The boosters who respond with yells of "M," "I," "N," "N" may do so with no modification, interpretation, or relating the communication to any other events. *Repetition* of an habitual response requires no processing of the stimulus that brings it about.

When the human brain processes information, change occurs because of perception. Perception is the process of assigning meaning to an incoming stimulus. Whether perception sometimes occurs in responding to the cheerleader's request is debatable. Certainly, no perception is required to yell "M" in response to the request "Gimme an M." Habit can easily take over in situations like those associated with responding to a cheerleader. Perhaps perception does occur in appreciation of the cheerleader's abbreviated costume, her shapely figure, and her skill in choreographed maneuvers.

Once perception takes place, processing interprets and evaluates the message and decides what, if anything, to do about it. This is done holistically or analytically, or by combining these two methods.

Holistic information processing is out-of-awareness. "Mulling over" is an example of holistic processing. We file the topic in our heads and call it to the surface to think about it from time to time. Sometimes we go to sleep thinking about it and wake up with a new insight. That this is not random or coincidental is shown by recent brain research.

When subjects in some recent brain research were given a problem, there followed within 0.3 of a second a decision wave on the screen of an electroencephalograph. The subjects were not conscious of any purposive or systematic activity, but their reported decisions confirm that their cerebral information processing yielded something new.

Analytic information processing is another way to use our critical faculties. When we analyze we operate consciously, dividing the problem or situation into its constituent parts, inspecting these to find what needs changing and so forth. We proceed in the fashion we outlined in Chapter 4 when we discussed the conscious analytic methods of organizing a presentation such as the state your case and prove it and the inductive exploration of possibilities. The disadvantages of the analytic method are its slowness, its necessarily fragmentary nature, and its frequent dependence on counting things and relying on numerical data. Its advantages are precision and understanding of the step-by-step procedures involved.

A presenter can choose to precipitate automatic or thoughtful responses. Relying on suggestion emphasizes reflexive automated responses that often interfere with information processing. If the presenter chooses to encourage cerebral information processing (CIP), either holistic or analytic methods, or both, can be facilitated. A short rule of thumb is that if the heart of the matter is quantitative, analysis is appropriate, and if the heart of the matter is qualitative, holistic processing is usually more productive.

The integration of reasoning and suggestion depends on whether the persuader wishes the audience to respond thoughtfully or impulsively. The reader may have trouble imagining a situation in which a presenter would be promoting a proposal which, if pondered thoughtfully by the audience, would die a sudden death. We, too, are hard put to come up with examples; nonetheless, if bypassing critical faculties is desired, then reasoning should be minimized and suggestion exploited.

In the more usual circumstances, however, wherein a soundly reasoned case is submitted for holistic and analytic examination, suggestive elements are invaluable aids to gaining and maintaining attention and helping the audience to visualize present and future circumstances. These can be used ethically, that is, in ways that encourage the audience to be deliberative. Drawing fine lines to guarantee ethical use of suggestion is discussed in the last section of this chapter.

CONSTRUCTIVE USE OF EMOTIONS

In popular usage, "emotion" and "suggestion" are hopelessly confused. The basic error found in much writing about communication is to label all use of suggestion as "emotional appeal." Since the great majority of suggestion produces an *un*emotional response, to call it "emotional appeal" makes little sense.

The emotional condition is an upset physio-psychological state. People behave differently when they are emotional than when they are calm. People can respond to suggestion and reason with a great deal of or with very little emotion. An individual is capable of four modes of response to a message:

1	2	3	4
Reasoned Unemotional	Reasoned Emotional	Suggestive Unemotional	Suggestive Emotional

The sophisticated presenter will select one of the four modes as the desired dominant response pattern for a presentation.

Why do we speak of "emotional condition" instead of naming emotions? Part of the reason is that dozens of emotions are listed in the literature, and psychologists are not in agreement as to a finite list. But the main reason is that no matter what emotion is experienced the physio-psychological symptoms are the same. This leads us to the "emotional condition" perspective and to consider that the particular emotion is a learned way to express the general emotional condition, in context. In order to discuss emotions, we need to name a few; we will therefore use three basic emotions on whose names most psychologists seem to agree: love, fear, and anger.

When a calm person becomes emotional, what changes occur? Internally, breathing, heartbeat, blood pressure, endocrine secretions change, and adrenalin increases. These physical modifications take time, so emotion is slow to build and slow to normalize. Perhaps you have had the experience of a close call in an automobile during which you were perfectly relaxed. Then you sat on the curb and "went to pieces," and it took the passage of considerable time before you were calm again.

Behaviorally, an emotional person exhibits three symptoms: shock, diffusion, and transference. Shock is a matter of degree. To some extent, a person in shock loses control of critical faculties. Such a person tends to make bad decisions. Diffusion is a matter of physical coordination. The emotional person loses the ability to make fine and accurate movements and tends to use excessive physical activity. An angry person shouts, paces the floor, increases the number and amplitude of his or her gestures.

Transference is often explained as "psychological spillover." It is the tendency to treat objects and people unrelated to one's emotional condition as though they were involved in it. The woman who is scolded at the end of the work day for something she did not do comes home, shouts at her husband, ejects the kids from the house, and kicks the dog.

If the reader at this point has concluded that the emotional condition is of no help in doing rewarding work, the authors agree. Probably the most constructive use of knowledge about emotions is to keep people from becoming emotional. Shock, diffusion, and transference reduce the availability of human resources. Imagine two identical working organizations. The one in which the personnel spend fewer total hours in an emotional condition will be the more productive.

There are some circumstances, however, under which people *should* become emotional. The subject of a presentation may be one that creates righteous indignation in the audience. The presenter causes them to think about the situation critically, and the better they understand it the more angry they become. Justified anger energizes response, and when it is a result of thoughtful deliberation, it becomes a valuable asset to the persuasive process.

The reasoned emotional mode of response can be constructive as in the above illustration, but it should be used sparingly. A presenter should be reluctant to create circumstances that prevent the audience members from thinking clearly and that make them more impulsive. Trying for a suggestive emotional response is seldom constructive, for a solid base of evidence and reasoning is missing. Impulsive responses then may be quite irrational and possibly harmful.

The constructive use of emotion in presentational speaking is possible but not prevalent. The presenter restricts it to those few instances when such emotions as fear, anger, or love are logical consequences of the facts of the case. Caution is doubly indicated because the emotional condition not only takes time to subside, but may feed on itself, increasing its intensity in an ascending spiral over days, weeks, or months. Experimenting with people's emotions is risky business.

ETHICAL CONSIDERATIONS

Ethical considerations stem largely from the act of choice. People doing the inevitable do not raise ethical concerns. We ought not hold people responsible for communication over which they have no control. Choice implies both the freedom and the ability to understand and do the ethical thing. We can and should hold people responsible for what they deliberately choose to do. When a presenter intentionally chooses to break the rules, conventions, customs, and norms of the communication event in order to gain a personal advantage over the others, we have a right to hold the speaker responsible for that communication.

Most people want to be ethical. That is, they want to choose to "do the right thing," *in context*. There is that phrase "in context" again. It implies that the "right thing" at one time and place might be the wrong thing in another context. Because ethics are a function of context, at least to some degree, dealing with the boundary separating the ethical from the unethical becomes complicated but vital to the making of wise communication decisions.

In recent years scholars studying organizational communication have referred more and more frequently to "corporate or organizational culture." Parke Burgess, a respected rhetorician, defined *culture* as a system of moral demands. Since cultures are unique—no one quite replicates another—this insightful observation suggests that it is normal for ethical standards to vary from place to place and from time to time. Del Hastings, a man with a lifetime of experience in international projects, states that the main difficulties in multinational ventures are the different ideas people have of what is right and wrong depending on their cultural background.

The first ethical consideration, then, is *do not expect the same ethical standards to prevail all the time, everywhere.*

But there are general norms that prevail—in fact, predominate—in homogeneous cultures. In twentieth-century North America, the following general rules apply to the making of presentations.

1. The presentation should be factually accurate and representative of conditions. It should contain no significant omissions or distortions as to facts. In common-sense language it should be truthful.
2. The intent of the presenter should be revealed to the audience.
3. Pseudo-logic, the use of logical forms and language to camouflage unsound material, is to be avoided.
4. The presenters should not rely on arousing intense emotions to facilitate persuasion.
5. Presenters should accept full responsibility for the changes they are attempting to bring about.
6. Presenters should be open; that is, all relevant points of view should be welcomed and discussed fairly in an atmosphere of free inquiry.

We believe that the above list is both reasonable and clear. But we recognize that the interpretation of key phrases in each of the six standards such as what is "accurate and representative" or what is the "presenter's intent" will be decided largely by the judgment of the speaker, given the particular circumstances surrounding the presentation. Two different presenters may interpret these criteria differently. So even when reasonable and clear ethical standards are applied, they often become less than definite.

It is important to understand that two hypothetical presenters who interpret these ethical criteria differently do *not* necessarily differ in their desire to be scrupulously ethical. They may just view the world from somewhat different perspectives, even when they agree on ethical standards in the abstract. The important thing is to have the rules and the desire to be ethical. Interpretation of the rules is beyond any control that can be exerted by the culture. However, talking about the rules and how these are to be applied can increase uniformity in their interpretation.

Applying rules is an analytic procedure, and on the whole ethical decisions are more qualitative than quantitative. So we now supply a holistic guide to being ethical that can be used by any agent of change. It does not replace the analytical rules approach when that is in any way applicable. The holistic method should be used in addition to the six prescriptive criteria, so both analytical and holistic processes contribute to the making of ethical decisions. With ethical problems we need all the help we can get.

The holistic criterion we suggest is *social utility*. The usefulness of a presentation is measured by real and probable consequences to individuals and groups. Presenters "mull over" what they intend to do and, drawing on tangibles and intangibles, facts and feelings, attempt to answer two questions: (1) Will what I propose to do benefit groups and the organization affected? and (2) will any individual be harmed by this action? If after conscientiously and holistically working through variables, hunches, feelings, and other relevant information presenters can honestly answer the first question "Yes" and the second question "No," they can proceed, assured that they have met an important ethical standard.

An advantage of the social utility criterion is that it is completely "in context." The holistic processing of information provides a "big picture" gestalt interpretation of all complex elements and their relationships. The presenter's final holistic ethical conclusion is a product of unique circumstances, at one time, in their totality.

We conclude this brief section on ethical considerations by noting that much unethical communication is caused by careless neglect. If we do not think about being ethical, we may well be unintentionally unethical. A basic prerequisite to being ethical is to be concerned about responsible communicative behavior. A famous business consultant once said that if he were a CEO (Chief Executive Officer of an organization) who wanted to improve ethics in his corporation, he would publish far and wide the policy that anyone in the corporation found to be doing something unethical would be fired immediately. People would then worry about ethics, and that worry would contribute to ethical behavior.

SUMMARY

Persuasion is defined and examined as a process that intends to influence choice. When successful, it leads to willing cooperation, in contrast to coercion which relies on force or threat of force to limit options and gain compliance.

Fallacies, unsound, and deceptive units of argument, may be used unintentionally or intentionally to increase the power of a presentation. Three prevalent fallacies are *post hoc,* hasty generalization, and either-or analysis.

Suggestion and reasoned appeals supplement each other in creating powerful persuasion. Suggestion secures signal response which is automatic, unprocessed, and reflexive, while reasoned appeals produce delayed, thoughtful symbol responses.

Suggestion is accomplished both verbally and nonverbally. Nonverbal elements are environmental and personal, whereas verbal techniques are direct and indirect. Popular formulas that employ verbal indirect suggestion are common ground, yes response, transfer, multiple options, and team play. Presentation of self involves both direct and indirect suggestion.

Integrating reason and suggestion is complicated because their contrasting responses, deliberative and impulsive, often interfere with each other. Similarly, constructive use of emotions is difficult to control. Assuming that presenters wish to be ethical, we supply analytic and holistic suggestions designed to increase the ethical quality of the presentation event.

Effective persuasion rests on a foundation of sound reasoning. Chapter 6 demonstrates how the presenter can be perceived as sensible and logical.

QUESTIONS FOR DISCUSSION AND REVIEW

1. How does persuasion differ from coercion?
2. What are the three "fallacies"? Give an example of each.
3. What are some examples that illustrate "The Process of Persuasion" diagram (Figure 5.1) and that show how reasoned appeal to a particular audience might produce a signal reaction?
4. In your experience, which environmental elements of nonverbal suggestion are managed least effectively by presentational speakers?
5. What are some of your recent experiences in communication that provide examples of the four verbal techniques of indirect suggestion?
6. Why do formulas of persuasion become ineffective when identified by the receiver?
7. What are some examples from your own experience that distinguish between holistic and analytic information processing?
8. What is the nature of the emotional condition, and how does it inhibit the discretionary use of human resources?
9. What are some arguments for and against the existence of a universal standard of ethics?
10. What is meant by the "social utility" criterion of ethics in a presentation? Why is it holistic?

REFERENCES AND SUGGESTED READINGS

The quotation from the Minneapolis columnist is from:

Sherman, John K. "Conversation Droops Too, When Tongue Hangs Out," *Minneapolis Sunday Tribune,* August 2, 1964, p. 6.

For more on the deceptive possibilities of persuasion, see:

Simons, Herbert W. *Persuasion: Understanding, Practice, and Analysis.* 2nd ed. New York: Random House, 1986, Chapter 15.

For a compact analysis of ethical considerations in the use of persuasion, see:

Johannesen, Richard L. "Perspectives on Ethics in Persuasion." In Charles U. Larson. *Persuasion: Reception and Responsibility.* 4th ed. Belmont, Calif.: Wadsworth, 1986, Chapter 11.

For a detailed examination of holistic and analytic information processing, see:

Howell, William S. *The Empathic Communicator.* Prospect Heights, Ill.: Waveland Press, 1986.

For a thoughtful and well-illustrated inventory of ways we interpret nonverbal cues, see:

Taylor, Anita, Teresa Rosegrant, Arthur Meyer, and B. Thomas Samples. *Communicating.* 4th ed. Englewood Cliffs, N.J.: Prentice-Hall, 1986, Chapter 4.

For general treatments of nonverbal communication, see:

Hickson, Mark L., III, and Don W. Stacks. *NVC: Nonverbal Communication Studies and Applications.* Dubuque, Iowa: William C. Brown, 1985.

Knapp, Mark L. *Essentials of Nonverbal Communication, Brief Edition.* 2d ed. New York: Holt, Rinehart and Winston, 1980.

Mehrabian, Albert. *Silent Messages: Implicit Communication of Emotions and Attitudes.* 2d ed. Belmont, Calif.: Wadsworth, 1981.

For the overall process of persuasion in modern society, see:

Brembeck, Winston L., and William S. Howell. *Persuasion: A Means of Social Influence.* 2d ed. Englewood Cliffs, N.J.: Prentice-Hall, 1976.

chapter *6*

Achieving a Reasoned Response

In Chapter 4 we defined perception as assigning meaning to an incoming stimulus. Obviously, this is a key element in the process of presentation. Our goal is to generate a *perceived reality* for our audiences to inspect and interpret. We begin our analysis of perception with a look at the nature of reality as we perceive it.

THE NATURE OF PERCEIVED REALITY

Two kinds of information processing occur in the human mind that together tell us what is going on and what, if anything, we should do about it. We place these independent and different processes in the context of presentational speaking to see how they supplement each other. What does the presenter need to know about perceptual control?

Perception is independent of physical phenomena to a significant degree. For human beings, perception *is* meaning. Different people perceive the same circumstances differently, and hence develop different meanings. From another perspective, what you and I "read into" incoming stimuli is real, to us. Whatever is actually out there, physically, becomes incidental. What we *perceive* to be there is what we have to work with; consequently, our possibly unique perception determines our response. Perhaps the question in the reader's mind right now is expressed in the title of a once-popular song: "Is That All There Is?" To understand ourselves and others, why do we do what we do, the answer has to be, for the most part, "Yes." Figure 6.1 indicates the two major ways of perceiving reality.

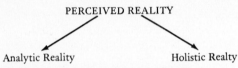

Figure 6.1 Factors in Perceived Reality

Why do we choose the terms *analytic* and *holistic* to designate the two contrasting ways by which we perceive reality? The source of these terms is found in the study of ways in which the human brain processes information. When information makes possible a conclusion or the solution to a problem, the brain may consciously inspect bits of evidence and thoughtfully construct what these imply. This procedure is the process of analysis. Or the brain may survey the overall pattern of items without awareness of the parts of the picture and reach a conclusion from the arrangement rather than from looking at the pieces composing the pattern. This procedure is the holistic process of perception.

The analytic procedure involves analyzing a problem and finding its central or core idea, dividing it up into its component parts, judging which parts are most important and which are subsidiary, and relating the parts to the central idea and to each other. In using the analytic process, we develop a perception by identifying certain stimuli explicitly and consciously and interpreting these logically (within our own system of logic, of course). When meeting a person for the first time, we may be aware of certain details of appearance, perhaps width of coat lapels, hair style, makeup, color and pattern of tie, facial expression, and vocal style. We think about these few selected features of the person specifically, and, after considering this information thoughtfully, we build a partial impression, an analytic reality. Such games as bridge and chess provide a focus for what is relevant and what is not. Therefore, the players often find it useful to break the game into small parts and ponder the implications of a specific bridge play or chess move by conscious analysis.

The second information processing procedure involves assimilating the impact of the whole without awareness of particular component parts. It is a global grasp of the gestalt of the situation by intuition in which the processes of analysis and synthesis, if any, are out of our awareness. As we interact with our new acquaintance, feelings about her or him accumulate that go far beyond what we can infer from the list of consciously noted features. Perhaps "red flags" go up in our nervous system, warning us against placing trust in this individual. Or perhaps we begin to feel a warm receptivity to the stranger. We "just know" that this person is a congenial companion, good to be with, bright, informed, and competent. These emerging characterizations are just as real as our conscious interpretation of items of which we are aware. But these are impressions of the second kind, difficult or impossible to explain. The holistic reality stems from our more global out-of-awareness intuitions. Even such an elementary matter as hitting a tennis ball with a racket requires us to process a vast amount of sensory information, including the sound of the ball hitting the court, the sight of the ball moving in our direction, the feel of the wind on our skin for strength and direction, the feel of our shoes on the court surface, and so forth. We not only must process much information to hit the ball successfully, but we must do so very quickly and we often act without consciously attempting to analyze and synthesize the information. Indeed, we generally play better when we process this information holistically than when we try to be analytical in our approach.

The first process, analysis, proceeds sequentially, step by step, with the brain always aware of what is going on and how one step leads to another. The second process illustrates a fundamental principle of gestalt psychology, that the human mind can make sense out of a complex pattern without consciously inspecting its constituent items.

Why should a book on making powerful presentations be concerned about perceived reality and the two ways of constructing it? *Because the most important—and most difficult—task of a presenter is predicting response.* If you know your audience in context so well that you can predict how it will respond to a certain stimulus, you can provide that stimulus and influence its behavior. Thus, true power in a presentation requires accurate prediction of response, as well as ability to provide the messages sufficient to trigger it.

If you fail to recognize that perceived reality differs from objective reality, you cannot be an effective predictor. In addition, if you assume that people respond only analytically and logically to the evidence you present, you will go further astray. And the effective presentational speaker understands that a strong holistic response to patterns, particularly in dealing with complex issues, often outweighs any necessarily fragmentary, objective analysis. So it behooves the presenter to assess the perceptual realities of an audience as affected by circumstances, past experiences, and vested interests. Treating your audience as a group of impartial, logical computers responding to your message uniformly and without bias is a prescription for failure.

At this point, we must call attention to our deviation in this section of the book from cultural norms in much of Western society. The cultures predominant in Western Europe and North America north of Mexico stress analytical processing of information and put less emphasis on holistic methods. The Western attitude is to minimize the holistic way of perceiving reality by labeling it "intuition" and not treating it seriously. Many of the predominant cultures in the rest of the world emphasize the holistic process while neglecting the analytic. In non-Western cultures, responses to a total situation, a complex field or pattern, has the status that analytical analysis has in the West.

In the non-Western world, analytic problem-solving was almost nonexistent until introduced by Western visitors and technical specialists and by foreign students coming to schools in Europe or North America. Only one Eastern nation, Japan, has largely succeeded in adding analytic methods to its holistic base. Analysis in Japan, however, is largely confined to communication related to science and commerce.

Although Western schools teach analytic methods for the most part, effective processing of information in the West requires both analytic and holistic procedures. Innovators and other creative people in particular rely heavily on holistic data processing. Because we see both ways of creating a social reality as important in our culture, we treat both in detail in this book. We believe that the scholarly community must come to realize that the competent thinker is one who is adept in using both the tools of analysis and the methods of holistic information processing.

In earlier chapters we have assigned importance to one form of holistic information processing, "mulling over." The insights an audience generates by "mulling over" an issue are just as real and important to them as are conclusions drawn from their analysis of trends in rates of taxation or figures of profit and loss. Both ways of perceiving reality are reasoned responses. The social reality of the audience for a presentation includes both. If the presenters are to control the listeners' perceptions of reality, they must communicate in ways that encourage both the analytic and holistic processing of information.

THE PROPOSITION: A KEY ELEMENT IN THE PRESENTATION

A point to be established by a message unit is generally known as a *proposition*. A presentation typically has a central proposition and one or more subordinate propositions. When the subordinate propositions are supported and accepted, they in turn become support for the central proposition. Great importance attaches to the formulation and arrangement of propositions. Language choices become critical.

The decision to use relatively abstract or relatively specific language is a particularly difficult one. To improve our ability to structure propositions for optimum effectiveness in a particular situation, we need to know how to word a recommendation in a relatively more abstract or in a relatively more concrete form.

Language and Abstraction-Concreteness.   Abstraction-concreteness is an important dimension of language. Because complete knowledge of all events is impossible to transmit or obtain, any sample of language will fall somewhere on the continuum between abstraction (bits of information sacrificed for applicability to a large number of events, e.g., "Many fools run for public office") and concreteness (number of applicable events sacrificed for inclusion of many bits of information, e.g., "Mr. Gulch, who couldn't pass the eighth grade and who spends 90 percent of his income on drinking and gambling, is running for the state legislature from the sixteenth district").

As we move to more abstract expression, we include:

1. More events.
2. Less information.

As we move to more concrete expression, we include:

1. Fewer events.
2. More information.

Thus, we might say:

1. Abstraction is less about more.
2. Concreteness is more about less.

Support of a proposition is more concrete than either the purpose or the proposition. Although relatively more abstract material may appear to support a proposition, it is not support unless it is made more concrete than the proposition. For example, the proposition "Taxes on business are unreasonably high" is *not* supported by the generalization "government is robbing the entrepreneur."

A proposition is related to a message unit by being only as abstract as is necessary to summarize the unit. It should be as concrete as possible without being as concrete as the support.

To summarize:

1. The purpose of a message is the manner in which the persuaders want the audience to respond to the overall message—their intent.
2. Propositions summarize the significance of message units as concretely as possible.

THE EFFECTIVE WORDING OF PERSUASIVE PROPOSITIONS

Reasoned elements in a message depend on clearly worded propositions. The proposition or claim is a concise and precise statement of what the persuader wishes the receiver to believe or to do as a result of his or her persuasion. Eight criteria of a good proposition are helpful guidelines toward realizing maximum benefit from thoughtful use of propositions to this end.

A Good Proposition Is a Complete Declarative Sentence.   While fragments of sentences may have headline value, a phrase only suggests an idea
while a sentence says something about it.

   "Inefficient committees" suggests in a vague and general way that the
speaker will indict the use of committees in some manner, but it fails to tell
us, for example, whether he or she will criticize the committee system in
general, or committees as used for certain purposes in an organization.
"Poor planning makes committees inefficient in Research and Development
at ABC Corporation" pins down the point the speaker may wish to make
much more satisfactorily.

A Good Proposition Is as Concrete as Possible.   Some complete declarative sentences are little better than fragments. "We need to pay teachers
according to merit" is indeed complete as a sentence, but it fails to meet
the requirement of specificity or concreteness. Before the desirability of
merit pay can be considered seriously, it must be placed in a limited context
of real people and situations. "Merit evaluations should be made of all
public school teachers at all levels of education" is much more concrete
than the first statement and much more likely to contribute to a meeting
of minds of people discussing the issues involved.

A Properly Worded Proposition Expresses a Single Idea.   The principle
of concentrating on one idea at a time to maximize clear thinking and
minimize confusion explains this criterion for writing propositions. "Air
pollution and organized crime are major problems in U.S. cities" is a double
proposition because two essentially unrelated topics are combined. Such a
duality should be divided into two separate statements. A series of single
claims is easier to present and easier to follow than a shorter list of multiple
propositions.

   The temptation to write multiple propositions is great when the ideas
involved are closely related. "If you want to lose weight safely, don't go to
a 'fat doctor' who prescribes sacks of potent pills that are dangerous, but
rather see your family doctor." This statement seems to many at first
reading to be a single idea. It incorporates many nonessential elements that
prevent clear reception of the message. Actually, only one idea is needed
for the argument. "Your family doctor can help you plan a safe weight
reduction program" covers this area of discussion and permits the persuader to talk about "fat doctors" as evidence that at least most overweight
people should turn to family physicians for help.

Propositions should Be Written in Report Language.   The double proposition about losing weight cited above contains several terms that violate this
criterion. For example, "fat doctors" and "sacks of potent pills that are
dangerous" are connotative phrases and tend to produce an immediate,

unthinking response of rejection. In contrast, "report language" is carefully selected to be objective and avoid triggering prejudices and emotions.

Extremes in slanting are not likely to occur in presentations designed to be reasoned and thoughtful. However, the zeal that produces eloquence often generates either an unconscious loading or a slanting that seems justifiable and necessary to its author. "The high price of food is caused by unwarranted farm price supports." "The cities of St. Paul and Minneapolis should purchase the inefficient Twin City Rapid Transit Company." In these propositions the words "unwarranted" and "inefficient" can be said to "beg the question." Accepting them predisposes acceptance of the propositions, regardless of the merit of arguments pro and con. Loading factors like these create difficulties as great as the problem of answering the well-known trick question, "Have you stopped beating your wife?"

Propositions should Omit Reasons and Explanation.　Since the claim or proposition is the most economical statement of intended belief or action, reasoning, evidence, and elaboration are never included. But these tend to intrude, as shown in this example: "The great humanitarian stance of many members of the moral majority is fallacious because it is the result of fear, hate, and lack of citizen responsibility on the part of its advocates."

The major defect in the example is inclusion of the "because" clause, which consists of material in support of the proposition. A second defect is intentional or accidental loading caused by including the unnecessary adjective "great." If this proposition were reworded to put it into acceptable form, it would read simply, "The humanitarian stance of many members of the moral majority is fallacious."

Figurative or Colloquial Language Is Inappropriate in a Proposition. Many a heated discussion has been unproductive because its subject was expressed in figurative or colloquial terms. "Communism is like a colony of ants" is an attractive analogy that evaporates when one attempts to ascertain precisely what it means. "Only a Yuppy can truly appreciate the good life in today's America" is a statement couched in terms that fluctuate in meaning from person to person, time to time, and place to place.

Even subtle figurative usages blur the meaning in an otherwise definite proposition. Consider "Philosophy courses are more than a mental exercise" and "The U.S. will be doomed unless it reverses its traditional self-view as the world's savior." Mental exercises are a loose entity, and reversing a traditional self-view is difficult to envision, particularly when it is of the United States as world savior. Metaphors make these propositions unclear.

The reason any figure or colloquialism is undesirable in a proposition is that the statement is more abstract with it than without it. Since good propositions are as concrete as possible, the use of colloquial and figurative language in them is seldom, if ever, justified.

A Well-worded Proposition Assumes a Definite Burden of Proof.   As a statement of intent, a proposition in persuasion must necessarily specify a belief or an action that is not currently acceptable to its receivers. If the objective of communicators is something their audience already believes or would do anyway, without their message, they cannot be said to be persuading. The obligation to word a proposition so it requires a change of belief or action is called "burden of proof."

Burden of proof is always in terms of a particular topic, audience, and situation. Typically, persuaders first study the current attitude of the audience toward their recommendation. Then they estimate how far they can reasonably expect to "move" it (change its attitudes and beliefs) with their appeal. They then word their proposition to express this calculated goal. If their's is an action recommendation, they design the nature of the requested act by deciding what they can reasonably expect their audience to be willing to do, once it has understood their message. They word their claims to state this action objective.

An ever-present pitfall is the tendency of many persuaders to assign themselves an excessive burden of proof. A recommendation should be examined thoughtfully to assure that, for a particular audience and circumstance, its burden of proof is substantial but not beyond reason. Trying to do more than can be done accomplishes little. And since persuaders define their own goals, failure from overestimating one's persuasive potential can be particularly punishing.

Propositions should Be Worded Positively.   One good reason for avoiding the word "not" in a proposition is the tendency people have when told *not* to do something to want to do it. This probably explains why positive suggestion is generally conceded to be more persuasive than negative suggestion. Wording a recommendation in the affirmative thus removes at least one roadblock to its acceptance.

But is it possible to word all claims positively? By and large it is possible, although in a few instances converting a negative wording to a positive form may be prohibitively awkward. Let us see how some sample propositions, originally worded in the negative, can "accent the positive."

"The United States should not expand its space program" becomes "The United States should restrict its space program to present levels."

"Capital punishment is not a deterrent to crime" can be worded "Capital punishment should be abolished."

With ingenuity almost all negative propositions can be changed to positive wordings with negligible distortion. In addition to the benefits of positive suggestion, the change avoids some confusion should the recommendation be disputed. When one argues against a "not" proposition, one contends that the negative position is not the case, and "not not" phrasings muddy the arena of argument. It is much cleaner and neater to advance an affirmative position and make it possible for the contrasting view to be designated by a single negation.

THE ROLE OF SUPPORTING MATERIAL

When we discuss the concept of *supporting material,* we must remember that one cannot tell whether or not a given bit of speech material is supportive until it is examined in its relation to the statement to be supported. Just as an architect must examine a column for a building in terms of the beam or rafter that is to be supported, considering weight, aesthetic relationship, and proportioning, so must a speaker evaluate supporting material for a presentation in terms of the point that it is to enhance.

The best way to view the development of ideas, therefore, is in terms of message units. Each unit, to be complete, must contain the point or proposition and the material that amplifies the proposition. Although our discussion of various kinds of supporting material does not always fit the devices into context, the student should remember that material which would be excellent support for one idea might not be logically related to another.

USING STATISTICS AS SUPPORT

Statistics are numerical descriptions of facts. When statistics are appropriate and the numerical descriptions actually represent quantitative and qualitative differences, they provide the most precise information about factual matters that is available to the presentational speaker. Because of the precision of statistical data, they are the single most important type of supporting material used in presentational speaking for business and the professions.

Since statistical statements often concentrate on presenting selected relational information, they are open to distortions and may prove more misleading than helpful. The use of statistical support in persuasive messages to mislead or hoodwink the general public by pleaders for special interests has often been documented. All of us understand and are justifiably suspicious of statistical assertions in such obviously self-serving situations as the television commercial or the paid political advertisement.

Our discussion of statistics will examine both the usefulness of and dangers in supporting ideas with numerical descriptions of the facts.

Statistical Indexes of Typicality.   One of the most important uses of statistical statements is to give an indication of the typical instance in a large population of events or of the general drift of affairs.

The arithmetic average, probably the most common indicator of typicality, is the *mean.* In instances where a distribution of the statistical information reveals a few extremely large numbers at one end or a few extremely small ones at the other, another index of central tendency such as the *median* may be more accurate. To determine the median, the scores must be ordered as to size. The median is discovered by finding the score that is in the middle of the range. The number with half of the scores above and half below is the median.

On occasion, neither average nor median is an appropriate indicator of the typical or important central tendency in the information.

The third index of central position is the *mode*. The mode is the value that occurs most often in a distribution. For example, the dress length that occurs most often in a given season is called the "modish" length. The mode does not necessarily have to fall in the middle of the distribution and is not always a single number. On occasion, a distribution may have two or more modes.

By careful use of the measures of central tendency such as the mean, the mode, and the median, a person making a presentation can convey a great amount of accurate information in a few words.

Statistical Indexes of Variability.   One way to discover the variation in events is to take the numerical data and arrange them in a distribution as to magnitude. The statistician can then divide the distribution into one hundred parts so that 1 percent of the events fall in each part. Each division is called a *percentile*. The median is the fiftieth percentile since it falls at the midpoint. The point where 1 percent of the cases have smaller values (99 percent have larger values) is the first percentile. The value that falls on a point where 75 percent of the cases have smaller values (25 percent have larger values) is the seventy-fifth percentile.

Students are probably most familiar with the use of percentiles in relation to test scores and grade-point averages. A student's position in a high school graduating class may be described by a percentile mark. If the grade point of each student in a class of five hundred is computed and then distributed according to magnitude, the resulting distribution forms the basis for discovering percentiles. The first percentile includes the five students with the lowest grade points, the second the ten with the lowest grade points, on up to the last percentile, which includes the five students with the highest grade points. Each individual student can get a rank that indicates his or her standing in the class. A student whose rank was in the twenty-fourth percentile stood in the lowest quartile of the class, with 76 percent above and 23 percent below him.

Percentiles can be used to discover how tightly the statistical data are clustered around the measure of central tendency and thus indicate how similar are the events described by the median, mode, or mean. The entire *range* of the scores or statistics is the value resulting from subtracting the lowest number from the highest in the distribution.

In a case where an arithmetic average (mean) is the indicated measure of central tendency, statisticians often compute a *standard deviation* as an index to variability. Although to figure the standard deviation one must incorporate the concept of square root for computational convenience, the concept itself is no more difficult to grasp than that of the interpercentile range. Recall that the purpose of the standard deviation is to get some index as to the amount of variation in the statistical distribution. The technique in the instance of the standard deviation is to first discover the average (mean) of the entire distribution and then compute the distance of each individual statistic from the average, add up all the resulting variances, and divide by the total number of scores. The result of such figuring is the average deviation from the mean of all the scores.

When one subtracts the average from each statistic, some of the remainders are plus and some are minus values. Adding them up will always result in a total of 0. To overcome the problem with the figuring of the average deviation, statisticians may ignore the signs. Another way to overcome the problem is to square the values that result from subtracting the average from each score; the process of squaring results in having all positive values for the variation. Squaring the differences, adding them, and dividing by the total number of items results in another figure indicating the size of the variation around the average. The technical name for that figure is the *variance*.

Statisticians seldom use the variance as a way to describe variability, because it cannot be represented graphically. They have discovered, however, that the square root of the variance can be graphed as a measure along a scale of scores. Thus, the most useful measure of variability related to averages is the square root of the variance, a figure that is called the *standard deviation*.

The standard deviation provides an index to the dispersion of values similar to the interpercentile range and is an excellent summary of variability or variety in a set of statistical scores. The middle two-thirds of the distribution will fall in a range one standard deviation above and one below the mean. Approximately the middle 95 percent of the range will fall between two standard deviations either side of the mean.

The modern organization assembles large masses of statistics in the normal course of events. Today's management is often inundated by an excess of numerical information because professional researchers and statisticians, buttressed with the latest data processing systems, can provide it in abundance. It is often far easier to gather and present statistical information than it is to determine its meaning and discover the realities that lie behind the numbers. Quite often, the basic information required for wise decision-making is an estimation of relationships. The realities under discussion can often be described in such simple relational terms as *enough, too much, on time, gaining, out of reach, leveling off, losing ground steadily, the weakest region, our strongest line, too slow, ahead of schedule,* and *above-average performance.*

The basic mental process involved in developing relations is that of comparison. One of the most important ways the presentational speaker has of making accurate comparisons is by means of statistical statements. Comparisons make figures meaningful and significant. The basic relationship that statistics describe in comparative terms is that of more or less. The refinements of more or less relate to the concepts of simultaneous observations and to trends through time of consecutive observations.

Among the most important ways of preparing and interpreting statistical data are the table and the graph. Indeed, one factor in the rise of presentational speaking with its emphasis on visual aids is that so much information related to matters such as items produced, labor used in production, sales, profits, losses, and time of distribution is statistical. Every student of presentational speaking must have a good grasp of the use of tables and graphs to display comparative statistics and reveal basic relationships.

The Summary Table. A summary table presents major conclusions derived from analysis of the raw data in such a way that it makes clear important relationships relevant to the purpose of the presentation. Several different summary tables can be developed from the same statistical data for different purposes. We remind the reader of the relationship between supporting material and the proposition it amplifies.

Both tables and graphs can be arranged to exaggerate or attenuate the effects of the same numerical data. If the information is processed analytically, the impact of arrangement is lost because analysis in computer fashion responds only to number. But the human responds holistically, appreciating the quantitative distinctions but maximizing or minimizing their

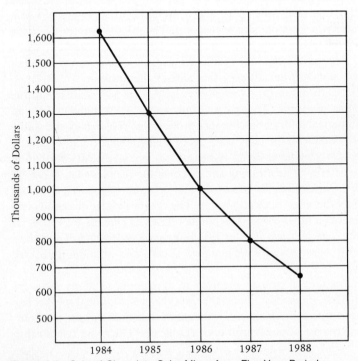

Figure 6.2 Sale of Chocolate Cake Mixes for a Five-Year Period

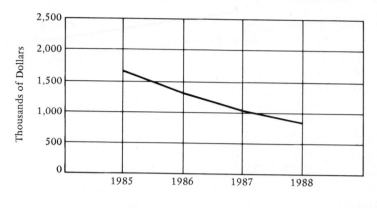

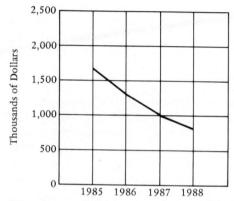

Figure 6.3   Two Graphs Presenting Same Data on Chocolate Cake Mixes

significance because of the "big picture" impact of their total presentation. The overall perception of the gestalt is influenced by the arrangement of the person making the presentation.

The overall management of response can be accomplished by the strategic arrangement of numbers in a table, but graphs provide more striking (we were tempted to write "graphic") examples. So rather than attempt to illustrate both, we will provide a sampling of graphic methods for presenting statistical summaries.

To provide concrete data for the graphs, we will return to the hypothetical milling company used for the John Jamison case study in Chapter 1. Chocolate cake mix sales have distressed the parent company in recent years, and the resulting predicament is summarized in varied graphic forms.

GRAPHIC METHODS FOR PRESENTING STATISTICAL SUMMARIES

The main purpose of translating tabular statistics in graphic form is to make them more vivid and to present relationships in a way that is easier to grasp. A *graph* is a representation of numbers by geometric figures drawn to scale.

The Line Graph.   Perhaps the most widely used means of presenting statistical data visually is the line graph. Line graphs are particularly useful for clarifying comparative relationships through time. Since many business and professional presentations deal with information relating to time-based trends—for example, comparing profits, production, wages, or market potential from quarter to quarter or year to year—the line graph is one of the more important tools of the presentational speaker.

If we take chocolate cake mix sales, we can construct a line graph as in Figure 6.2. Drawing a line graph requires that scales are laid out at right angles to each other. Often there is little relationship between the horizontal and vertical scales to be selected. The magnitude of a trend can be distorted by compressing or elongating the space allotted to time periods while keeping the scale for the other axis constant. Figure 6.3 presents two line graphs, each indicating a decrease in sales of chocolate cake mixes over a four-year period. The graphs have the same magnitude, but because of the difference in scale selected to represent an interval of a year, the lower graph makes the decrease appear much more dramatic.

Placing more than one curve on a graph facilitates the communication of relationships by quick visual inspection. Figure 6.4 indicates the sales of chocolate cake mixes for a five-year period with the supermarket sales compared to the independent retail outlets. The supermarket sales continued to rise, while the sales at independent outlets dropped. The decline of cake mix sales is here revealed to be primarily a function of independent outlet sales. A person preparing a presentation ought not graph more than one comparison for each visual.

Occasionally the comparisons to be graphed are of such widely different magnitudes that equal-interval scales cannot be used. For example, if the presentation about cake mixes required a comparison on the rate of

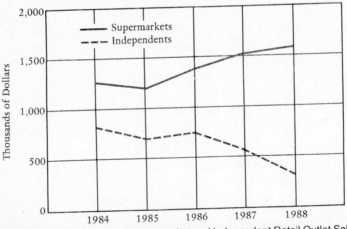

Figure 6.4   Comparison of Supermarket and Independent Retail Outlet Sales of Chocolate Cake Mixes for a Five-Year Period

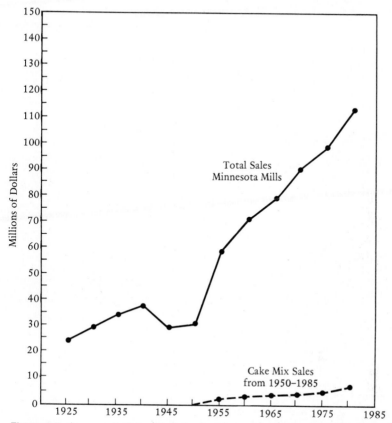

Figure 6.5   Increase in Cake Mix Sales for Minnesota Mills Compared to Gross Sales

increase in cake mix sales as compared to total income for Minnesota Mills, the share of the total income attributable to cake mixes might be such a small fraction of the total income of the corporation that graphing the two sets of data might not reveal the accurate information. Figure 6.5 indicates the comparison graphed on equal-interval scales (also called *arithmetic scales*). According to this figure, one might assume that while total sales for Minnesota Mills were rapidly increasing, the cake mix sales have only grown slightly. In terms of dollar volume the graph is accurate. In terms of the rate of increase, however, the graph is misleading. An accurate representation of percentage or rate of increase is provided by a vertical scale which would represent a 10 percent increase in total sales, with the same amount of distance on the vertical axis as a 10 percent increase in cake mix volume. The scale that reveals proportionate increases is called *logarithmic*. A graph that has one arithmetic (equal-interval) scale and another logarithmic (proportional-interval) scale is called a *semilogarithmic* graph. Figure 6.6 presents the same comparative data as Figure 6.5 but in a semilogarithmic graph that reveals that cake mix sales have risen at about the same rate as total corporate sales.

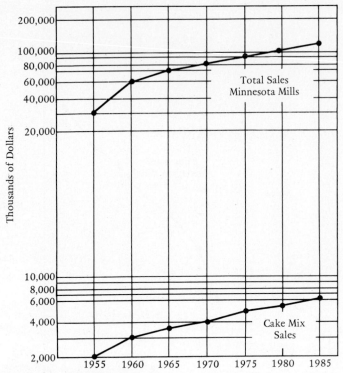

Figure 6.6 Increase in Cake Mix Sales for Minnesota Mills Compared to Gross Sales on Semilogarithmic Graph

The Bar Graph.   In a bar graph numerical dimensions are visualized in terms of bars of varying lengths drawn to scale. A bar graph is illustrated in Figure 6.7.

The bar graph is also well suited to depicting comparative statistics. Figure 6.8 displays the proportionate percentage of supermarket to independent retail stores in the sample.

Bar graphs can present comparisons among many different statistics. Figure 6.9 illustrates a bar graph that compares year-by-year three different cake mixes, and each bar is divided to show further comparative data.

While bar graphs of the complexity of Figure 6.9 are often useful in written reports where the reader has ample time to decipher the various keys and discover the meaning of solid bars versus hatched bars and the units along the side of the graph, a speaker making a presentation would not use such a complicated visual. Again, the principle of restricting the information on each visual to one or two basic relationships clearly graphed so the audience can quickly grasp the essence of the information must be applied. Figure 6.7 represents a good bar graph for oral presentations.

In general, the bar graph should have all scale values beginning with

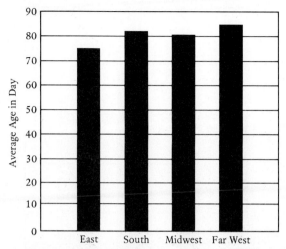

Figure 6.7 Age of Cake Mixes of Minnesota Mills on Retail Outlet Shelves: A Survey of 200 Retail Outlets in Four Major Geographical Regions

the zero point. Because the relationship is based on a geometric comparison, starting the graph at some other point will result in misleading the viewer. For example, if the information graphed on Figure 6.7 were presented as in Figure 6.10 starting at fifty days rather than at the zero point, the differences among the regions would be exaggerated.

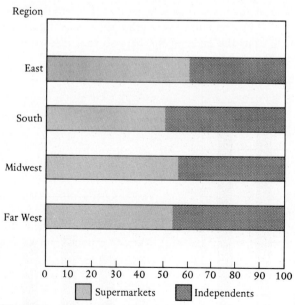

Figure 6.8 Proportions of Independent Retail Outlets in Cake Mix Survey: A Breakdown of 200 Retail Outlets in Four Major Geographical Regions for Minnesota Mills

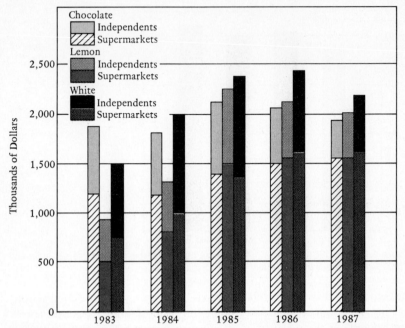

Figure 6.9 Sales of Chocolate, Lemon, and White Cake Mixes for a Five-Year Period

The eye may be misled by graphic material if the numbers that the bars represent are added at the ends, thus exaggerating the length of the bars, as in Figure 6.11. The best technique is to place the needed figures at the left and far enough from the ends of the bars so that distortion is unlikely as in Figure 6.12.

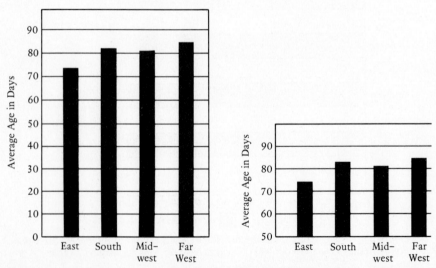

Figure 6.10 Distortion of Comparative Statistical Data Resulting from Not Starting from Zero Index

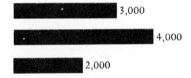

3,000

4,000

2,000

Figure 6.11 Incorrect Labeling of Bars May Mislead Viewer by Making the Bar Appear Unduly Long

Bar graphs have several obvious virtues for the individual preparing a presentation. Because they reveal basic relationships in geometrical fashion, they can be made large enough for the audience to read and grasp the essential point quickly and easily. A table that presents a relatively simple relationship often requires some translation by the speaker or listener in gross terms such as "that is approximately twice as much in a ten-year period" or "that is about one-third of the projected sales." A well-constructed graph reveals such relationships as one-half, one-third, and so on, in visual terms.

Other Graphic Techniques.   The pie chart reveals proportional divisions of a whole set of data in such easy-to-grasp form that it deserves special consideration. The pie chart is often used to show the distribution of total income among various sources, or the total budgetary allocation to various divisions or departments.

Although speakers might hesitate to use a pie chart in a presentation about cake mixes for fear of being accused of using a mixed metaphor, they might do so to indicate the percentage of sales for various departments within the pastry division. Figure 6.13 shows percentage of income from various products within that division of Minnesota Mills.

Notice that Figure 6.13 starts with a radius drawn vertically from the center. The other parts are then laid off clockwise beginning with the largest slice of the pie and continuing with the next largest and down to the smallest component. Unless the data divide logically in another fashion, the procedure used in Figure 6.13 is the usual one.

A person making a presentation to an audience that may be unfamiliar with the data or relatively uninterested in the subject may want to use a *pictograph*. The pictograph represents the statistical information in terms of cartoon pictures, with quantitative relationships shown by areas or heights of pictured figures. Using height of figures to indicate quantity is a distortion, since a taller figure has increased area and suggests greater magnitude.

Pictographs often add interest to a visual and make abstract statistical comparisons more concrete. Drawing symbols requires time and skill, and

4,000

3,000

2,000

Figure 6.12   Correct Way to Label Bars in Bar Graph

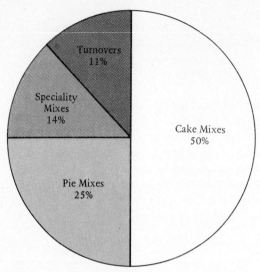

Figure 6.13 Pie Chart of Total Sales of Pastry Division of Minnesota Mills, All Departments

often the added interest may not be commensurate with the expense of preparing good pictographs. When pictographs are used, the symbols must be simple and depend primarily on their outline. Often, the symbols are prepared in silhouette rather than including detail in the drawings. The data must be such that gross differences in the size of the pictures will convey the intended message. The pictograph is relatively inflexible and can only be used with very simple data. Most of the data in Figures 6.2–6.13 could not be easily illustrated with a pictograph. (Pictures that would readily distinguish between chocolate cake mixes and lemon cake mixes are not easy to come by.)

The Use of Graphs for Presentational Speaking. The decision as to whether to use a table or a graph to present statistical information and comparisons is one that needs to be made with an eye to the audience, the graphic resources available to the speaker, and the amount of time available for the speech. As a general rule, the graph will serve the speaker's purpose better than a table because it is less difficult to decipher and presents relationships visually in terms that can be readily understood.

On occasion, to be sure, an audience that is used to interpreting statistics in tabular form will appreciate the added information that tables can provide. Tables do require less time to prepare and less skill and artistry.

Graphs must be large enough so that they can be easily deciphered by all members of the audience, a problem that is easily solved by use of the overhead projector. With the projector, a pencil can serve as a pointer to indicate crucial parts of the graph and their relationships.

The presentational speaker should be highly selective in deciding what statistical information to present in graphic form. Only a few of the more important data should be developed into visual aids and incorporated into the speech.

Each graph ought to contain only one or two basic comparisons and ought not be shown to the audience for more than twenty or thirty seconds at one time. Important graphs may be shown again a second or third time.

All in all, the graph is one of the most important and useful tools for the presentation of statistical data in business and professional speaking. Every student of presentational speaking should become adept at developing, interpreting, and using graphs as visual aids.

NONSTATISTICAL FORMS OF SUPPORT

Nonstatistical forms of support for the contentions in a presentation may be divided into two main categories: (1) evidence and (2) clarification. *Evidence* is supporting material designed to furnish grounds for belief or to make evident the truth or falsity, rightness or wrongness, wisdom or folly, of a proposition. Evidence is a technical legal term that refers to material furnished by lawyers in support of their briefs. In the courts, evidence may consist of both testimony of witnesses and factual exhibits such as pistols, knives, and clothing. *Proof* is the sufficient marshaling of evidence to achieve conviction or acceptance of the proposition from the judge or jury. Evidence carries weight as proof with the members of the audience. For the student of presentational speaking, evidence includes both oral and written testimony (verbal evidence) and things such as prototypes of new products, models of buildings and bridges, and demonstrations. Our emphasis in this chapter will be on verbal evidence, which includes, in addition to the statistical information treated earlier, case studies and the testimony of eyewitnesses and experts.

Clarification is supporting material designed to enlighten the listener. Clarification is primarily aimed at achieving understanding. Clarification consists solely of verbal devices. *Understanding* is achieved when sufficient clarification results in a meeting of the minds among those involved in the communication.

NONSTATISTICAL EVIDENCE

The Case Study.   The virtue of numerical descriptions of facts is that they have precision and scope. Statistics suffer, however, from lack of qualitative material, human interest, and concreteness. Statistical descriptions of factual situations tend to be cold, dull, and dry. Some business people and professionals deal with situations that are so idiosyncratic that statistical descriptions of central tendency or range of variability are essentially meaningless. The most useful complement for statistics when they are appropriate and the best substitute for them when they are not is the form of evidence known as the case study.

The *case study* (sometimes called real-life example) is a detailed observation and analysis of a given event. Case studies used for evidence in support of an argumentive position are always based on observations of actual events and should not be confused with hypothetical case studies such as the ones we have been using in this book for clarification. Hypothetical cases are fictions dreamed up by communicators to help clarify their ideas and gain understanding. We deal with hypothetical cases later, in our discussion of clarification.

When case studies are used to supplement, clarify, and humanize statistical descriptions, they ought to be selected in order to complement the basic statistical analysis. Several cases that are typical of the most common or usual events integrated with such statistical indexes as averages, means, or modes will help support the statistical evidence.

Case studies are often appropriate in clinical professions such as medicine, social work, psychology, and psychiatry. Careful case studies of welfare clients may prove to be the best evidence for a change in the welfare program of a given city.

Case studies must be based on careful and accurate observations. If the features of the case that are crucial to the decision are falsified, then the actions based on the evidence may be unwise. Even accurate case studies may be poor evidence for a given proposition, however, if they are not typical of the category they represent. While case studies serve to humanize conditions and provide understanding of the qualitative detail of a problem, they do so at a considerable sacrifice of scope and generality. The danger of drawing a conclusion from too few cases and applying it indiscriminately to new situations is thus increased when arguing from case studies.

Testimony.   The most convincing evidence is often that of the senses. When people see for themselves, they are often convinced. Direct verification of factual assertions is the ultimate test of truth or falsity. Thus, in the law courts witnesses testifying to what they have personally experienced are evaluated as a source of good evidence. In scholarship the primary document is one that contains the account of a person who can testify from his or her own experience. The lawyer or scholar developing an argument to prove a proposition about something that he or she does not know firsthand must often turn to the words of those who have directly observed the facts in question. The testimony of eyewitnesses thus becomes another important form of evidence.

The basic strength of the modern corporation is its ability to utilize narrowly and highly trained specialists. Minnesota Mills can undertake such a complicated project as launching a new cake mix because it has among its employees specialists in flour milling, nutrition, home economics, marketing, production, advertising, distribution, sales, and so on. The corporate structures make it possible for all of these experts to focus their energies on the development of a new product. Thus, by having talented people do a small part of the task very well and by integrating these specialized functions, the entire project can reach a level of excellence that no one person no matter how great a genius could hope to match.

Under ideal conditions, when the decision-making group has gathered the relevant factual information, heard the authorities draw their expert conclusions, and listened to the recommendations of the specialists on all questions relating to their specialties, the next step should be the previously mentioned free-for-all discussion in which everyone tests and challenges everyone else's conclusions and recommendations. A major difficulty in achieving the ideal condition is the tendency for experts to be defensive about their special prerogatives. If someone challenges an electronic engineer about electronics, the expert tends to brush off the challenge on the basis that only a fellow engineer is competent to discuss technical problems, for example. What often happens, therefore, is that a norm of behavior is established in an organization that "if you do not challenge my expertness by questioning my professional recommendations, I will recognize your authority in your area of specialization and not challenge you."

CLARIFICATION AS SUPPORTING MATERIAL

Hypothetical Cases. Hypothetical case studies resemble real cases in all respects save that they are fictitious. The speaker creates imaginary situations to illustrate a point, clarify a complex analysis, or present abstract and esoteric principles or theories in concrete terms. Just as a good novel may illuminate human nature and human experience, even though it contains characters who do not resemble any real persons living or dead and its plot consists of incidents that never happened, so can a good hypothetical case clarify a speaker's ideas. Since hypothetical cases are fictitious, they are not evidence and thus cannot be considered as proof. Hypothetical cases can, however, dramatize a central tendency or a general trend if they are developed by people who know the real facts intimately. If a speaker is using a hypothetical case in order to make concrete the general information already presented in statistical form, this should be made known to the audience. The case is then more than a fiction and becomes a technique to enable the audience to grasp the significance of the evidence it exemplifies. Often, a hypothetical case can reveal the implications of statistical data more accurately than a real case because a truly typical real case might be difficult to find.

Hypothetical cases are also useful for clarifying and adding interest because speakers can tailor them to their purposes. The hypothetical case is often the best choice to clarify a concept because it does not require as extensive a search of materials as does the real case study and because the speaker may add or subtract details, depending on the point to be made and the time available, without fear of distorting the facts. The hypothetical case is probably the most useful clarifying device available to the presentational speaker.

Analogy.   Another important technique useful in refining and clarifying ideas for an audience is the *analogy*. An analogy is a similarity between two individuals, facts, things, or events on which a comparison can be based. Analogies may be found by comparing and contrasting events drawn from the same class. Thus, an analogy might be found between the sales pattern of the Chocolate Delight Cake Mix and the Lemon Taffeta Cake Mix. Top management officials might discover an analogy in their experience with the merger with Timkin Toy and the proposed merger with Consolidated Electronics. A literal analogy is one in which the similarity is discovered to hold between two individuals, facts, things, or events drawn from the same class. Analogies can also be invented by rearranging unlikely individuals, facts, things, or events into patterns that reveal an unexpected or unusual similarity. When the ad agency copywriter named the new lemon cake "taffeta," he invented a similarity between the cake and a piece of cloth and asserted in his copy that the cake was "rich as taffeta." The fictitious or invented similarity between two things that are not, in fact, similar (the copywriter did not seriously suggest that anyone try to make a dress out of the lemon cake) is called a *figurative analogy*.

The figurative analogy has much less validity as a means of prediction. An executive may argue that for Minnesota Mills to merge with an electronics firm is like a major league ball player going on an African safari to hunt lions with his baseball bat. She may say that Minnesota Mills is in the big leagues as a milling company and has hit its share of home runs. She may urge Minnesota Mills to keep on doing what it knows best. She may suggest that if a ball player takes off for Africa with a ball bat trying to hit lions instead of baseballs, he is likely to get badly mauled. She may conclude, "As I see it, we'd be a lot better off if we didn't go hunting any lions like General Electric on a safari run by a little two-bit outfit like Consolidated Electronics and stick to hitting more home runs in our own ball park." The figurative analogy about ball players and lions compared to a merger of Minnesota Mills and Consolidated Electronics may add interest to the meeting and clarify the rigidity of the speaker's position, but as a bit of argument against the merger it does not have the stature of a literal comparison of the Timkin Toy and Consolidated Electronics capital structure, product lines, growth potential, and so on.

Figurative analogies are used sparingly in contemporary presentations. The spare shorthand style of today's business speaking does not lend itself to inventing colorful and unusual comparisons. Figurative analogies must be used with skill and good taste, or they degenerate into the laughable as did the analogy about mergers and lion hunts. However, the paucity of figurative analogy in business and professional speeches is perhaps unfortunate. Used with discretion, they add spice and sparkle to what might otherwise be a relatively grim and dull message. Often a good figurative analogy will clarify a difficult argument or concept more effectively than can any other rhetorical device.

Narratives.   Another important clarifying device is the *narrative*. Narratives are stories of events or experiences either true or fictitious. They may be long or short and deal with past events, present situations, or future possibilities. Generally in the presentation, narratives are used to clarify and to add interest. On occasion, however, the purpose of a narrative may be primarily amusement.

Good narratives for presentational speaking contain characterization, conflict, suspense, and a point directly applicable to the topic under discussion. A story requires characters to play the various parts. Stories usually concentrate on one central character who is sympathetic and draws the audience's interest. Usually, the main character has a clear object in view and his attempts to achieve his goal dictate the selection of incidents for the story. As the character strives to gain his objective, he meets obstacles that he does not expect. Some of the obstacles are of natural origin and some may be placed in his way by an antagonist, a bad guy who is working against the hero, and the result is a conflict which arouses suspense. In a good narrative the forces of good and evil ought to be equally balanced so the hero has a fighting chance, but a slight tipping of the scales in either direction can carry the day.

Narratives may recount a factual event. True stories carry conviction and are often more impressive than fiction in a presentational speech. Quite often, however, actual events do not fall neatly into a good narrative pattern, and the speaker may wish to modify the details of the story to improve its narrative quality. When telling of actual events, the speaker may base the story on personal experience or recount events as an experience of someone else. Only conscience limits the amount of distortion introduced to make a good story. The personal-experience narrative is one of the most widely used and effective clarifying and amplifying techniques. A personal experience, if it is told well, can amuse, illustrate, clarify, convince, and present the speaker in an attractive light as a person of insight and humor.

A danger in using personal-experience narratives is that they may make the speaker appear egotistical and self-centered. A secondary problem is that personal-experience stories often require more time for the telling than the point they make will justify. Speakers tend to include unnecessary incidents and expressive detail in relating narratives.

Parables are narratives about events seemingly unrelated to the topic but with an unusual appropriateness when the speaker points out the application. A famous lecturer at the turn of the century, Russell Conwell, gave a speech called "Acres of Diamonds" thousands of times. The basic narrative that formed the spine of the lecture was the story of an ancient Persian named Ali Hafed who was wealthy but grew discontented when he heard that with one diamond the size of his thumb he could purchase his entire country and that if he had nine diamonds he could place his children on thrones through the influence of his great wealth. Ali Hafed sold all of his holdings and, taking the proceeds, traveled all over the world searching for diamonds. He wandered the earth without success until he had reduced himself to poverty. He then drowned himself in the bay at Barcelona in Spain. Meanwhile, the man who bought Ali Hafed's farm led his camel one day into the garden for a drink, and as the camel drank, the farmer noticed a flash of light from the sand in the bottom of the stream. He had discovered the diamond mine of Golcanda which exceded Kimberly itself. When delivering the lecture in Philadelphia Conwell drew the lesson from his parable that "you have 'acres of diamonds' in Philadelphia right where you now live." He told his audience that "the opportunity to get rich, to attain unto great wealth, is here in Philadelphia now, within the reach of almost every man and woman who hears me speak tonight, and I mean just what I say."

Clarification by Stylistic Devices. An interesting paradox of business and professional communication results from the claim of many organizations that their communications should be utilitarian. Business and professional people often praise brevity, clarity, and objectivity as the best characteristics of good communication. They often, therefore, shun elegance, aptness, or beauty of language in oral and written reports, memorandums, and presentations. The paradox is that the same people who talk down stylistic flourishes in messages seem to crave verbal elegance. They often repeat the apt slogan or a memorable aphorism. They may hang a particularly striking maxim on the wall of the office or print it on their letterheads. An extreme example of this paradox is the archetype of the modern presentation, the television commercial. It exploits every avenue of visual communication, aims at being persuasive in the most economical fashion, yet best illustrates the advantages of stylistic artistry. Almost without exception television commercial copy relies on the catchy jingle with reiteration and restatement or a swinging slogan and alliterative word play to reinforce the message.

Certainly one of the basic devices for amplification of oral messages and clarifying their meaning is the use of reiteration. Reiteration is the device of repeating the same idea in another way either by presenting another case, supplementing the case with testimony, making the same point with narrative material, or simply repeating the idea in slightly different words.

Another of the highly effective devices of oral communication is repeating elements of the message in a rhythmic or patterned way. The child is charmed by a story or poem that repeats the same phrases or comments by characters over and over again. Music and poetry illustrate the charm of echoing sounds. The refrain in a song and the repetition of the last line of each stanza in certain poetic forms is a common form of repetition.

While reiteration and repetition may be ineffective in a written message, seeming to constitute unnecessary verbiage, these are necessary and useful parts of the spoken communication. Reiteration serves to give the audience time to absorb an idea and see some of its many implications and ramifications. Since the listener cannot go back over the material and read it again and again as can someone studying a written paragraph, the speaker can provide for somewhat the same effect by reiterating and repeating an idea several times.

Another stylistic supporting device is to borrow particularly apt sayings, sentiments, or verbal pronouncements from philosophers, poets, theologians, and novelists. In one sense the use of quotations is a form of testimony. But quotations primarily function as stylistic devices of support. Speakers are using the talents of another to provide them with their material, but the function is much the same as if they themselves had originated the material. (Of course, we must recognize that some positive suggestion about speakers results from their quoting Aristotle or Confucius or Emerson.)

A final important stylistic way to support and clarify ideas in presentational speeches is by the use of distinctive phrases, catchwords, and terse sayings. An *aphorism* is a brief apt statement that embodies a general truth such as, "Nobody can make your mistakes for you." The test of a good aphorism is how often it is repeated and appreciated subsequently. Barnum's assertion that "there is a sucker born every minute" has proved itself an aphorism according to that standard. Other examples of aphorism would include: "The greatest enemy of communication is the illusion of it." "See it big and keep it simple." A *maxim* is an aphorism that contains advice as to how one should conduct oneself. Organizations thrive on maxims and often display them prominently in offices, on letterheads, and on buildings. Examples of maxims would include: "Don't say it—display it." "Never say it—write it." "Talk it over—jot it down."

Aphorisms and maxims are often used to inspire to greater effort or to add meaning and significance to the organization's efforts. They are excellent for presentations of an inspirational nature.

MANAGING THE REASONED CONTENT OF A PRESENTATION

Hit-or-miss arranging of logically related information is the result of myopic planning procedures. The author of such a message is unable to see beyond one piece of information and its interpretation. The speaker cites an example and draws a conclusion, gives some numerical data and another conclusion to interpret the numbers, and after projecting a trend into the future, concludes once again. Each fragment may be closely reasoned while the overall impact is negligible, because the parts are not clearly inter-related. A series of effective subpoints results, but the big picture fails to emerge. For evidence and reasoning to attain a cumulative effect, the ingredients in a reasoned appeal must be articulated so that one point builds on another, and these in turn serve as foundation for a third. The structure of the presentation should be assembled without a missing or unneeded building block.

To build a logic-tight structure that incorporates a variety of subpoints and supporting materials requires a *system* for arranging in a visible and orderly fashion every element needed to advance a major point. The layout presented in Figure 6.14, which often requires an outsized sheet of paper, permits the builder of a message to see the relationships among all parts of an argument. The speaker can then eliminate the nonessential, emphasize the relatively more important, and improve the integration of all elements in a complex rational unit. The skeleton of the unit plan reveals the basic strategy of the system. After a few suggestions for applying the layout, we will look at a sample structure that shows how diverse elements in the network of reasoning become unified.

HOW TO USE THE UNIT PLAN FOR RATIONAL PRESENTATION

Perhaps the most important suggestion for using the unit plan effectively is this: Begin with the proposition. The claim or proposition states the desired outcome of the presentation in terms of an action response or a specific belief. Above all else, effective persuasion is goal-oriented, so specifying the intended result rather precisely at the beginning of planning creates a frame of reference in which all materials used can be related and focused.

Essential Information   **Reasons and Support**   **Qualified Proposition**
                                    for Reasons

                                                                      Exceptions

Necessary Explanation
1.
2.
3.
4.

Figure 6.14 Unit Plan for Rational Presentation

"Qualifying" the proposition increases its precision. The difference between "each and every" and "by and large" claims is shown by the qualifiers used. "Probably" and "certainly" are qualifiers, as are "always" and "usually." A properly worded proposition always incorporates a qualifier that is carefully chosen to assume a sufficient burden of proof without going beyond available means of support. The good qualifier makes a claim both believable and provable to the contemplated audience.

When the message builders are satisfied with their qualified proposition, they set about accumulating essential information. They ask what evidence will best contribute to the credibility of their proposition in the minds of their listeners. Attempting to be extremely selective, they note on their planning sheet a minimum number of facts and assumptions. Later, if more information is needed, they can collect only what is required to complete their pattern. The selective, "bare bones" approach to listing items of essential information is recommended because of a universal tendency to assemble unneeded information and the confusion caused by a surplus of little-related facts.

The next step is to check out the adequacy of essential information by filling in the middle column, "reasons and support for reasons." Reasons interpret information. Whenever a reason is not self-evident, support for it is supplied, attached to the reason by "because." If essential information is adequate and the reasons are properly structured, the qualified proposition will follow as a conclusion, without other basic elements of communication having to be supplied.

As the arrangement of proposition, reasons, and information is gradually improved by selecting better evidence and rearranging and rewording reasons and their support, planners ask themselves repeatedly, "What will be unclear or difficult for my audience?" By assuming the point of view of a listener, they find that certain explanatory materials add significance and make basic points easier to grasp. They note these items as "necessary explanation" in their plan.

Now the authors of the messages turn back to their starting points. Can the qualified proposition be improved so that it states their points better and has more persuasive potential? Usually the process of building a unit of rational presentation changes the authors' perspective of their assignment enough so that they find it desirable to reword the proposition. The perfect proposition is not likely to be achieved. Other things being equal, the more a proposition is rewritten, the better the final product will be. Simplicity and clarity are particularly enhanced by rewriting.

Finally, the plan is completed by noting any exceptions that might invalidate the conclusion. Often there are possibilities, usually of an unlikely nature, which if true would negate the entire line of reasoning in the unit. The thoughtful planners may or may not wish to include them in their presentations. But they certainly make them a part of their plan, to protect against being unpleasantly surprised by an unanticipated and damaging exception at the time of the presentation.

To make the unit concrete we are including in Figure 6.15 a sample structure designed to argue that cigarette manufacturers should be permitted to omit health warnings on their packages. Read the plan in the order of its preparation: first the Qualified Proposition, then the Essential Information, then the Reasons and Support for Reasons, and finally, the Exception and Necessary Explanation items. The parts of the structure will fall into place neatly, each related to every other part and to the whole.

Most presentations incorporate several units of approximately this level of complexity. Occasionally, a single unit will encompass the evidence and reasoning involved. More often two or three, or as many as four or five such layouts, are necessary. These become the central themes and the foundation pillars on which the presentation rests. When these are arranged so that interlocking takes place, the resulting structure is indeed impressive. The unit plan is a specialized form of the brief, one that has great utility as an aid in preparing closely reasoned presentations.

Speakers with a completed unit plan will proceed to implement it by first selecting a pattern of organization, then evolving it into a speech of presentation by arranging and balancing their statistical and nonstatistical means of support, incorporating appropriate devices of suggestion, and finally, deciding on audiovisual materials to be utilized. The well-built unit plan protects the speaker against loose ends and unsupported conclusions.

Essential Information	Reasons and Support for Reasons	Qualified Proposition
1. Liquor bottles carry no warning. 2. Cola bottles carry no warning. 3. Cigarette packages carry a warning. 4. U.S. agencies should be consistent in requiring warnings on harmful products.	1. Liquor is potentially harmful because of alcoholism, heart trouble, loss of control. 2. Cola is potentially harmful because it is addictive and causes diabetes. 3. If cigarettes should carry a warning, then cola and liquor should also. 4. But cola and liquor carry no warning: Therefore: Qualified Proposition	Cigarette manufacturers should probably be permitted to omit health warnings from their packages. **Exception** Unless cigarettes are substantially more harmful than other products without warnings.

Necessary Explanation

1. The federal government has no obligation to protect citizens from any and all harmful products.
2. Information about the damage done by harmful products is unreliable and scarce.

Figure 6.15   Unit Plan for Rational Presentation of Argument That Cigarette Manufacturers Should Probably Be Permitted to Omit Health Warnings from Their Packages

It guarantees that all major points are dealt with sensibly and arranged in a proper sequence. Unity, coherence, and selective emphasis are the consequence, yielding a speech that is easy to follow and understand.

REASONING AND MOTIVATION

At this point in the discussion of reasoning in presentation, it is necessary to confront a popular belief that poses a dilemma. Are motive appeals and appeals to critical thinking incompatible? Can common sense and personal desire coexist? Do logical and nonlogical messages activate separate segments of the human psyche or does the receiving mechanism process all incoming signals in a single integrating and blending operation?

Probably most people envision reasons and motives as distinct and separate phenomena. The notion that human beings tend to become thoughtful about something they want fervently does not occur to most of us. Still, we know that in many instances only rigorous problem-solving can lead us to our heart's desire. And we *do* "reason about our wants." This suggests strongly that reason and desire cannot be separated and that their constant interaction is the usual rather than the exceptional case.

Our position with respect to the reason-motivation dichotomy is simple and clear: The dichotomy does not exist. The presentation, as we noted at the beginning of this chapter, is a predominantly rational form, *but in the frame of reference of the listener's motives.* This interaction was described several decades ago by William Norwood Brigance, who summarized his analysis when he wrote that "arguments which appeal to 'human reason' without touching human wants will be ineffective." Thus, reasoning is seen to be one method of triggering motives, a thoughtful, reflective method useful in meeting the needs of people. Indeed, rational units are often the most effective motive appeals.

If we grant that being reasonable is an effective means of helping people get what they want, we then ponder what is meant by "being reasonable." Since modes of critical thinking vary from culture to culture, we must conclude that logics are relative. Whatever provokes a listener to pause and reflect is, for that person, logical. In North America people tend to become thoughtful about assertions of cause and effect. In the Middle East similar statements have little meaning, since, there, causation is not a significant part of problem-solving procedures. In Japan the possibility of losing face promotes considerably more reflective thinking about a business problem than does the prospect of losing money. Hence, loss-of-face logic is more reasonable than profit and loss—to the Japanese.

Necessarily, by definition, what is reasonable to the listener *is* reasonable. The implications for communicators are clear. We must understand the habits of critical thinking possessed by our receivers and know the values assigned to preferred patterns. Only then can we be "reasonable" in a way that makes the most sense to our listeners.

Because perception is congruent with people's needs, the ultimate extension of meaning for the concept "reasonable" is that nonreason may be perceived as reason. This does indeed occur. When people's prejudices drive them furiously enough, they become capable of seeing an emotional, unsupported argument as carefully reasoned and conservatively stated. Truly, one person's suggestion is another's reasoned discourse, and vice versa. Hence, "good" reasons that are not important to the receiver of the message are functionally bad reasons, since they fail to generate reflective thought.

CRITERIA OF REASONED APPEAL

It is useful to the makers of presentations to have definite means of assessing the quality of their reasoned materials. This takes the form of three criteria. The first is derived from knowledge of members of the audience and of their systems of logical thought. The second and third are absolutes, in that they can be applied to a message independent of its intended receivers.

1. *Will the selected evidence and its interpretation be thought-provoking to this particular audience?* Concerns of the listeners are weighed and shrewd guesses made as to their problem-solving behavior in response to stimulation from the message. To the extent that the audience will probably be intrigued by information, topics, facts, and conclusions, the message is judged to satisfy the first criterion. Habits, needs, interests, desires, and goals, the entire motive structure of people who will be responding, enter into this evaluation of the rational elements in the presentation.

2. *How concrete and specific is the reasoned content?* Truly, concreteness is the basis of rationality. The more specific and definite a presentation is, the more reasonable it may be said to be. "Facts of the case" presentations are the most concrete, and nothing gets people thinking like involving them in real situations where they need to make decisions. Examples and illustrations, given in detail, contribute to this desirable characteristic of a message.

3. *Is the reasoned appeal valid and true?* A message is true when its verifiable elements correspond to reality, and a message is valid when its form violates none of the generally agreed-upon patterns of sound thinking. Using representative and comprehensive statistics and avoiding fallacies are matters of validity. False information, such as assuming a consensus that does not exist, is a matter of truth. The truth test is generally understood, although many slight distortions are difficult to detect and confirm. But criteria of validity in reasoning are many and complicated. The following tests of validity will be useful in producing soundly reasoned presentations.

1. Is all wording simple and clear?
2. Are opposing points of view recognized?

3. Are units compared really comparable?
4. Are statistics representative?
5. Are bases of all percentages supplied?
6. Do examples and case studies represent the situation fairly?
7. Are generalizations adequately supported?
8. Are quoted authorities reliable and qualified?
9. Are concealment and other deception avoided?
10. Are all relevant facts of the case acknowledged?
11. Is appropriate documentation supplied?

Truth and validity are criteria to be continuously applied during the planning and the building of a message. But when the presentation is substantially complete, a reworking in an effort to make all parts of it even more true and valid often pays rich dividends.

SUMMARY

When we attempt to achieve a reasoned response to a presentation, it is essential to know that we are working with *perceived reality,* not objective reality. A perceived reality is a social product of both analytic and holistic information processing in the minds of people with strong interests and firm preconceptions who are presented with communication that engages both. The social reality of the audience is only partially a product of their analytic processing of verifiable data.

The proposition states the central purpose of a reasoned presentation. Proper wording of the proposition is a vital step that precedes selection of reasons and evidence.

Supporting material is statistical and nonstatistical. Graphic methods are often effective ways to present statistical data. Nonstatistical support includes case studies, testimony, hypothetical cases, analogy, narratives, and stylistic devices.

Good reasoned content for a presentation is ineffective unless it is arranged optimally. Managing reasoned content requires an overall logical plan that classifies the ingredients of the message and shows how each part of the structure is related to every other part. The "Unit Plan for Rational Presentation" helps the presenter to attain this important objective.

Reasoning and motivation, often thought to be separate entities, are shown to be interactive and inseparable.

Three criteria serve as a final test of the reasonableness of a presentation:

1. Will the selected evidence and its interpretation be thought-provoking to this particular audience?
2. How concrete and specific is the reasoned content?
3. Is the reasoned appeal valid and true?

The readiness of an audience to accept and appreciate a presentation depends to a significant degree on how it feels about the speaker as a person. We refer to this all-important factor as "source credibility" and it is the subject of Chapter 7.

QUESTIONS FOR DISCUSSION AND REVIEW

1. Why is it necessary for the presenter to distinguish perceived from objective reality in order to predict response?

2. How can "mulling over" be a reasoned reaction?

3. What are the characteristics of a properly worded proposition?

4. What are some examples that distinguish statistical from nonstatistical support materials?

5. What are the definitions of the statistical indices of typicality and variability?

6. How may changing the space allotted to one of the scales change the visual impact of a line graph?

7. What are some advantages of the bar graph as a visual aid in presentations?

8. How can cases, analogies, narratives, and stylistic devices serve as support material?

9. What is the purpose of the "Unit plan for Rational Presentation?"

10. How are reasoning and motivation, often thought to be separable, actually interactive and inseparable?

REFERENCES AND SUGGESTED READINGS

For an interesting examination of perception as influenced by self-concept and sets of expectations, see:

Adler, Ronald B., and George Rodman. *Understanding Human Communication.* 2d ed. New York: Holt, Rinehart and Winston, 1985, pp. 23–47.

For the neurological foundation of reasoning, holistic processes, and motivation, see:

Gazzaniga, Michael S., and Joseph E. LeDoux. *The Integrated Mind.* New York: Plenum Press, 1978.

For a novel approach to enhancing creative competencies, see:

Samples, Bob. *The Metaphoric Mind: A Celebration of Creative Consciousness.* New York: Addison-Wesley, 1976.

For a less serious but equally insightful treatment of applying holistic methods, see:

Golde, Roger A. *Muddling Through: The Art of Properly Unbusinesslike Management.* New York: AMACOM, 1976.

For an application of analytic and holistic skills to management, see:

Agor, Weston H. *Intuitive Management: Integrating Left and Right Brain Management Skills.* Englewood Cliffs, N.J.: Prentice-Hall, 1984.

The quotation from Conwell's speech is from:

Conwell, Russell H. *Acres of Diamonds.* New York: Harper, 1915, pp. 16–17.

The Unit Plan for Rational Presentation is an adaptation of the model of argument in:

Toulmin, Stephen. *The Uses of Argument.* Cambridge: Cambridge University Press, 1958, Chapter 5.

The quotation from Brigance is from:

Brigance, William Norwood. *Speech Composition.* New York: Appleton-Century-Crofts, 1937, p. 182.

For an examination of reasoning as it is applied in communication in varied institutions in our contemporary culture, see:

Toulmin, Stephen, Richard Rieke, and Allan Janik. *An Introduction to Reasoning.* 2d ed. New York: Macmillan Co., 1984.

See also:

Cox, J. Robert, Malcolm O. Sillars, and Gregg B. Walker, eds. *Argument and Social Practice: Proceedings of the Fourth SCA/AFA Conference on Argumentation.* Annandale, Va.: Speech Communication Association, 1986.

Wilson Barrie. *The Anatomy of Argument.* Lanham, Md.: University Press of America, 1980.

chapter *7*

Maximizing Your Credibility

Since the times of ancient Greece, we have records that indicate students of communication have known and understood the persuasive power of the human personality, and the truth in the saying that "What you *are* speaks more loudly than what you say." Aristotle wrote several thousand years ago:

> The character *(ethos)* of the speaker is a cause of persuasion when the speech is so uttered as to make him worthy of belief; for as a rule we trust men of probity more, and more quickly, about things in general, while on points outside the realm of exact knowledge, where opinion is divided, we trust them absolutely. . . . We might almost affirm that his character *(ethos)* is the most potent of all means of persuasion.

RESEARCH INTO SOURCE CREDIBILITY

In the late 1940s, Franklyn Haiman investigated the concept of ethos by attributing the same speech on medical care to three different sources. For some audiences he said the speech was by the Surgeon General of the United States, for others he attributed the speech to the secretary of the Communist party in America, and for the third audience he said the speech was by a student at Northwestern University. He had tested the audience members' attitudes toward the question prior to hearing the speech and retested them afterward. He discovered that the audience members changed their opinions more when the speech was attributed to the Surgeon General than when attributed to either of the other speakers.

With the growing acceptance of the ideal model of source-encoding messages to transmit through channels to receivers came a growing interest in the question of why some sources seemed more credible than others. The result was an increasing amount of empirical research into the question. These investigators used the term *source credibility* to describe the focus of their studies.

Studies of source credibility tend to support Aristotle's discovery, and we can consider the persuasive power of personality to be empirically demonstrated. Indeed, the fact that Aristotle could discover the principle in a culture as remote from ours in time and space as classical Greece, as well as the fact that the Roman theorists of rhetoric made the same observations, is evidence that source credibility may be an important universal variable in human interaction, anytime, anywhere.

We know that some people are more believable than others, for certain people, in certain contexts. We know, in general, that the personality of the individual who utters the message is an important part of the persuasive context. What we do not yet know much about are specific ways in which source credibility functions. Some investigators have searched for specific factors (character traits) that account for a speaker's credibility. They have found such general factors as a speaker's qualification, dynamism, authoritativeness, objectivity, expertness, and so forth to be related to credibility. However, attempts to find some small set of general factors that explain source credibility have failed. The holistic perspective on presentations suggests that the factors that go into source credibility are so complex and tied so strongly to specific context that a small set of factors cannot explain the phenomenon.

The sorts of people who are credible within a general community or within the subcultures of an organization will be different from those in other groups and subcultures. For some audiences, topics, and occasions, a female speaker might be more credible than a male and not for others. For some audiences, topics, and occasions, the president of an organization might be more credible, whereas a member of the secretarial pool might be more believable in other contexts.

In this chapter, we will present information about the general nature of ethos or source credibility as it pertains to presentational speaking. Two definite factors influence the credibility of the presentational speaker: the individual's reputation and the impression made by the unfolding of a given presentation. When we examine the credibility of presentational speakers, therefore, we must study both the effect of the speaker's reputation, including organizational position, and the reactions to the moment-by-moment delivery of the message.

CREDIBILITY AND THE PRESENTATIONAL SPEAKER'S REPUTATION

Most politicians have professional help in building a credible reputation (often called *image*) that will result in votes. Business firms, motion picture stars, rock musicians, government agencies, and other institutions often try to create a favorable image for themselves by means of institutional advertising.

A presentational speaker's credibility is not static. Rather, when people talk with one another they develop an evolving intuition of one another's credibility, a holistic reaction rather than an analytic response. A given message source does not project one image now and forever, nor is the persuasive impact of an image independent of the receivers of the message.

The listeners' initial opinion of a speaker comes from many sources: previous in-person communications between them; what the listeners have read about the speaker, and biographic information the listener may know about the speaker. Sources of information need not be individuals, of course. We receive communication from organizations as well, and they too have prior reputations. The Defense Department has a reputation that affects all the messages which that particular unit of the government sends out, just as do business corporations and religious organizations, and radical groups. In addition, we often know the formal organizational position of the presentational speaker. We know, therefore, that the speaker not only represents Minnesota Mills but that she is the manager of the training division.

As an individual, you are projecting a public image every day. You can learn much about how your own image appears to others and how you can improve your credibility by studying the techniques of the professional advertising and public relations specialists. What are they doing primarily? Professional persuaders often go to great lengths to discover attractive images for clients. Obviously, as a presentational speaker you are also trying to project a credible image for your listeners.

Credibility varies from audience to audience and from culture to culture. Teenagers will certainly try to project a most responsible image to their fathers should they want to use the family car, but ten minutes later, on the telephone to a possible date they may try to project an exciting, devil-may-care image.

Psychologists tell us that we identify with people with whom we feel we have much in common. In this instance, the word *identification* refers to the feeling that you and another person have similar interests, attitudes, and values. Consider a candidate for public office who is black, was raised in an urban ghetto, went to college on a basketball scholarship, became a star in the National Basketball Association, and subsequently worked with ghetto youths and became a militant advocate of black rights. Would you find such a candidate attractive? Or consider a candidate for public office who is white, was raised in an upper middle-class home and went to an Ivy League school on a basketball scholarship, became a Rhodes Scholar and then a star in the National Basketball Association, and subsequently worked for conservative political groups. Would you find such a candidate attractive? Persons studying presentational speaking should take a closer look at their own images and work hard to analyze what their potential bases for source credibility might be.

From all of this, however, you must not conclude that image-makers are always, or even usually, successful in creating false impressions of candidates or institutions. Persuasion must work within the limits of the facts. The basic background and personality of the candidate or the nature of the institution in question form the framework within which the persuaders must operate. The best public relations firm in the world cannot make the black candidate discussed above into an Ivy League Rhodes scholar nor the white candidate into a ghetto-wise individual with an understanding of black teenagers and a burning desire to improve their lot.

All the persuaders can do—and this is of considerable value to candidates and to you as an individual—is to learn what is attractive and credible in your personality, background, and position, helping you to stress the attractive portions of your image and to minimize the less attractive elements.

Biographical Detail as a Source of Credibility.   Just as the historical record shapes the future, so do the reminiscences, memories, and legends about the speaker affect the audience's response. A person who sees a twisted pile of steel and wire in a storage room at a local art institute and inquires about it may be told that it is some discarded junk from the basement waiting to be carted to the dump ground. One may then dismiss the artifact and attend to other matters. If, however, we are told that the thing is the artistic work of one of our most gifted artists and that it was recently purchased at auction for $100,000, we may well have a different response. With increased interest we may circle it, view it from all angles, and it may now evoke a feeling of aesthetic pleasure, of amusement, of anger, or of disbelief. Someone may glance at an individual at another table in a restaurant without much notice until told that the person is an astronaut who has orbited the earth many times. The bit of biographical information may well cause considerable interest in and study of the individual.

Stereotypes as a Source of Credibility.   If a person has had a series of unpleasant experiences trying to buy a secondhand automobile and if some intimate acquaintances report similar experiences, certain stereotypical details may be inferred about used car salespeople. As a result, the prospect approaches the salesperson with a set of expectations that influence the response to the sales pitch.

A number of professional fields require such long periods of education and training that certification requirements are standardized. Thus, a medical doctor, a professor of mathematics, a certified public accountant, a dentist, an engineer, and a lawyer, to name but a few professions, will have gone through a prescribed course of study and certain practical apprenticeships. When a speaker is identified as a medical doctor, therefore, the audience will expect that the person has graduated from an accredited medical school, served a period of internship, and, perhaps, a residency. The credibility of a medical doctor giving a presentation on health matters, all other things being equal, will be higher than that of someone without such qualifications.

Just as members of a given culture or subculture will have stereotypes for certain important functionaries such as medicine men, priests, fakirs, physicists, astronauts, movie stars, and football quarterbacks, so will they understand the importance of certain key institutional, organizational, or corporate positions.

Formal Organizational Position as a Source of Credibility. While the king, chief, or shaman of a nation or clan or tribe may be unknown to the listeners, the biography of anyone who reaches such a position can be partially inferred by the informed listener. Many times the individual who holds a certain formal organizational position must give the presentation in order to achieve maximum source credibility. In Chapter 2 we noted that the formal organizational positions of the speaker and the listeners are an important part of the context of any presentation. The credibility of the source for a presentation is typically closely tied to the formal organizational position. One reason that banking institutions have so many formal positions named *senior vice-president, vice-president,* or *assistant vice-president* is that the bank personnel must make many presentations and meet many clients in situations where a high-level official must represent the institution. Persons discussing important financial affairs find it more satisfying to communicate with an assistant vice-president or a vice-president than with a bookkeeper or teller.

Increasingly, the leadership community gives public speeches to groups within the organization for inspirational purposes and to groups outside the organization for public relations purposes. Such speeches cannot be given by an administrative aide or a public relations person, but must be given by a formal leader of the organization. Indeed, the last decade has seen an increasing use of the chief executive officers of business and industry as announcers in television commercials. Inspirational public relations, or public service speeches, are usually prepared by professional speechwriters and typically do not use audiovisual aids to support them.

Presentations are often made to peers or superiors, as well as to subordinates in crucial situations. Presentations are given in a context where the individual is judged as to skill, understanding, and competence on the basis of the presentation. Typically, presentations are developed at the request of a supervisor or employer who has the power to authorize them. One reason for the assignment of presentations is that they require audio or visual support, or both, and thus are expensive. On some occasions, presentations may be given repeatedly to different groups, but the most common situation is one in which a presentation is prepared with a definite persuasive purpose for a specific audience. A key element in the crucial presentation is always the persona of the presenter.

Presentations are usually the most carefully prepared, structured, developed, tested, and rehearsed speech messages given by a member of an institution, organization, or corporation. Quite often, the organization's specialists and managers become involved in reviewing presentations in advance of their delivery. The "dry run" is often the rule rather than the exception. On occasion, a presentation is prepared in a way that resembles a professional theatrical production or a television feature. Within the trade such elaborate presentations are sometimes characterized as "dog and pony" shows.

When presentations are given within the organization, the formal organizational structure often dictates who will be selected to make the speech. Since presentations are formal messages, they require the proper formal source to maximize their credibility. Although public relations departments can prepare public speeches for the general public, when presentations are made the situation changes. A person usually gets organizational help in preparing a presentation, but the speaker often cannot rely on a ghostwritten effort. The presentational speaker cannot adapt to listener response moment by moment and handle questions competently with secondhand information and ideas. Nor can a person delegate the reading of the presentation to a professional speaker or actor because the source credibility demands of the situation require that a person holding a specific formal position give the presentation. Advancing important ideas and proposals is often a key assignment that cannot be delegated satisfactorily. To state it plainly, for maximum source credibility, individuals in the proper formal positions have to accept responsibility for preparing and delivering their own presentations.

When representatives from several organizations meet in joint endeavor, one or more presentations may be needed to facilitate business. When one organization seeks to sell another a part, a program, or a product, the stakes are high for both organizations and the problems are often technical. For example, if Information Systems, Incorporated, a manufacturer of computerized office communication equipment, needs to subcontract a component to another firm, the contract is not let without considerable negotiations. If Linking Networks, Incorporated, wishes the contract, they will usually send a team to meet with a similar team from Information Systems. Again, the formal position of the team members and the selection of the right spokespersons with appropriate authority and responsibility to give the presentation become important for source credibility.

CREDIBILITY AND THE PRESENTATIONAL SPEAKER'S PERSONA

In our discussion of such things as likability, competence, and conviction as elements of credibility, we are probably reflecting a predominant North American culture rather than providing features that are universal. Nonetheless, our approach in analyzing elements of credibility in one culture should provide guidelines for you to follow should you find yourself making presentations to minority or foreign cultures. Noting various contextual factors that affect source credibility may help you to be more flexible, able to adjust to different audiences and circumstances.

Credibility and Personal Relationships. One of the important contextual features of a presentation is the quality of personal relationships that have been and are established before and during the communication. If people who are participating in the presentation like and trust one another, attempts to influence each other are more likely to succeed than if people are suspicious and dislike one another.

Presentational speakers often give advice. When the choices are risky and we need advice, we tend to turn to someone we can trust. Trust assumes that the presentational speakers will give us advice that is the best for us. When we trust speakers, we assume that we can count on their strength, integrity, sincerity, and expertness, and on their concern for us and our group or community.

Credibility and Likability. Good relationships and trust are often based on liking the other person, but they are not always necessarily connected. We might find some people likable but not trustworthy in important matters because we know they are forgetful, unreliable, easily swayed by emotions, heavily biased, or uninformed. On the other hand, we may find some people whose advice we would take in a presentational setting and whom we trust even though they are not likable. We might trust the advice in a presentational speech given by a certain engineer because we know she is well trained, sober, level-headed, and talented—even though we do not like her much as a person.

If we like certain persons, however, we are tempted to believe and accept their ideas and their advice. We often feel better about taking the advice of someone we like than about accepting the recommendation of someone we dislike. An important part of the study of presentational speaking, therefore, concerns how people who communicate come to like or dislike one another.

Physical beauty is a factor in being likable. Peoples' ideas about what is beautiful or handsome are as individual as people. Just the same, Americans spend billions of dollars each year in the search for beauty because, for many, physical attractiveness is the key to popularity and friendship. As a study of cultures around the world will indicate, Americans are not alone in this preoccupation with physical attractiveness. Physical beauty is not enough by itself to assure likability, but it is an advantage. Advertisers often use the persuasive power of handsome men and beautiful women shown using a product or simply being present in the same picture or sequence of images as the product or advertising slogan.

Speaking ability is another factor in being likable and trustworthy. A pleasant, flexible, resonant voice quality communicates a dynamic personality. The person who can find the right word at the right time and who can express an idea clearly and with interesting examples or analogies draws attention and interest. The person with a lively and vivid imagination, who can make small talk, spin out dreams or fantasies, dramatize characters, tell interesting stories, and ask unusual questions, is interesting and likeable and given credit for being competent.

Listening ability is yet another factor in being likable. Listening is a real talent and is often underestimated as we explained in Chapter 3. The person who is willing to listen to others and find out who they are, what they are interested in, and what they are worried about is often liked and respected. Genuinely good listeners are always welcome.

Credibility and Attitude Toward Others.   All of the basic personality characteristics mentioned above enter into our presentational speaking, but equally important is the attitude toward others that we bring to the situation. Most important is our demonstrated attitude of wanting to create a *joint venture* in which everyone participates for the good of all. If we have an exploitative attitude of trying to win the meeting, getting our way at the expense of members of the audience, or climbing in the organization by chicanery and skullduggery, it will be very difficult to earn credibility as a message source. Manipulators out to exploit others in face-to-face communication may succeed in the short run, but over time they usually find that persuasive tricks fail and their credibility takes a nose dive.

An attitude of willingness to help creates feelings of trust and liking in others. A genuine offer of help is a powerful force for credibility. A good salesperson often has a sincere and dedicated desire to help the customer. The opposite request also works to build trust. "I need your help" is another message that often builds a good relationship between speaker and audience members.

Credibility and Source Competence.   In addition to being likable and working to engender trust, the presentational speaker should suggest competence, expertness, and mastery of the situation if the advice is to be persuasive. We expect a competent person's presentation to contain a wealth of good and relevant information about the topic under discussion. Respect is granted the speaker who demonstrates expertise. The speaker who is clear, whose comments are easy to follow because they are well organized, whose language is precise, and who has a fluent and expressive way of speaking further suggests competence to the audience.

CREDIBILITY AS INFLUENCED DURING THE PRESENTATION

A great deal of any presentational speaker's ethos is generated by how the person talks and what is said. Any speaker can do much to increase credibility right at the moment of communication.

Credibility and Communication Apprehension. Presentational speakers should strive to behave in such a manner that they project an image of being in control of the situation. If their eye contact, gestures, vocal inflections, and so on, give the audience the impression that they are extremely nervous, embarrassed, or unsure, the impact will be negative. If a speaker is unable to meet the problems posed by a presentational speaking situation, why should the audience members suppose this person is more able under other conditions of stress?

Why do we feel tense and excited when we anticipate giving a presentation? Tension comes when much is at stake, when we feel failure will be unpleasant, perhaps even punishing to us, and when success will be pleasant and rewarding. The body alerts itself for verbal battle or for flight.

The fight or flight response is an old one that we have inherited from our prehistoric ancestors, who often faced personal danger. Whether they stood and fought or turned and ran, their bodies needed to be keyed up for maximum physical effort.

Our bodily symptoms when we become alerted to a communication situation where much is at stake tend to vary from person to person. They usually include such things as sweaty palms, increased heartbeat, dryness in the mouth, and shortness of breath. We often report these feelings in such terms as "I had butterflies in my stomach," or "My heart was in my mouth."

A number of investigators have studied the relationship between the emotional feeling people report they have and physical measures of bodily changes, such as increased heartbeats. These investigations reveal that some subjects will interpret such arousal as a positive and pleasurable emotion, while others will interpret the same physical changes as anxiety, fear, or dread. In short, communication excitement need not be interpreted as communication apprehension.

We will define *communication apprehension* as mental distress, worry, or uneasiness brought about by the fear of punishment or misfortune as a result of a given communication.

The emotional arousal that goes along with presentational speaking prepares people for either going ahead and meeting the situation or taking flight from it. One common response is to avoid communicating if possible. However, as we have seen in earlier chapters and above in this chapter, when you are the person who should give a presentation because of your organizational position there is really no way you can avoid the responsibility. The proper course of action is to go ahead and meet the situation.

The odds are that as a student of presentational speaking you experience the normal and understandable anxiety that is a response to the exciting and important situation of making a presentational speech which means a great deal to you. Such feelings of tension are to be expected, and people who do not feel them are probably the abnormal ones.

One of the authors was coaching an executive in a major financial institution on communication skills related to giving presentations to clients about the investment of funds involving millions of dollars. The executive's position required that he give frequent presentations of complicated financial material to influential clients. To an observer he seemed to be fluent, articulate, and poised.

During a private meeting in which we were playing back a videotape of a presentation for evaluation and coaching, he confessed that he suffered from communication apprehension whenever he had to give a presentation. He testified that his apprehension made his life miserable. He was not going to give up an excellent position, but he did want to do something about what he perceived of as a problem.

Discussing his situation revealed that the executive did not suffer from *trait apprehension* (abnormal continual anxiety about communication of all kinds) but had fallen into the habit of working himself into a *state of apprehension* (normal feelings of anxiety focused on a specific communication situation) about this one particular kind of recurring presentation. When we talked about the situation and changed his attitude, he was able to break the habit of how he thought about the opportunity of giving a presentation. He began to feel better about his communication both before and during the presentation.

Some years ago a nationwide survey of American adults discovered that the most frequently reported fear was of speaking in public. Of course, the results of such surveys often change over time, but the fact that communication apprehension was so high on the list is interesting and is consistent with our own experiences in teaching students and working in management training programs with organizational leaders.

In our culture there is a widespread idea that if you are going to give a presentation you should feel nervous and dread the experience. Your friends may kid you about it as though you were going to a torture chamber. Since some people suggest you should be apprehensive, you are encouraged to interpret the excitement that is a normal reaction to thinking about an important event in your life as anxiety or apprehension.

We do not have to follow the suggestion that the usual response to giving a presentation is to be anxious. We can interpret our aroused state as excitement, as pleasurable anticipation. A good skier standing at the top of a long slope may have the same feelings of butterflies in the stomach, pounding heart, and dry mouth as the speaker waiting to begin a presentation, but the skier may find the excitement pleasurable while the speaker may interpret the same arousal as apprehension.

A good way to manage the physical tension surrounding a presentation is to develop a positive interpretation of what it means. If we are interested in sports cars, we may have a daydream in which we drive our favorite model. On one hand, we could anticipate the skid of our dream car as we hit a bad spot on the road, the terrible crash, and the pain following the accident. On the other hand, we could anticipate the thrill of handling the car and the enjoyment we would get from driving it. When preparing for a presentational speaking situation, you can daydream about the coming event in positive fashion. You can choose your own daydreams. You can see yourself before the audience—poised, trying out an interesting line of thought, holding the audience's attention, and receiving the hoped-for results. If you begin to dramatize your speaking in positive fashion, you may interpret your tension prior to speaking as a heady excitement similar to that felt by the skier at the top of the slope. Indeed, in our experience, giving a successful presentation can be as exciting and pleasant as making a good run down a ski slope.

In addition to anticipating the presentation in a positive way, there are some rules you can keep in mind to make productive use of speech excitement while giving the presentation.

The first rule is to emphasize the excitement of the topic to you. You have been selected to make the presentation because you are the best person to do so. You are the expert on this topic and have the proper organizational position to make the greatest impact on behalf of the material. Interest in what you are saying can take your mind off yourself and how you are doing.

The second rule is to prepare thoroughly. A good way to get the tension under control is to feel confident that you are well prepared. A thorough preparation serves to put your mind at ease about that common bugaboo of speakers—forgetting what you want to say. We have stressed that the best way to prepare is extemporaneously, and certainly that mode of preparation is the best for providing you with confidence that you can handle the unexpected.

The third rule is to develop an audience-centered approach to speaking. Keep your mind on the listeners and their responses. Watch individuals. Did the audience like some example you used? Did a chart work particularly well in getting one of your points across? Was there nodding of heads in agreement for an example or analogy that you used? Is the audience getting bored? Do any members look confused? By concentrating on the audience, you can take your mind off yourself and your performance. Self-centered attitudes are primary reasons for communication apprehension.

The fourth rule is to act as though you were confident both before and during your presentation. An audience is quick to pick out cues about the way you feel about yourself. If you interpret your nonverbal cues as showing worry, the audience will often form the same impression. Interestingly enough, the same body motions—if you perceive them as symptoms of intense involvement with, and high regard for, the subject and the occasion —can make a positive impression on the audience. The perception of yourself is the first thing you communicate to any audience.

While waiting to give the presentation, force yourself to sit erect and gaze about with confidence. Pick a spot in front of the audience, and when you are introduced get up from your chair, pause, pull yourself erect, and firmly and calmly force yourself to walk purposefully to that spot. When you reach the spot, pause again, stand erect, and with the weight balanced comfortably on both feet, look out at the audience and, for just a moment, let your eyes run over the listeners. Be sure and look at the people in the audience *until you can see them.*

Some beginners are unwilling to look at the audience. Since they do not know what the people look like or what they are doing, they find themselves growing more and more nervous as they proceed. We are all afraid of the unknown, and, if the speaker is not watching the audience, there is no way of knowing what it is doing. You should look at your audience, see the friendly faces, the smiles, the frowns, the questioning looks so that you can realize that an audience is made up of human beings much like yourself, that they usually wish you well, and that they want you to do a good job with your presentation.

The point is that you do not want to stop feeling excited and keyed up about giving a presentation. You want to learn to use this tension to make your mind sharper and less likely to forget, and to give your whole body more focus and concentration in communicating with your audience.

Credibility and Nonverbal Communication.   The speaker who projects an image of calm confidence and assurance, who seems sincerely and honestly convinced of the wisdom and truth of the message or product, will benefit from transfer. Successful salespersons often testify that the first person to whom they sell a new product is themselves, on the assumption that unless they are sold they will not be able to sell anyone else.

In general, credibility is enhanced by nonverbal cues for the audience that the speaker is audience-centered rather than self-centered. If the speaker appears to be convinced of the importance of the topic and the occasion, and, above all, if interest in listeners seems strong, then the result is often an increase in trust, belief, and liking.

If in the question-and-answer period after the formal presentation the speaker's manner of fielding questions, dealing with disagreements, and handling challenges is confident, open, and fair, the presenter's credibility is increased. If, moreover, the speaker communicates nonverbally to the listeners a genuine appreciation of questions and respect for the questioners and projects fairness and candor, admitting honestly when stumped, the result is an increase in audience feelings of good will. On the other hand, if presentational speakers suggest by their manner that they have something to hide, if they hedge in such a way that they appear insecure and afraid of making a mistake, then their ethos is damaged. Dodging difficult questions is a short cut to loss of respect.

Finally, presentational speakers should communicate nonverbally the tone and manner appropriate to their formal organizational positions. They should make it clear by their style when they are speaking for themselves and when they are speaking in an official capacity. If John Jamison speaks for all of his associates in his capacity as head of the New Products Division, that should be made clear nonverbally as well as verbally. If he speaks for John Jamison personally rather than officially, that should be made clear as well.

A presentational speaker's nonverbal cues sometimes create a wrong impression, so that the speaker fails to establish friendship and trust without knowing why. When people are having trouble talking with one another because of unintended nonverbal mannerisms, discussing the things that bother them may enable them to come to an understanding.

Credibility and Verbal Content.   Speakers' messages have a considerable effect on whether we like and trust them, on whether we accept what they are saying, and on whether we are persuaded by their advice. If the speakers are to be trusted, they must say things that reveal them to be unselfish, interested in us, and guided by a suitable code of ethics.

Presentational speakers may well create credibility by reminding their audiences of factors in their background, experience, and training that make them particularly competent to discuss the topic. A speaker might comment, for example, that in fifteen years as manager of the New Products Division he has never presided over a more technically careful and thorough analysis of the potential of an addition to the product line. A speaker might also imply her status by commenting, for example, that the recommendation is the result of extensive study by a special departmental task force investigating sites for the new plant, that the study was carefully reviewed by all units of the department, and that the recommendation is a unanimous one. Comments about personal experience, competence, and status should not be made in a boastful way, of course.

One final element that, wisely employed, is most helpful in building credibility is humor. We all like to laugh, even in the midst of a most serious presentation. Humor is not for every speaker because an inept attempt at humor will backfire, and sarcasm or humor at the expense of others will surely damage the speaker's credibility. However, if presentational speakers can amuse us, if they can share their sense of humor with us, we are going to find them more likable. If they can communicate to us that they take the subject but not themselves seriously, we will be drawn toward them. If their humor is gentle rather than cutting or sarcastic, if they turn their humor back on themselves rather than using it against others, we will trust them more. Speakers who can amuse their audiences in this way seem secure, at ease, and in command of the situation.

As noted earlier, you must be careful not to overdo the use of humor, particularly if you have a serious point to make. People love comics and clowns and try to place people in those roles if they have some talent for comedy (and if you do not have some talent you ought not try to be humorous). The rewards for amusing speakers are great—laughter, congeniality, and the knowledge they are well liked. But just as experts should stay within their area of expertness when giving advice, so the comic is expected to stay the comic. If the clown tries to make a serious point, to give advice about important matters, we feel uncomfortable and tend to ignore the advice. If you have the talent to do so, use humor in your presentations to build your credibility as a source, but keep in mind your overall purpose. Humor in presentations is like explosives in building a road through mountains: skillfully used both are invaluable, but improperly used both are dangerous and potentially damaging.

If the presentational speakers can rise above the self-absorption that comes when they are the focus of attention and can work to raise the status of their listeners with genuine compliments about the organizations or organizational units they represent, can make warm comments about individuals in the audience (I know that Marsha Everding has her pocket computer and is ready to whip it out, and I respect that), can request help and advice (giving every indication that they plan to take suggestions seriously), can use humor in the right amount with a light touch, can demonstrate the ability to create and maintain a joint communicative venture—then they will build good will and increase their credibility during the course of their remarks.

SUMMARY

From the times of ancient Greece we have known that how a speaker is perceived as a person influences audience response to what is said. As Aristotle phrased it, ". . . character (ethos) is the most potent of all means of persuasion."

We now term this effect of character on communication *source credibility.* Modern studies have supported Aristotle's discovery. Some people are more believable than others for certain people and in particular contexts, but we have only partial understanding of why this is so. We have found no small, neat set of items to explain these differences. However, two clusters of variables have been shown to influence the credibility of a speaker: the individual's reputation and what happens during the presentation.

A speaker's image as perceived by an audience comes from many sources, including personal contact, what listeners have seen, heard, and read about the speaker, and biographic information. Professional speakers and organizations attempt to project a credible image, using all available devices of public relations and varied means of publicity. But what constitutes a credible image varies from audience to audience and from situation to situation. Because of the complexity of ever-changing circumstances, the credibility of a source is usually beyond the control of an image-maker.

Three contributors to credibility—trust, respect, and liking—have been shown to occur more frequently with similar people, that is, those who share interests, attitudes, and values. An empathic relationship, requiring mutually perceived high credibility, is more probable with persons who have many common characteristics than it is with persons who differ in such convictions as political and religious preferences.

Stereotypes associated with vocations and cultures contribute to negative or positive source credibility. Status accorded to the person with a high position in an organization is a typical stereotype.

Manifest personality, often called personal style, generates confidence or lack of it during a speaker's interaction with an audience. In particular, a speaker's ability or inability to handle open disagreement fairly and comfortably builds or destroys credibility.

Credibility and likability are often but not always connected. We do tend to be influenced by people we like. However, integrity and competence may make highly credible a person toward whom we feel no affection.

Some attributes that increase likability are physical ability, attractiveness, speaking skill, and ability to listen to others effectively and with appreciation. Appreciative listening, or lack of it, reveals much of a person's attitude toward fellow human beings. Does the individual show a liking for people and enjoyment of being with them? A sincere offer to help builds credibility. Willingness to receive help and show gratitude for it also causes others to view one more favorably.

Both nonverbal and verbal behaviors communicate confidence and competence. Appropriate personal style fits both speaker and situation. Well-chosen verbal messages satisfy the analytic and holistic critical faculties of listeners. And humor, tastefully used, is a valuable asset to source credibility.

You can maximize your credibility in presentational speaking by developing two kinds of competence: mastery of your subject and mastery of the situation. An audience perceiving these attributes in action cannot but be favorably impressed.

An often misunderstood but valid bit of advice to presentational speakers who would maximize their credibility is, "don't take yourself too seriously."

Audio and visual aids can help or hinder the process of presentation. We examine these and their use in some detail in Chapter 8.

QUESTIONS FOR DISCUSSION AND REVIEW

1. What was the ancient concept of ethos and how does it relate to the modern concept of source credibility?
2. What evidence do we have to believe that source credibility may be an important factor in human communication anytime, anywhere?
3. What are some of the leading conclusions that have emerged from studies of source credibility?
4. How can the speaker's reputation relate to his or her source credibility?
5. How does formal organizational position relate to source credibility?
6. How do personal relationships relate to a speaker's credibility?
7. How does the speaker's attitude to others relate to the creation of a joint venture and to credibility?
8. How does the speaker's positive attitude relating to communication apprehension relate to source credibility?
9. How does the presentational speaker's nonverbal communication relate to her or his credibility?
10. How does what the presentational speaker says, the message, relate to his or her credibility?

REFERENCES AND SUGGESTED READINGS

The source for the quotation from Aristotle is:

Cooper, Lane, trans. *The Rhetoric of Aristotle.* Englewood Cliffs, N.J.: Prentice-Hall, 1932, pp. 8–9.

For Franklyn Haiman's study, see:

Haiman, Franklyn. "An Experimental Study of the Effects of Ethos in Public Speaking." *Speech Monographs* 16 (1949): 190–202.

For early studies of *source credibility,* see:

Andersen, Kenneth, and Theodore Clevenger, Jr. "A Summary of Experimental Research in Ethos." *Speech Monographs* 30 (1963): 59–78.

Hovland, Carl, and Walter Weiss. "The Influence of Source Credibility on Communication Effectiveness." *Public Opinion Quarterly* 15 (1951): 635–650.

Simons, Herbert W., N. Berkowitz, and J. R. Moyer. "Similarity, Credibility, and Attitude Change: A Review and a Theory." *Psychological Bulletin* 73 (1970): 1–16.

For some typical studies reflecting the search for specific factors that account for source credibility, see:

Berlo, David K., James B. Lemert, and Robert J. Mertz. "Dimensions for Evaluating the Acceptability of Message Sources." *Public Opinion Quarterly* 33 (1969–1970): 563–576.

McCroskey, James C. "Scales for Measurement of Ethos." *Speech Monographs* 33 (1966): 65–72.

For a study that discovered that students asked to rank ten religious, political, and social groups in terms of general credibility, ranked doctors, physicists, and civic leaders at the top, and labor union members, high school dropouts, and sexual deviates at the bottom, see:

Goldberg, Alvin, Lloyd Crisp, Evelyn Sieburg, and Michele Tolea. "Subordinate Ethos and Leadership Attitudes." *Quarterly Journal of Speech* 53 (1967): 354–360.

Of course, such polling results are subject to change through time and would probably differ with different populations of subjects. These studies do indicate, however, how the stereotyping of biographical details results in credibility estimates. For a work that summarizes studies demonstrating the importance of physical beauty in terms of likability, see:

Kleinke, Chris L. *First Impressions: The Psychology of Encountering Others.* Englewood Cliffs, N.J.: Prentice-Hall, 1975.

For a summary of studies on trust and credibility, see:

Giffin, Kim. "The Contribution of Studies in Source Credibility to a Theory of Interpersonal Trust in the Communication Process." *Psychological Bulletin* 68 (1967): 104–120.

The disillusionment with further studies of factors in personal style that account for credibility is indicated by the paucity of recent studies of that question. For an analysis on the entire line of research that points out the shortcomings, see:

Delia, Jesse. "Constructivism and the Study of Human Communication." *Quarterly Journal of Communication* 63 (1977): 66–83.

For material relating to communication apprehension, see:

Daly, John A., and James C. McCroskey, eds. *Avoiding Communication: Shyness, Reticence and Communication Apprehension.* Beverly Hills, Calif.: Sage, 1984.

Fremouw, William J., and Michael D. Scott. "Cognitive Restructuring: An Alternative Method for the Treatment of Communication Apprehension." *Communication Education* 28 (1979): 129–133.

McCroskey, James C. "Oral Communication Apprehension: A Summary of Recent Theory and Research." *Human Communication Research* 4 (1977): 78–96.

Phillips, Gerald M. "Rhetoritherapy Versus the Medical Model: Dealing with Reticence." *Communication Education* 26 (1977): 34–43.

chapter 8

Audio and Visual Aids to the Presentation

Planning and implementing the productive use of available aids require both knowledge and skill. However, presenters are not always mechanically inclined or competent in operating electronic devices. This chapter attempts to supply helpful guidance in these matters, something presentational speakers often find in short supply. Many a presentation of commendable substance has collapsed because of the failure of one or more mechanical details. Only if the presenter chooses and uses the appropriate gadgets, adapted to the unique situation, will the objective of the presentation be facilitated.

To stress the importance of these matters, we revise a legendary maxim: "For want of a bulb, the overhead projector was lost; for want of an overhead projector the message was lost; and for want of the message, the battle, war, cause, or whatever was at stake, went down the tube."

Mechanical devices used in presentations are increasingly electronic and complex. We believe that the competent presenter should know what is available, their capabilities and limitations. For this reason the first section of this chapter is a review of modern audiovisual devices. If you know the tools that may be helpful and what they can and cannot do, you are more likely to succeed in utilizing equipment productively in your presentation.

WHAT THE PRESENTER NEEDS TO KNOW: TECHNICAL BASICS

Audio

Audible sounds, their production, and distribution, constitute the audio elements of a presentation. Key factors include acoustical conditions, loudspeakers, microphones, and recording and playback devices. We now look at these components and how they serve the presentational speaker.

Microphones.   Microphones convert sound waves into electrical impulses that can be amplified and transmitted along wires or via radio frequency waves in the atmosphere, and that actuate loudspeakers or recording devices. Microphones are classified by their pattern of sensitivity, the directions in which they pick up sound. These patterns are nondirectional, cardioid (basically unidirectional), bidirectional, and shotgun (designed to focus on a distant sound source).

Wireless microphones contain or are hooked to pocketed small-frequency modulation transmitters, which broadcast to a nearby FM receiver that is plugged into an amplifier or recorder. The wireless microphone is usually of the cardioid type. Football referees use wireless microphones to announce their decisions.

For presentations, microphones are mounted on a stand, or a podium, or are hand-held, or are attached to a person with a lavalier around-the-neck cord, or a clip on a lapel, necktie, or other bit of clothing. The obvious advantage of attaching a microphone to a speaker is to hold constant the distance from mouth to microphone. Speakers tend to forget stand- or podium-mounted microphones, with the result that their movement causes the transmitted signal to vary from loud to soft. A disadvantage of lavalier or lapel locations is the microphone cord, which restricts movement and distracts the speaker. The wireless microphone frees the speaker to move about. A difficulty with the wireless microphone is electrical interference, which prevents its use in some locations.

For optimum voice pickup, a normal mouth to microphone distance is 10 to 12 inches. The speaker is well advised to speak over the top of the microphone rather than directly into it.

Loudspeakers.   Loudspeakers convert electrical impulses to audible sound. As the name suggests, their purpose is to convert the output of a microphone (or radio or playback) which has been strengthened by electronic reinforcement into a sound louder than the original.

Since loudspeakers are the means by which wired or wireless communication reaches the ears of listeners, they are found in many places: in recorders, television monitors, speaker's stands, mounted in ceilings or in front of the room, at the sides of a platform, or above the center of a stage or platform. Generally, it is better to have the sound come from the same direction as the actual source, although better sound distribution results from in-the-ceiling speakers, equally spaced and covering the room.

When used for public address (PA), to amplify a present program or speaker so that all the audience can hear, how loud should the loudspeakers be? An ideal is to adjust the level of loudness so that a remote listener has difficulty in deciding whether what is being heard is the unaided or the amplified speaker's voice.

Sound Recording and Playback Devices. Conventional record players using 33 ⅓ or 45 rpm prerecorded materials are seldom a part of presentations. Tape recorders and playbacks are available almost everywhere. The tape width of ¼ inch is standard, but the thickness of the tape may be 1.5, 1.0, or 0.5 mil (thousandth of an inch). The reel-to-reel tape recorders have been replaced almost completely by cassette recorders. A cassette-enclosed tape does not need to be threaded into the machine, and the reels have been eliminated.

Because of standard-sized cassettes, the thickness of the tape determines recording and playback time. Typically, a cassette is recorded forward and back, with half of the tape used in each direction. With 1.5 mil tape, time is thirty minutes per side, with 1.0 mil tape, forty-five minutes per side, and with 0.5 mil tape, one hour per side. The 0.5 mil tape is not recommended for general use because it is delicate and tends to jam in some machines. Both the 1.0 mil and the 1.5 mil thicknesses are widely used and seem to be equally satisfactory.

Tape speed in the typical inexpensive cassette recorder is 1 ⅞ inch per second. This provides relatively low fidelity, but is satisfactory for most voice recordings, less satisfactory for music. Professional audiotape recording uses higher speeds, possibly 3 ¾ inch per second, but usually 7 ½ or 15 inches per second.

Tape recordings are monaural or stereophonic. Stereo is recorded from two separated microphones, so that two separate recordings are side by side on the tape. When played back through separate channels with independent amplifiers and loudspeakers, the stereophonic effect is achieved. That is, a person with two good ears hears the sound much as one would if present at the original event. For this to work properly, the two loudspeakers in the stereo reproduction should be spaced the same distance as were the two recording microphones.

Cassette audiotape recording is cheap and easy, and recorded tapes can be edited and duplicated quickly. Microphones built into the recorder can be used, but much better results are obtained with remote mikes close to the source of sound. However, a single speaker talking directly into a machine-mounted microphone at a distance of not over 12 inches can be recorded satisfactorily.

As we will explain later, cassette tape recordings can be integrated with filmstrip and slide presentations, combining narration and sound effects with a sequence of images. The audiotape recorder-playback is one of the more flexible and useful devices available to the presentational speaker.

Visual

Microcomputer Graphics.   With the proper software, most microcomputers have graphic capabilities. Microcomputers can produce a variety of type faces and styles for printing titles and other visual aids. They can also generate professional-appearing line graphs, bar graphs, pie charts, and pictographs. Microcomputers can be used to develop a host of additional artwork suitable for visual aids. Computer-generated graphs, charts, pictures, illustrations, and designs can easily be reproduced for projection on a screen or for integration into films or videotapes. With some practice on a microcomputer, most people can develop professional-looking visuals to supplement their presentations.

The 35 mm Slide Projector.   The 35 mm slide projector with a magazine for holding a hundred or more slides and a remote control that can be operated by the speaker is a valuable aid to the process of presentation. Slide film is available for the popular 35 mm cameras and, owing to its color-reversible characteristic, can be developed and placed in 2 inch by 2 inch cardboard or plastic mounts for projection, avoiding the printing process.

The projected picture can fill a large screen and provide excellent detail and color. Slides are inexpensive, can be duplicated easily, and conventional prints can be made from them. Slide projection requires a darkened room, which is a distinct disadvantage for the speaker who would maintain eye contact with the audience. While a large number of slides can be arranged in sequence, retrieval of a slide shown earlier is difficult, and doubly so because the speaker is usually up front beside the screen using a remote control device to change slides. If the speaker chooses to talk from a location in the middle of the audience beside the slide projector, the noise of the motor in the projector becomes annoying and prevents the speaker from hearing audience responses.

When slides are projected from a booth at the rear of the room, the noise problem is solved, but the possibility of retrieving a slide or making machine adjustments is reduced. Booth projection is more satisfactory with a separate operator at the machine to follow the speaker's instructions.

Use of multiple slide projection with special fade and dissolve capabilities makes possible elaborate and aesthetically pleasing productions. Such a program can be transferred to videotape and copied, if its distribution is desired. These operations require special equipment and significant expertise. The amateur should obtain professional help in a project that goes beyond simple sequencing of slides in a single projector.

The major error in using slides in presentations is probably showing too many. Just as a tourist returning from a trip abroad wants the guests to see all pictures taken en route, so, too, a presenter is often reluctant to edit out good but unneeded frames. A few carefully selected slides, together with exposition and interaction about them, usually succeed better than a profusion of pictures. Many pictures projected in a darkened room have a soporific effect. The jokes about how boring it is to watch a friend's slides have a basis in fact. Another consideration is that the speaker, not the picture show, should be the focus of interest.

Inexperienced presenters will often use a group of attractive slides to organize their speeches. They simply show the slides and talk about each in turn. Using the slides as a crutch, they fail to analyze the topic, the audience, or the occasion and to select an organizational pattern with suitable supporting material adapted to their audience. Listeners often emerge from such presentations with a feeling of confusion, aware that something was amiss but not sure why the apparently smooth flow of attractive images with innocuous commentary by the speaker has failed to communicate effectively.

Filmstrips. A sequence of 35 mm shots can be mounted as slides or assembled in a single roll of 35 mm film called a filmstrip. The filmstrip projector advances the film from frame to frame, one click at a time, using the perforation on the film much as a motion picture projector would control film progress. The result is equivalent to slide projection except that frames cannot be rearranged or omitted.

Filmstrips can be duplicated easily, are economical, and can be filed in rolls in small cans; hence, they can be stored conveniently. When the strip is made into a continuous loop, an automatic projection of the sequence is possible. This is most frequently used in a compact rear projection unit, incorporating a synchronized audiotape playback. One push of the button starts the audiovisual presentation, which stops automatically at the end. The screen on such a device is usually small, making it suitable for individuals or small groups, perhaps six to a maximum of ten persons.

An audible or inaudible signal to advance the filmstrip makes possible the synchronization of the strip projector and a separate audio cassette player. This combination is more flexible than the single unit audio-filmstrip machine, for either filmstrip or audiotape can be modified without affecting the other.

The nature of the filmstrip dictates that it should be used where it is needed for many repetitions over a period of time. It also determines whether a number of copies are to be sent to various locations. For the one-shot presentation, 35 mm slides are definitely preferable to a filmstrip.

Overhead Projector. The overhead projector throws an image from a 10 inch by 10 inch (approximate) transparency on a screen 6 to 10 feet away. Typically, the speaker stands by the machine changing transparencies, writing on them with a felt tip pen when appropriate, all the while maintaining eye contact with the audience. The room does not need to be darkened.

There is no need to turn to the screen because a pencil or pointer aimed at the transparency appears on the screen. Limited only by screen size, a large image is possible.

Individual sheets of transparent acetate or acetate on rollers that can be cranked over the lighted glass surface of the machine carry the messages and images to be projected. Individual sheets may be unmounted or mounted in cardboard frames. Individual transparencies provide great flexibility for the speaker, for items can be added, deleted, or repeated easily. Overlays, sheets that are superimposed on an original sheet, can be used to develop a concept, drawing, or message. Abundant light makes possible the use of as many as a half dozen overlays. By covering part of a transparency with a sheet of paper, sequential revelation of its content is possible.

Pens for writing on the acetate are water based (temporary) or permanent. Water-based writing can be removed from a transparency with a damp cloth, making reuse possible. Instead of using a blackboard or flip chart, many presenters write on blank transparencies. They thus avoid turning their backs to the audience, they can maintain eye contact, they can use pens of various colors, and, instead of erasing past writing, they use another transparency sheet. Previously written sheets, not having been erased, are also available if needed.

A great variety of preprepared transparencies is available. The simplest are transparencies handmade with felt pens. More complicated are the thermal and electrostatic film products and the diazo film color transparencies. The most complicated of all are the various cold and hot laminator methods of copying printed pictures, camera-processed images with or without size change, and computer-generated transparencies. The variety of ways available to make transparencies suggests that, with the help of professionals, an overhead projected program can be as elaborate, artistic, and aesthetic as desired. Many organizations either hire outside professionals or have professional people on the staff to help the presentational speaker by preparing suitable transparencies for overhead projection. The more elaborate transparencies can be written on with water-based pens during the course of a presentation and then cleaned up with a damp kleenex for reuse.

Mounted transparencies fit in a file drawer, so the special reusable items can be easily catalogued and kept.

Flip Chart. A simple, easy-to-use extension of the conventional classroom blackboard is the flip chart. This consists of a pad of large-size paper (usually blank newsprint stock) on an easel. Either sheets on the pad are prepared ahead of time to be revealed at the proper time, or the speaker writes on the paper with variously colored felt-tipped marker pens while speaking. Prior preparation is often combined with writing on the flip chart during the presentation. To stimulate audience participation, the speaker and the listeners together may decide what should be written on the flip chart. Perhaps a member of the audience will be invited to come up and diagram or illustrate an idea on the chart. In order to achieve audience involvement, it is usually preferable to have little, if any, material placed ahead of time on the flip chart.

When a page of the chart is used up, it is flipped over the top of the easel. Any page that might be referred to later can be torn off and taped to the wall of the room. Papering the walls of the room with the pages from the flip chart makes it possible to review efficiently what has been done. And after the presentation, important pages can be preserved.

Audiovisual

Sixteen mm Movie Projector.   The 16 mm movie projector is universally available, produces high-quality pictures and sound, and accommodates large audiences, but films for it are relatively expensive. An extensive library of films for many purposes exists, and through commercial agencies these can be purchased or rented. Usually such films are professionally made with accuracy and artistry.

Although videotape undeniably produces an image of lower quality, the 16 mm motion picture for education and business uses is losing ground in the competition between them. Because videotaping is inexpensive and videotape units are readily available, many 16 mm films are being copied on videotape. Most film catalogs offer the renter or buyer the option of 16 mm movie or videotape of VHS or Beta format. Videotape is, of course, substantially cheaper to prepare and use than film.

Sixteen mm sound film, color or black and white, is no longer used for contingent, one-shot applications. Videotape can be played back immediately, no time-consuming and expensive developing and printing are involved, the tape can be reused, and it can be viewed in a lighted room. The sacrifice of picture detail and quality is, in most instances, unimportant.

However, durable items such as films showing scientific processes or historical events will continue to be popular. Standard metal containers make these films portable. Moreover, whenever there is an available 16 mm sound movie projector, the film will play on it. Videotape in different widths and formats lacks this feature of compatibility, and large groups will continue to be better served by film than by videotape.

Videotape Recorders, Monitors, and Projectors.   The videotape, a by-product of television, is rapidly evolving into new and flexible forms. It is becoming the most important audiovisual aid available to the presenter.

Among the advantages of videotape are immediate viewing, reusable tape, and no need to darken the room for good viewing. But compared to the 16 mm movie the videotape picture is distressingly small. Currently, most videotape presentations utilize direct view monitors, which resemble home television sets with 19 inch or 26 inch screens. A single screen serves a maximum of twenty people. For larger audiences more monitors are necessary. Monitors are often mounted high on the side walls of the viewing room, and in still larger rooms they may be suspended from the ceiling. The individual auditor is expected to watch the nearest monitor.

An improvement currently emerging from the laboratory is projection TV. At present, front projection (like a movie projector) can illuminate a 5 foot by 6 foot screen, and rear projection (through ground glass) gives approximately a 3 foot by 4 foot picture. More viewers are accommodated by projection TV than by direct view TV monitors, but picture quality leaves much to be desired. But day-by-day television is getting better and better (technically, that is), and so we can anticipate that projected pictures from videotape and from broadcast television will soon approach the film-projected pictures in size and quality.

Many variables in the world of videotape challenge the presentational speaker. The width of the tape itself varies. Currently, 2 inch, 1 inch, ¾ inch, ½ inch, and ¼ inch (8 mm) tapes are in use. The format in which signals are recorded on tape also varies. Today, we have such formats as those used for Beta, VHS, and Super Beta video recorders; other formats are undoubtedly on the way. Tapes also run at different speeds—at present at least three. A recorder-playback system handles only one format, predominantly either Beta or VHS. Consumer model Beta units automatically adjust to one of three speeds, but most commercial and broadcast devices are single speed. Three-quarter inch, 1 inch, and 2 inch tapes have dual sound tracks as well as the picture track. Three-quarter inch, ½ inch, and ¼ inch videotape is usually in a cassette rather than on a reel, but not always.

Great confusion is caused by failure to match tape, format, and device. The user must be certain that a tape to be played or recorded is the right width, the correct format, the appropriate speed, and in reel or cassette to be compatible with a particular machine. While recorder-playback compatibility is critical, all videotape playback units can be accepted by a monitor, whether direct view or projected.

Narrower tape machines are less expensive, smaller, easier to use, and more available. They also produce lower quality pictures, that is, the narrower the tape the less detail is reproduced on the monitor. A sophisticated user decides what level of quality is satisfactory for the purpose of the presentation and uses equipment at that level. Fine quality is wasted when that refinement is unnecessary. Three-quarter inch tape provides quality satisfactory for most commercial and educational applications but is insufficient for broadcast. Most television stations specify 1 inch tapes, which permits editing and dubbing, both of which processes sacrifice some detail.

Video cameras are becoming increasingly portable and are powered by fairly small batteries, sometimes self-contained. These can be hand-held for most videotaping from actuality. Automatic adjustment to light conditions and automatic focus simplify the making of videotapes. The camera is usually capable of recording both picture and sound, but, because a microphone attached to the videotape recorder is usually too far from the source of sound, it is desirable to use a separate microphone. When persons are videotaped while speaking, having each wear a lavalier or lapel microphone provides optimum voice pickup. Sound is just as important as pictures, but amateurs making videotapes tend to be concerned with the visual image and neglect sound. Because the microphone is built into the camera, they assume no other audio pickup is needed, with often disappointing results.

Producing videotapes suitable for presentations usually requires production that goes beyond point and shoot. Multiple microphones require a mixer, to blend and balance their outputs. Editing, which is necessary to achieve smooth transitions, requires an editing machine. A third basic device to make effective videotape possible is a character generator, which adds titles, labeling, and expository printed messages to picture and sound.

The major disappointment experienced by the beginning user of videotape comes from expectations exceeding possibilities. We are all accustomed to professionally produced television, which uses fades and dissolves effortlessly and is carefully edited. The contrast of the broadcast tape and the product of a single-camera unedited effort is discouraging. The presenter who would use locally produced videotapes must assess minimum technical requirements for the proposed application, know the limitations of the available equipment, and be willing to call in professional assistance when appropriate.

With all the complexities and problems that accompany video, still in presentations as in broadcast journalism, videotape has become the most flexible and powerful aid to communication currently available.

Videodisc.   A specialized device for electronic audiovisual recording and playback is the videodisc. Originally intended for home use, it has been replaced there by the VCR, the video cassette recorder, but it remains valuable in commercial and educational applications.

The videodisc stores huge amounts of data, both audio and visual. It provides two sound tracks, and, while expensive to make, the original disc can be replicated by a process analogous to duplicating phonograph records. Playback uses a laser beam that does not wear the record, so the videodisc recording can be said to be permanent.

A single disc can store 64,000 still pictures that can be retrieved in any sequence. Retrieval is fast, the longest interval of seconds occurring when an item on the inside of the disc follows an item on the periphery. A library of materials on a topic can be recorded on a disc and duplicates sent to remote branches of an organization. In this way, a tremendous amount of information can be transmitted in compact, easily stored form.

The videodisc lacks recording capability. In addition, taking advantage of its sequencing, rapid retrieval feature requires that the playback unit be equipped with a programming device. A presentational speaker can program a sequence from a videodisc, transfer it to videotape, and have a custom-made feature for a presentation. The disc provides an abundance of options with no worries about sound and picture synchronization. In combination with videotape, it suggests solutions to many problems of presentations.

MANAGING THE MECHANICAL AND TECHNICAL DETAILS OF PRESENTATIONS

We conclude this technical section with a bit of practical advice we learned in the school of hard knocks: *never* expect untested devices to function. So *always* give each piece of audiovisual equipment an operational check, in place, just before the time of the presentation. This includes items often taken for granted, such as the flip chart (Do the pens write? Is there plenty of paper?). Murphy's Law, that if anything can go wrong it will, should be taken seriously when preparing to give a presentation. There is, of course, the possibility that the carefully checked gadget may break down later (projector bulbs seem to choose awkward times to burn out), but the checking ahead process reduces the number of possible disasters during the event. And the precheck always includes verifying a supply of replacement bulbs.

From the mechanical and electric, we turn to the nitty-gritty of managing gadgets, situations, and environmental circumstances to achieve the purposes of the presentation. The devices we reviewed technically are used mainly to contribute to passive involvement experiences. However, the presenter can create participative and passive involvement experiences that interest and convey information to the audience members. Perhaps more important, the more personal involvement that results from the presentation, the more likely is the creation of a joint venture rather than relying on the speaker sending and the listeners receiving.

PARTICIPATIVE INVOLVEMENT EXPERIENCES

The most effective and the least used aids to presentation are those that provide an experience of active personal involvement. They are impressive and interesting because they are multisensory in their stimulation and have an actuality that pictorial or linguistic representations of events cannot approach. They are little used because they require more ingenuity and effort than the simpler devices such as pictures, charts, and words. In addition, most speakers and audiences are unaccustomed to participative experiences in presentations. We tend to imitate our predecessors and to expect others to stay within the boundaries of the familiar.

Participative experience as an aid to communication can be classified as direct or contrived. In direct experiences the audience participates in an actual event, complete and undistorted. Contrived experiences result when the presentation incorporates imitations of actuality that are purposefully simplified to highlight important elements. Although the speaker manipulates and controls the participation of the audience, the experience still creates an effect very similar to direct experience.

Direct Participative Experiences.   Actual participation in an activity is possible in two forms, either by the speaker taking the audience to the event in a field trip or by transporting the event to the audience. If presentational speakers are proposing modification of a manufacturing operation, they can secure fullest understanding of the present method and of the nature of the change by taking their audiences to the assembly line, showing them the old and new methods in action, having them try their hand at the jobs to be done under current and under recommended procedures. If the presentation proposes a new cake mix to the Board of Control at Minnesota Mills, the members of the board might well go to the experimental kitchens and individually or in groups of two or three follow the directions on the box. Ideally, they would complete the baking process and taste their own final product, but if that plan takes too much time, they could mix the cakes, then sample others previously baked. The sales presentation frequently permits direct participation. The salespersons trying to get farm implement dealers to add new corn pickers to their lines should take the dealers to a harvest field and have them operate the machine themselves.

A speaker who has the audience manipulate, feel, see, hear, smell, and even taste "where the action is" creates involvement that cannot be duplicated in any other way. The makers of presentations should aggressively seek out opportunities to build a field trip into their planned activities.

When the field trip is impractical, a speaker can sometimes transport devices and processes into the room where the audience is assembled. Instead of relying on pictures and words to make the point, the speaker recommending the use of videotaped role-playing in the training of salespeople can set up a videotape machine, have volunteer audience members play roles, and another member operate the recorder. Any demonstration of equipment becomes participatory involvement when operated by members of the audience.

If the purpose of the presentation is to sell a new product and if the product is sufficiently portable, the people planning the speech should have some samples in finished functioning form for audience members to study, handle, and operate. For example, if speakers are presenting the advantages of a new machine for taking dictation, they might set up a typical secretarial installation of desk, chair, electric typewriter, and dictation machine and have one of the audience members dictate a memo. A secretary could then transcribe the memo to illustrate the way the new installation works. If speakers take some pains, they can develop a lively interchange among the observing members of the group, the performers, and themselves which will generate interest in the new device and its potential.

Admittedly, direct and realistic participative involvement is possible in only a minority of presentations. The important consideration is that the student of presentational speaking ought not overlook participative involvement whenever it *is* possible. Often, with a little ingenuity the speaker can discover ways to move the persons to the scene of action or the equipment to the people with gratifying, dynamic, and impressive consequences.

Contrived Participative Experiences.   The person who contrives participation for the audience ordinarily uses objects that are three-dimensional, such as specimens, cutaway machines, models, and mockups. Less used but still valuable is the simulation of processes that are largely symbolic and two-dimensional.

Specimens are representative parts of a machine or process that can be isolated, handled, and inspected. A new valve that is the heart of an oil-pumping system can be used in the presentation about the complex system.

Cutaways are usually full-sized devices, modified by having parts eliminated and housings "cut away" to reveal the details of how some complex machine functions. The automatic transmission cutaway is typically mounted on a stand and driven at a slow speed by a small electric motor. As controls are adjusted, the operator can see precisely how neutral, reverse, and varied forward speeds are accomplished.

The models used as audiovisual aids may be classified as *theoretical* and *physical*. Theoretical models are usually two-dimensional drawings representing fairly abstract concepts in some structural relationship to provide an explanation for a complicated phenomenon. Typical of theoretical models are those explaining the process of communication. What we referred to as "models" of person-to-machine and person-to-person communication in Chapter 2 are theoretical models, and Figures 2.1 and 2.2 in that chapter represent typical two-dimensional drawings of models in the theoretical sense. Occasionally, a model of theoretical relationships is three-dimensional, as in the instance when the structure of a molecule is represented by a rod-and-ball three-dimensional structure.

One kind of physical model is the person who poses for pictures and displays of clothing and other merchandise. Human models are seldom used as aids to presentations. The physical model the presentational speaker finds most helpful is a literal simulation of reality, and quite often it is a physical representation to scale of another physical entity. When we speak of a "model" as an audiovisual aid in the remainder of the chapter, we will be using the term to refer to physical models.

In this limited sense, models are

. . . recognizable three-dimensional representations of real things. The thing represented may be infinitely large, like the earth, or small as an atom. It may be an inanimate object such as a building, a monument, or a mine shaft; or it may be a living organism such as a paramecium, or the

human heart. The model may represent something as intricate as a jet engine, a nuclear powered submarine, or a spacecraft, or as simple as a number of spools on a string. It may be complete in every detail or considerably more simplified than the original (Walter Wittich and Charles Schuller, p. 173).

By a wide margin, models are the most flexible representations of physical relationships.

Advantages of using models are apparent in this list of characteristics supplied by Wittich and Schuller (pp. 174–177):

Models are three dimensional . . .

Models reduce or enlarge objects to an observable size . . .

Models provide interior views of objects . . .

Models eliminate the nonessentials of objects . . .

Models employ colors and texture to accent important features . . .

Many models can be disassembled and reassembled . . .

Models can be created. . . .

A mockup is an elaborate, functioning model, often full size, designed to clarify complex interdependent processes or to train people in skills and techniques of operation, maintenance, and repair. The mockup of a telephone, for example, could consist of the essential components spread over a demonstration board with labels that identify parts and describe their functions. The speaker using such a mockup could easily measure voltages at all parts of the circuit and trace the voice signal with an oscilloscope. A presentation based on steps in a manufacturing process condensed and clarified in a mockup would be useful to the orientation of new employees. Devices that simulate an automobile moving through traffic to train and test drivers are complicated mockups, as are the famous Link Trainers used to sharpen the flying skills of military and airline pilots.

Mockups are useful in presentations whenever a dynamic, complex operation can be simplified and arranged so that the "how" of its operation becomes readily apparent. A danger is that the mockups may become unproductively elaborate. Often, restricting the mockups to an absolute minimum of essentials, and assembling them of cheap, disposable materials, will produce a working unit that is easy to operate and to understand.

The mockup is a *literal* simulation device. Often, more *symbolic* simulations are helpful to the presentational speaker. The planners of an important presentation might devise variations of computerized business games to check out the probable consequences of a proposed change in company policy, or to explore the market for a new product, or to predict the effect of a price change on profits. Speakers could use the computerized game to compare their recommendations to current practices in various hypothetical situations. They could involve the audience by having it play the game and try to outguess the machine.

Of course, development of the simulated situation does not require a computer or other data processing equipment. Realistic hypothetical situations that pose perplexing problems familiar to the participants will provide incentive for thoughtful evaluation of the related proposal.

Other Techniques for Audience Participation.   The effectiveness of all audiovisual aids increases when the audience participates actively in the presentation. A rough rule-of-thumb is that the increase in audience interest and learning is roughly proportional to the amount of audience activity. The presentational speaker should know the ways and means of increasing the active involvement of the audience in audiovisual experiences. When appropriate, speakers should consciously "draw the audience in," converting passive participation into active participation by having its members do or say something.

Research into the uses of audiovisual materials in education supplies proven techniques for gaining audience participation. If the audience is carefully prepared for a particular audiovisual experience, more will be learned than if its members are surprised by it. Preparing the audience consists of overviewing what is to come, telling what to watch and listen for, explaining what is nonessential or possibly confusing, defining strange vocabulary or unfamiliar processes, and answering questions. Only when the audience is informed of general procedure and specific purpose of the coming experience is it ready to benefit maximally from it.

Frequently, it is desirable to pause along the way to talk with the audience about what is going on. For example, stopping a film and letting people ask questions will increase learning. If a discussion develops over what has been seen and what is to come, learning will be considerably greater than if only questions are asked. A summary after using any audiovisual aid makes it more effective. When speakers lead the audience members to help them summarize, results are much superior to those from a summary done by the speaker alone.

A basic principle to help speakers plan audience involvement is this: They should never do by themselves what members of their audiences can do as well. This applies particularly to demonstrations, when members of the audience can aid the speaker, as volunteers from a magician's audience contribute to the show by assisting.

Where there is no equipment to manipulate or materials for audience members to help arrange and manage, participation can take the form of *verbalizing content.* Skilled demonstrators can make their points by asking the right questions. Probably the best guarantee of high audience interest is to move the demonstration along with a series of thought-provoking and leading questions. The audience is encouraged to do some guessing and to call out answers. The developing presentation provides feedback to check each guess. Studies show that audiences like this feedback and that the process of making choices and finding that they are right or wrong increases learning. The questioning technique can be carried on into the final summary, with the audience being asked to recall the main points made and their significance.

Providing mental practice to aid understanding and recall is possible with audiovisual aids. Much reiteration is built into films and filmstrips, and demonstrations repeat central points in various ways. Audience questions and discussion are certain to "hash over" familiar concepts and to focus on their application. All of these reiterative activities constitute mental practice, the "covert" or inner verbalization of response that fixes words and ideas in memory and makes them more important to the learner.

Finally, involvement of the audience causes a much more animated interaction between speaker and listeners. The result is a two-way communication that is clearer and more pleasurable than a one-way sending of a message. A "team" spirit tends to emerge as speaker and receivers pool their efforts to make the presentation a success. The *quality* of the speaker-audience relationship may well be the decisive factor determining the outcome of many presentations. A warm, mutual respect is usually an outcome of vigorous two-way communication.

PASSIVE INVOLVEMENT EXPERIENCES

Most audiovisual aids to the presentation produce a passive involvement, casting the listener in the role of witness or observer. Even though the speaker involves the audience only passively, the audiovisual aids can help the communicative process by using direct sensory experiences to supplement the words in the message.

Demonstrations. The passive involvement device that most closely resembles the direct participative experience is that of the demonstration. Although the speaker manipulates the things in a demonstration as the audience watches, the idea, fact, or process can still be made vivid and concrete. Demonstrations can consist of films, still pictures, objects, models, mockups, easel pads, or chalkboards, alone or in any combination.

Much careful preparation is required for an effective demonstration. The speaker must keep the demonstration simple and yet pace it so interest does not lag. The wise speaker sets the stage for a demonstration with explanation, discusses each step as the demonstration develops, and frequently checks audience response to assure that every step is understood. Every element in the demonstration must be visible and audible to each receiver. Major points to be made must emerge as more prominent than other details. The demonstration should summarize from time to time and conclude with a skeletonized, yet comprehensive, crystal-clear final summary.

A good way to prepare a demonstration is to view it as a dramatic unit. The speaker should meticulously outline or script the sequence of events to be included in the demonstration. When the show goes on, everything must be in its place, for no interruptions or miscues should be tolerated. A rehearsal or two is mandatory. The best way to refine and "tighten up" a demonstration is to rehearse it with a perceptive critic. Critics can represent the intended audience and attempt to see the demonstration through their eyes. The critics' reactions can help prevent the COIK fallacy that sabotages many demonstrations. COIK is translated "clear only if known," reminding us of the pitfall of assuming that the audience knows more than it does about our topic!

Written materials to supplement the demonstration are frequently helpful, but their use often interferes with the communication. A safe procedure is to distribute written matter only after the demonstration is over. Earlier distribution guarantees that most people will attempt to read and look and listen at the same time, doing each ineffectively.

Exhibits.   Displays that are intended to accomplish the objectives of a demonstration without concurrent human assistance are called exhibits. An exhibit could show the products of the pastry division of Minnesota Mills in a way that would highlight the gap in the product line that a proposed new pie mix would fill. Such an exhibit might well create a frame of reference for an entire presentation.

Usually, one thinks of exhibits as belonging to store windows, fairs, museums, art galleries, bulletin boards in government agencies, and schools. However, relatively simple displays can often make the circumstances surrounding a presentation vivid and clear.

Ingredients of an exhibit are almost unlimited in variety and include posters, models, mockups, objects, chalkboards, voice narration, and still or motion-projected pictures. Interval projection of a series of 35 mm slides is often part of an exhibit. Animated exhibits are more attention-compelling than a static display, so often a motorized process or changing lights justify added expense and effort by holding and directing a viewer's attention.

Exhibits, like demonstrations, can make clear complex relationships that cannot be adequately represented by two-dimensional graphs, diagrams, or pictures. The worldwide distribution of television by satellite can be quickly and accurately learned from a display. A diorama (a three-dimensional group of modeled objects) carefully scaled to give an impression of depth and blending into a painted background can be excitingly realistic. An audience can visualize a proposed new building in its setting by viewing a diorama more completely than by use of almost any other method of communication. An exhibit of this kind can be made highly artistic if talent is available.

The dominant principle governing the design and construction of an exhibit is to focus all elements on a single central idea. Too often people prepare exhibits with multiple themes, and the result is that the viewer becomes confused. As with the demonstration, the presentational speaker planning a display should remember: when in doubt, keep it single and simple.

Television and Videotape.   Among the aids to the presentation that deserve thoughtful consideration are television and videotape. One striking result of extensive research into the effectiveness of television as an instructional device is that television is found to be as effective as a live teacher. Actually, the evidence of television's effectiveness covers not only school situations of a great variety and at all levels, but also instruction of adults in the home and in the armed forces. Habits of TV viewing (most people spend about twenty hours a week watching their sets at home) cause members of an audience to spontaneously attend to and absorb televised messages.

Television as an aid to the presentation can incorporate and consolidate very nearly all the other "passive involvement" gadgetry. Should speakers wish to use a variety of aids without the trouble of managing them during the demonstration, they can put them on videotape. One roll of tape will carry everything they wish to show and demonstrate, and all the speaker will have to do is start and stop the videotape recorder. Photographs, diagrams, graphs, charts, filmstrips, slides, clips from motion pictures, models, mockups, actuality scenes recorded on the spot, posters, cartoons, interviews, excerpts from speeches, these and other elements can be planned in a scenario. Technicians can help the speaker record and edit the tape until it is properly paced and awkward junctures are eliminated. The persuasive impact of a well-produced variety of pertinent audiovisual aids on the television screen is considerable. Speakers can rehearse with their tape until they are letter perfect. Should they be operating in a well-equipped audiovisual room, their assistants in the control room can supply the television on signal, which might be given inconspicuously by pressing a button on the speaker's stand. The fringe benefits are improved timing and the likelihood of collecting more and better feedback from the listeners. Closed Circuit Television (CCTV) has freed them from the distractions of handling multiple objects and operating several machines.

Not the least of the services rendered to presentational speakers by the CCTV is the opportunity to look at and analyze their own presentations. As units of a presentation are assembled, they can be videotaped, polished, and perfected. Finally, the entire presentation may be taped and, preferably with the help of a friendly and knowledgeable critic, the speaker deliberately scrutinizes it, minute by minute. There is no better method of debugging a presentation. With the help of a few associates the speaker can stage a realistic question period so that all phases of the final event will have been experienced in advance. Speakers must take care not to memorize their message word for word, since their speaking will then lack spontaneity.

Rather, they should vary their sentences, experimenting with different wordings during the rehearsals. The extemporaneous "run throughs" will result in the speaker's language steadily improving in clarity and efficiency.

Building a consolidated program of aids on videotape offers temptations to insert related or not-so-related drama and entertainment. Most of these opportunities should be resisted. Research into uses of instructional television indicates that accent on the factual produces better results than stressing dramatic elements. A touch of humor at occasional but unpredictable intervals is sufficient to produce the light touch that increases interest without interfering with the process of learning.

Increasingly, organizations and enterprises of all sorts are wired for TV. Of some use in presentations will be the ability to look at what is going on elsewhere at the moment. In the not too distant future televised materials will be stored in central video banks and makers of presentations will select their audiovisual materials from microfilmed indexes. Their selections will be transferred to videotape by the worldwide satellite retrieval system. Television promises to make obsolete the firsthand use of objects, models, and exhibits by displaying them in full color on a wall-size television screen.

Motion Pictures.   The motion picture is probably the most expensive aid to communication. Producing a color film of professional quality costs a thousand or more dollars a minute. But because so many people see the same film, often over a period of several years, the per viewer cost may be the lowest of all audiovisual devices. Of course, the high initial costs make motion pictures prohibitive for presentations that reach a few people or for a one-shot situation.

No other audiovisual device can cope as well with the problems of motion, size, and time as can film. Film techniques include an almost unlimited magnification, zoom lenses, a nearly infinite range of speeding up and slowing down, the ability to recreate the past or explore the future, and integration of the arts of animation with all conventional audiovisual techniques. Because of its versatility, film can contribute significantly to the understanding of highly complex relationships and processes. Perhaps because of positive transfer from commercial movies, good instructional films are also aesthetically satisfying.

Generally, homemade movies as aids to presentation have not been very helpful because 16 mm equipment is expensive and complicated and use of 8 mm film provides an insufficiently detailed picture. Currently, improved films, cameras, and the Super 8 method of utilizing increased film area show some promise. But films made by the people who give the presentations usually look amateurish. Moviemaking is an exacting art requiring a mastery of many techniques and much knowledge of precise capabilities of the instruments used. Only skilled cinematographers should attempt to create their own filmed aids. For the foreseeable future, needs of this sort can be met more successfully by use of videotape.

For some presentations, however, particularly those that have educational objectives, instructional films available from film libraries and audiovisual services may be useful. Careful previewing of these standard films will enable the speaker to build the presentation around the films and utilize the strengths of a professionally produced film by adapting it to a specific audience.

Perhaps the major problem in using sound motion picture aids to the presentation is finding what appropriate films are available and where to get them. Even small cities have film sources and information listed in the Yellow Pages of the telephone book under "Audiovisual Equipment and Supplies" or "Audiovisual Services." Most of the films one would consider using are listed as "instructional" or "educational" motion pictures, so lists of these should be requested. Public libraries, high schools, colleges, and universities keep these listings up to date and are usually glad to share them with members of their community.

Previewing a film before deciding to use all or part of it is an absolute necessity. Names and descriptions give only a vague impression of a film's content. Commonly, a library, school or audiovisual service can obtain a movie for preview purposes cost free or at small expense. Purchasing a sound motion picture for a single presentation or for even a few showings is expensive. Usually, rental is more economical and convenient.

Help in locating a film-producing agency can best be obtained from the above-mentioned sources of films and information about films. Frequently, a college or university will include a film production unit that will do a limited amount of custom production work to provide laboratory experience for its students and to generate income to amortize its overhead costs.

STILL PICTURES AND RECORDINGS

A danger in the use of pictures is the "pitfall of projection," which in this instance is unrelated to malfunction of the projector. Speakers tend to assume without thinking that listeners will read into a picture the same meaning that they see in it. Communicators "project" their interpretation into the visual stimulus by assuming that other perceptions and reactions are identical to their own.

Suppose that a picture shows an automobile accident involving two cars that have had a glancing, head-on collision. Two apparently injured people are lying on the shoulder of the road near the heavily damaged cars. A policeman with a notebook is talking to two people, a man and a woman, who are neatly dressed.

A physician seeing the picture will likely note the appearance of the persons lying on the ground and by studying the damage to the cars will speculate concerning their injuries. She will also wonder about how long ago the accident happened and whether an ambulance is on the way. A mechanic will see the vehicles that have been damaged and think in terms of their repair. A lawyer might view the scene in the context of legal action, looking for evidence that one driver was at fault and wondering whether the people talking to the patrolman are eyewitnesses who could testify. A policeman might find himself thinking about what is being written in the patrolman's notebook, whether traffic violation tickets had been issued, and whether the accident had been reported by radio and an ambulance requested. He will also wonder how he could record details of the accident, paths of vehicles, measurements made, and diagrams to be entered into his report of the accident. A highway engineer might observe the conditions of the road surface, look for traffic signs, intersections, obstructions, and attempt to ascertain the probability that highway conditions helped cause the collision.

The point of the above example is that pictures, like words, are subject to widely varied interpretations. What is obvious and important in a picture to one person may be unnoticed or disregarded by another. We tend to think that responses to pictures are uniform, and we need to remind ourselves that with pictures, as with language, our interests and experiences shape our perceptions.

The "pitfall of projection" applies to other audiovisual aids as well as to still pictures. The uniformity of perception in an audience can be increased by appropriate setting-of-the-stage before and by concomitant commentary guiding responses along the way. With motion pictures, careful preparation for the film in the form of telling the audience what to look for and a summary of the film and the points it made immediately after the projector is turned off are helpful in preventing misconceptions.

Nonprojected Two-Dimensional Visual Aids.   The chief nonprojected visual aid to the presentation in both amount and tradition of use is the chalkboard. Some years ago, all chalkboards were made of slate and were termed "blackboards." Now chalkboards come in varied colors, matching room décor and serving different purposes. They are made of slate, moss-surfaced glass, plastic, paint-coated wood, or vitreous-coated steel. The last-named has magnetic properties that make possible considerably extended uses of the chalkboard. Here are a few techniques that exploit some of the potential of the modern chalkboard.

The speaker can prepare drawings and diagrams that are neat and accurate. Previously prepared visuals eliminate the major disadvantage of the chalkboard that comes from the necessity of drawing and talking at the same time, and may result in neither being done well. Here are several ways of preparing neat chalkboard displays.

1. Using slide, overhead, filmstrip, or opaque projector, project on the blackboard the picture, diagram, or chart and trace the desired outlines with chalk.

2. Make a pattern by tracing outlines of the drawing on heavy paper and punching ⅛ inch to ⅜ inch holes at ½ inch to 1 inch intervals along the lines. Rub an eraser bearing chalk dust over the pattern, leaving dots that can be easily connected to produce the finished drawing.

3. Hold template, or silhouette made of a stiff, lightweight material, against the chalkboard, while tracing its outline.

4. The grid method can enlarge a drawing accurately and easily. Draw the original on paper, perhaps 8½ by 11, which is blocked off into small squares. Lay off much larger squares on the chalkboard. Reproduce the drawing in enlarged form by duplicating the original, one square at a time.

5. With a magnetic chalkboard, attach two- and three-dimensional additions to the prepared visual to small magnets ready for use as the speaker talks about his or her drawing.

6. Cover any prepared chalkboard display until it is needed, thereby avoiding distracting the audience and permitting sequential development. Wrapping paper makes good cover material. It can be scotch-taped to the top frame of the chalkboard, held in place by "pinch clamps" used if the chalkboard has a map rail along the top, or secured by magnets on a magnetic chalkboard.

Prepared chalkboard displays are helpful but will probably never replace concurrent lettering or drawing and speaking. For speakers who are skillful at using the chalkboard to illustrate and develop their points along the way, simultaneous writing and speaking add movement and suspense to the presentation. Difficulties come because some people are inept at drawing or writing on the chalkboard, and from an inevitable loss of speaker contact with audience. When speakers are drawing diagrams, they have difficulty watching their audiences and for at least some of the time their backs may be turned to them. However, "along the way" lettering and drawing are essential to most presentations. Because this can be done on the overhead projector with less effort, greater visibility, and without turning from the audience, it may be wise for most speakers to use the chalkboard only for preprepared displays.

The flannel board, a rectangular surface as large as 4 feet by 8 feet, covered with a flannel-like fabric, is useful in situations where portability is not a factor. Display items, usually lettered or drawn on cardboard, are backed with a material that adheres to the flannel on the board. The speaker can build up a display, element by element, by simply touching the item to the board in the proper place at the right time. Items can then be pulled off and relocated, since the nature of the adhesion is such that neither of the surfaces involved is changed by the contact.

Projected Still Two-Dimensional Aids.   Projection adds flexibility to the use of all varieties of pictorial material. Taking a picture of something is generally easier and cheaper than having it drawn or painted in a size usable as a direct visual. Projection enables an easy adjustment of picture size to the size of the audience, being accomplished by changing the size of the screen and the distance of the projector from the screen. With modern zoom lenses, some projectors can now fill screens of different sizes from a constant screen to projector distance.

Two basically different means of projection of still pictorial materials are in current use: of light reflected from the pictorial to produce the picture, known as *opaque projection,* and use of light that passes through the picture, known as *transparency projection.* Opaque projection is accomplished by a machine called the opaque projector. It accepts any printed or written material up to approximately 10 inches by 10 inches and throws an enlarged image on the screen. It will also project images of three-dimensional objects, providing they are flat enough to present no great difficulties in achieving satisfactory focus. The major advantage of the opaque projector is that no processing is necessary; for example, a schematic in a book can be inserted directly into the machine, and its disadvantage is a picture lacking brilliance. Because the opaque projector puts relatively little light on the screen, the room must be darkened to the point where note taking becomes difficult or impossible. The low light level also limits the maximum size of an acceptable picture. A suggested rule of thumb is that opaque projection is not likely to be satisfactory for an audience of more than twenty-five people.

More than any other projection device, the overhead projector becomes an integral part of the presentation. The speaker has it at the front of the room, turns it on and off, writes and draws on it as on chalkboard or flip chart, prepared visuals can be added to or modified on the spot, the shadow of a pencil can be used as a pointer, and all this takes place without breaking eye contact with the audience or changing the lighting in the room. The "overhead" is economical to purchase and operate. Its flexibility and utility have resulted in its becoming the most universally used projector in presentations and lectures.

Because the machine and its operator obstruct the view of the screen to some extent, optimum placement of the screen locates it slightly off-

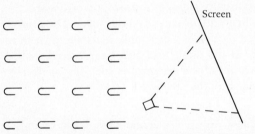

Figure 8.1 Proper Placement of an Overhead Projector

center and turned toward the projector, which is located toward the other side of the front of the room. A typical placement is illustrated in Figure 8.1. The overhead is close to the screen, and because the picture is considerably above the level of the projector, a phenomenon known as "keystoning" takes place, causing the picture to be distorted in the fashion illustrated by Figure 8.2. Consequently, the screen should be equipped with a "keystone correcting device," simply a means by which the top of the screen can be moved toward the projector, or the bottom of the screen can be moved away until the sides of the image are parallel to the edges of the screen.

Detailed instructions for use of any particular overhead projector can be obtained from makers of the machines, but some general advice relating to problems and techniques of using the overhead projector should be mentioned here. Typing for transparencies should be done with oversize type, since regular office sizes are difficult to see. A good size type for projection purposes is either $\frac{5}{32}$ inch or $\frac{8}{32}$ inch. A convenient way to build up a diagram is by overlays, four or five of which can be used without excessive dimming of the picture. A sheet of paper can be used to cover part of a transparency, and moving the paper will achieve successive revelation of a series of items. Transparency film is obtainable in colors, and various pictographs, figures, and so on, can be purchased in silhouette or contrasting colors, as can letters and numerals to aid in preparing visuals. A motorized, polarized disk attachment can give a prepared picture an illusion of movement. Audience members can write and draw on transparency sheets, and these can be immediately projected. Many more variations in application of the versatile overhead projector exist and will be devised. The enterprising presentational speaker will thoughtfully exploit this valuable device.

Audio Recording and Playback. In most presentations, sound is an adjunct to still or moving pictures. As such, it is produced by an audio channel added to the picture projector. The effective distribution of that sound is aided by good acoustics and by the proper placement of loudspeakers.

When sound without pictures is appropriate in a presentation, it is almost always provided by a tape recorder. The modern high-fidelity tape

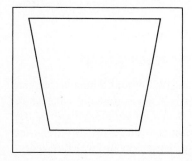

Figure 8.2 Keystoning Effect

recorder is reasonably inexpensive, it operates monophonically or stereophonically, and it can be operated with good results by a thoughtful layperson.

Usually, the audible component of audiovisual aids consists of prerecorded sounds and voices. Making a good recording requires elimination of unwanted noises, freedom from echoes and reverberation, never permitting microphone and recorder to rest on the same surface (the microphone picks up the motor noise of the recorder), and getting the microphone as close to the source of sound as possible. The last item is crucial and little understood. Sound energy diminishes as the square of the distance, so doubling the distance from the source results in the microphone getting one-fourth as much sound to record. Where people are recorded, the best possible microphone placement is to hang a lavalier mike around the neck of each, as is often the practice on radio and television panel programs.

Speakers can play tape recordings used in the presentation from the actual tape recorder on a table or stand beside them. Such direct playback is handicapped by the poor quality and low power of the playback-speaker circuit in the portable tape recorder. Much better results can be achieved if they connect or "patch in" the tape recorder to the sound system of the audiovisual room. The "patch" consists of an *electronic* connection from the recorder circuit to an input circuit of the room amplifier. *Never* play the tape recorder into a microphone, for the distortion introduced is substantial.

Spending time and effort to secure the highest fidelity audio possible and the best possible distribution of that high-fidelity sound is a good investment. Audience reaction to "hi-fi" sound is usually appreciative, and reaction to distorted sound is almost always bitter and uncharitable.

The tape recorder can make a faithful record of events that has many uses. In a well-equipped audiovisual room a tape recorder in the control booth should be used to record every presentation. With several ceiling microphones, audience comments and questions can be picked up as well as the speaker-initiated segments. After the event, speakers can review their efforts and be sure of what they actually said, and listeners can borrow the tape to freshen their memory of certain points. Often misunderstandings develop that can be cleared up by reference to the audio record. And, of course, any portion of the tape can be transcribed and converted to a written record.

A MULTIMEDIA SETTING FOR EFFECTIVE PRESENTATIONS

The setting for the presentation includes fixed audiovisual elements that can be crucial to its outcome. Some ingredients of environmental suggestion were discussed briefly in Chapter 5. We turn our attention here to the problem of providing surroundings and equipment for the presentation that will maximize positive transfer and minimize negative transfer. Admittedly, we will emphasize the creation of ideal conditions while recognizing that practical limitations will in most instances necessitate a compromise. Perhaps few of our readers will ever be able to design and construct an optimum room for presentations, reports, and instruction. Nevertheless, by sketching the ideal conditions, we hope to indicate the full potential of audiovisual aids to presentational speakers.

What are the characteristics of a room suitable for presentations? The ideal setting is large enough to accommodate the listeners comfortably, and no larger. Its design creates an atmosphere of informality and fosters comfortable concentration directed to the front of the room. Considerable attention has been paid to acoustical characteristics. The room is soundproofed, so outside noises cannot be a distraction, and sound-treated, so very little reverberation is possible within it. All of the ceiling and part of the wall space are surfaced with sound-absorbent material, and the floor is carpeted.

Lighting within the room is ample, glareless, and continuously controlled from darkness to maximum brilliance. Interior decoration has a variety of subdued colors. A tasteful harmony of furnishings, drapes, carpet, and wall treatment facilitates communication. Chairs are comfortable, movable, and provide a writing surface for each person. If more than twenty people are to be seated in the room, a low platform at the front is desirable, but the distance between listeners and speakers should be kept to a minimum.

Silent air conditioning is mandatory. Similarly, a built-in sound distribution system is an important part of the room. Loudspeakers, several of them, are flush with the ceiling, several microphones are suspended from the ceiling to permit recording of everyone in the room, and at the front of the room on the baseboard are plug-in connectors permitting use of lavalier, floor stand, hand-held and speaker's stand microphones, as well as television cameras, monitors, and receivers.

Magnetic chalkboards extend across the front wall of the room and halfway along the sidewalls. In the ceiling at the center of the front wall is a large pull-down projection screen, to be used with filmstrips, slides, and movies. To the side at the front another roll-up screen is suspended from the ceiling. This is angled slightly to permit locating the overhead projector a bit off-center to the opposite side of the room, and it is equipped with a screen-tilting device to prevent "keystoning" of the projected picture.

The "nerve center" of the multimedia room is its combined recording-playback-projection booth. This separate enclosed space is located behind the center of the rear wall, and it lies entirely outside of the main room. Slots are cut into the main room's rear wall for projection of slides, filmstrips, and movies, and for television cameras used in videotaping. Inside the projection booth, which is more accurately referred to as a "control room," are located slide and motion picture projectors, sound recording and distributing equipment, television cameras, a television monitor, and one or two videotaping machines. The control room is soundproofed and sound-treated. It is entered from the outside, so activities connected with projection and recording will not affect events in the main area. All lights can be controlled from the booth.

The room described above includes the basic features and equipment that are part of its construction and are permanent. More exotic and highly useful integral equipment might well be added. A telephone speaker could be installed that would permit everyone in the room to overhear and participate in a call from a remote person or persons. Audio and television lines from other rooms and buildings could connect to the control room switchboard. Remote controls for lights, the sound system, and for booth-located projectors could be installed in the speaker's stand and at the rear of the room. Built into the rear wall one could have shelf space for coffee, soft drinks, and snacks, supplied from the outside. Extra screens and projectors make multiple comparisons easy and may be justified. Every audiovisual room should be a product of particular requirements that are to some degree unique. The time to meet both general and specialized needs is when the room is being designed and built.

SUMMARY

Audiovisual aids to the presentation are necessary to provide a multisensory stimulus and to counter the influence of "verbalism," our tendency to place excessive reliance on words. Research in schools, the military services, and industry offers proof that concepts presented with audiovisual aids are more impressive and better remembered than when presented without.

Since devices used in the presentation are increasingly complicated, it is essential that the presenter know the tools that may be helpful and what they can and cannot do. The first major section of this chapter consists of "technical basics," information about available equipment, how it works, its capabilities and limitations.

These aids to presentation are classified as audio, visual, and audiovisual. Audio equipment includes microphones, loudspeakers, sound recording, and playback devices. The visual aids section provides detailed information about 35 mm slides and projectors, filmstrips, overhead projectors, and flip charts. The more complicated devices, those providing both audio and video elements, are covered in the final part of the technical section. These are the 16 mm motion picture projectors, videotape recorders, monitors, and projectors, and videodiscs.

Our word of advice to the user of electronic and mechanical aids is; *never* expect untested devices to function. *Always* be alert for possible malfunctions, even of tested equipment.

The goal of joint venture suggests that environment and equipment should be used to generate involvement. Audience involvement may be participative or passive. Audiovisual devices described in the technical section contribute primarily to passive involvement. Opportunities for participative involvement, however, are frequently overlooked.

QUESTIONS FOR DISCUSSION AND REVIEW

1. What advice would you give to a presenter concerning the use of audio devices?

2. How can the 35 mm slide projector and the overhead projector be compared as aids to the presentation? What are the specific advantages and disadvantages of each?

3. What are some recent improvements in videotape that are resulting in its gradually replacing the 16 mm motion picture in presentations?

4. What are some examples that illustrate how participative involvement experiences are direct and planned?

5. What are some ways in which audience participation can be increased by use of audiovisual aids?

6. How can the "pitfall of projection" often spoil a presenter's use of picture material?

7. What is the proper placement of the screen and projector to assure that keystoning is corrected and that maximum effectiveness of overhead visuals is obtained?

8. What are the desirable physical characteristics of a presentation room and its furnishings?

9. What are the functions of a multimedia room's recording-playback-projection booth?

10. How can a presenter avoid the overuse of gadgets?

REFERENCES AND SUGGESTED READINGS

For an overview of presentational aids and their use, see:

Applbaum, Ronald L., and Karl W.E. Anatol. *Effective Oral Communication for Business and the Professions.* Chicago: Science Research Associates, 1982, Chapter 9.

For a comprehensive treatment of audiovisual aids, their preparation, and use, see:

Kamp, Jerrold E., and Diane K. Dayton. *Planning and Producing Instructional Media.* 5th ed. New York: Harper and Row, 1985.

The quotations describing models and the advantages of using them are from:

Wittich, Walter A., and Charles Schuller, *Audio-Visual Materials. Their Nature and Use.* New York: Harper and Row, 1967.

Case Studies Applying Patterns of Organization

To illustrate the six patterns of organization for presentations, we present a case study for each. The case studies are rather elaborate, supplying background that places each *in context*. This is necessary because every situation for a presentation is unique. All the many persons and variables involved affect decisions made by the presenter.

The reader will recall that the presenting process includes all events from the introduction of an idea through the interaction of speaker and audience in the formal presentation. Representing this faithfully requires some history and a lot of context.

An advantage of the in context case study is the chance to demonstrate the three abilities required of competent presenters: adaptability, creativity, and flexibility. Note the efforts to create joint venture and analyze attempts to be adaptive, creative, and flexible.

The cases are hypothetical. No resemblance to actual situations or persons is intended.

CASE STUDY 1
THE STATE-THE-CASE-AND-PROVE-IT PATTERN

Context

Eric Bolton is the son of the founder of the Ira S. Bolton Publishing Company. He has an MBA degree from a respected business school. He has been with the company for two and one-half years, and this is his first job. He came in as assistant to the president (his father), worked hard, made both contributions and friends, and gained respect.

On the second anniversary of his employment, his father appointed him vice-president. This was a major change, there having been no previous vice-president. Within the Bolton Company the appointment was interpreted as formalizing succession in a family organization, giving Eric a substantial role as adviser and general helper to the president.

Eric knows the company well. He has become highly interested in marketing, particularly to educational institutions. He is convinced that here are promising opportunities to expand Bolton publications.

The Board of Directors, headed by President Ira Bolton, consists of the Editor of Trade Publications, the Editor of Textbooks, the head of Advertising and Marketing, the Comptroller, and Eric. The board is predominantly conservative, reluctant to change, but willing to review suggestions.

Eric, as the young, new member, is regarded as an apprentice, but as one with considerable potential for growth and development as a valuable contributing member. Personal relationships on the board are positive. Members like and respect one another. They are an effective team.

The Ira S. Bolton Publishing Company is reasonably prosperous but is in a plateau period, comfortably productive but not expanding.

Situation

For several years Bolton has provided a custom-printing service to college and university professors in nearby institutions. The service makes the professors' own writings available to their students in the form of softcover books. Students buy these books in college or university bookstores, securing texts that fit the courses better than would books written by outsiders. Responses to these publications have been favorable. Some have been reviewed in scholarly publications, resulting in a few orders from institutions scattered around the United States.

Eric believes that with special editing to make local books more suitable for general use, plus appropriate advertising, Bolton could merchandise a substantial number of these texts. To Eric, this appears to be a logical extension of a present operation.

To move toward a specific recommendation, boundaries must be set on what he wants to do and the direction advocated must be in sharp focus. A good way to accomplish this is to word a tentative proposition—tentative, because new information and the ideas of others may well produce revision.

Eric words the tentative proposition as follows: "The Ira S. Bolton Publishing Company should expand its custom-text operation to a national market."

Unit Plan and Qualified Proposition

To Eric the Board of Directors appears to be hard-nosed but fair, resistant to change but persuadable. The key to gaining acceptance of his proposal will be the reasonableness of his argument. He decides to prepare a Unit Plan, to be sure that he uses all essential information, no nonessential facts, that his reasoning supports his proposition and is based on that information, that necessary explanation is provided, and that possible exceptions which might invalidate his plan are recognized. He procures a large sheet of paper for his layout. His first entry is his tentative proposition.

Eric proceeds to list all facts he might possibly use in the Essential Information column. He asks himself which facts can directly support his proposition. The other facts he crosses out. Then he works on bridging the gap between facts and proposition by succinct reasoning. For the reasoning to be understood, some explanation is needed. He enters this under the Necessary Explanation column.

With the skeleton structure of argument complete, possible exceptions must be considered. What conceivable circumstances might invalidate the apparently conclusive logical sequence? Two unlikely but possible developments come to mind: (1) the text material may prove to be too localized to be widely attractive, and (2) bigger and richer publishers may move in and take over this market. Eric notes these possibilities in the Unit Plan under the Exceptions column. He knows that mentioning exceptions before his audience thinks of them makes the exceptions less obstructive.

Eric is ready to review his tentative proposition in light of the completed Unit Plan. Some of his early certainty has eroded now that he can see how few useful facts there are and he has worded the reasoning these will support. The exceptions also loom larger than he had anticipated. Common sense tells him his tentative proposition is overly ambitious.

Rather than a major national effort, a trial run might explore possibilities more economically, with less risk. Trial runs usually yield information helpful to later, larger ventures. Eric's qualified proposition becomes: "The Ira S. Bolton Publishing Company should explore expanding its custom-text operation by marketing current products to educational institutions in adjoining states."

Persuasion Before the Presentation

Eric begins sounding out reactions by discussing his idea casually with his father. The president is skeptical but agrees that a modest trial run would not be prohibitively expensive and might provide some answers concerning later expansion. Ira recommends that Eric check with the other members of the Board of Directors to get their opinions.

Eric goes first to the head of Advertising and Marketing. He begins by mentioning the favorable reviews and orders from remote places. Then he asks the head how marketing and advertising might increase the custom-text volume of business. Soon they are jointly developing possibilities, one of which is Eric's proposal. When Eric leaves the Advertising and Marketing office, he feels sure of the head's support. Furthermore, he suspects that the head thinks of the proposal as his own idea, rather than Eric's.

Eric opens his interview with the Textbook Editor by asking his opinion on the suitability of custom texts for wider distribution. The Editor has been thinking about this possibility. He lists for Eric the modifications necessary to remove features that restrict the books to local use. The changes include intensive editing, which is fairly expensive, requiring added editorial personnel. The trial run approach appeals to the Textbook Editor. Eric leaves, confident that the Editor of Textbooks understands his proposal and will support it.

The Comptroller and the Trade Book Editor are not directly affected by the change Eric wants to recommend, but it is as important that they be consulted as it is to talk to the others. Senior managerial personnel dislike surprises and value knowing what is going on. Moreover, Eric wants to discover any possible objections that the Trade Book Editor or the Comptroller might raise. Aside from the Comptroller's objection to spending money from the company's limited reserve, no obstacles emerge from Eric's discussions.

Information gathered during interviews with the Board of Directors enables Eric to make his proposition more specific. He now revises his statement as follows: "The Ira S. Bolton Publishing Company should budget $50,000 for a trial run of marketing its custom texts in the four adjoining states."

Since the audience understands that Eric will advocate an expansion of the custom-text business, the job to be done by the presentation is to state the recommendation precisely and to provide evidence and reasoning to support it conclusively. His purpose, of course, is to limit options to one. The state-the-case-and-prove-it pattern does this expeditiously.

Outline and Speaker's Notes

1.0 Introduction—Interest in custom texts outside present market.
2.0 Proposition: The Ira S. Bolton Publishing Company should budget $50,000 for a trial run of marketing its custom texts in four adjoining states. (Proposition is on preprepared flip chart sheet.)
3.0 Substantial potential market exists in the four adjoining states.
    3.1 Four overhead transparencies showing colleges, universities, and courses that could use Bolton custom texts in each of the four adjoining states.
    3.2 Responses of instructors of these courses to sample Bolton custom texts.
    3.3 Survey of instructors in these institutions who are possible authors of custom texts. (Survey results reported orally and on flip chart.)
4.0 A trial run is the economical way to assess possibilities of an expanded custom-text operation.
    4.1 Advertising can be by direct mail to prospects known to our field representatives.
    4.2 Our field people will be calling on these institutions and can follow up on the advertising.
    4.3 Probable allocation of $50,000 expenditure. (Overhead transparency chart to illustrate budget.)
5.0 The present custom-text program will benefit from this trial run.
    5.1 More intensive editing will improve quality.
    5.2 Some excellent authors will be discovered to add to our custom-text list.
    5.3 Present authors will be motivated by royalties and larger sales.
6.0 Bolton Publishing needs this innovation, now.
    6.1 For three years, same products, same markets, profits are on a plateau. (Overhead transparencies provide evidence of claims.)
    6.2 Competition in custom texts is relatively weak.
    6.3 Trial run may lead to a nationwide major market for Bolton Publishing.
7.0 Bolton has the personnel and financial resources to accomplish the trial run.
    7.1 Any added employees will be temporary.
    7.2 Only limited time, two years, is required.
8.0 Summary and repetition of proposal.

Comments

Eric plans a presentation of twenty or thirty minutes. He intends to make it a joint venture, securing verbal response within the first two minutes. His style will be informal. He is free to rearrange the sequence of the contentions in his outline if that seems indicated. Only after the audience has had its say will he conclude by summarizing and repeating the proposition.

You will recall that in the Unit Plan Eric had "Necessary Explanation" and "Exceptions." These do not appear in the outline, but they are available. Their inclusion in the Unit Plan guarantees that Eric can use them when and if his holistic (intuitive) judgment tells him they are needed.

CASE STUDY 2
IMPROMPTU 1

Context

Marilyn Gibson is president of the student body at Charlemaign College. She was elected at the close of the previous school year. She is now a senior, majoring in business administration.

The election was hotly contested because Marilyn advocated deemphasis of intercollegiate athletics through raising the grade point average necessary for participation, while her opponent, a talented and popular defensive back on the football team, ran on a platform of increased emphasis on athletic competition. Marilyn won by demonstrating that expansion of competitive athletics at Charlemaign would require extensive recruiting, a lot of money, and relaxation of academic standards.

The student publication, a thrice-weekly newspaper *The Clarion,* backed Marilyn, contending that the history of Charlemaign College and its basic orientation dictated strong scholarly priorities. Competitive athletics, said *The Clarion,* intrude inappropriately.

The student body was almost equally divided on the athletics versus scholarship issue. Nearly everyone voted in the election, with Marilyn winning by the narrowest of margins.

Situation

Now at the beginning of the fall semester the "Big Football" movement has apparently gained momentum over the summer. A well-organized movement to recall Marilyn, elect her opponent, and endorse athletic expansion is underway. When students return to the campus, posters are distributed each day, meetings are held, and one-to-one persuasion is aimed at key personnel. All departments of the college are being covered systematically.

The Clarion, with a new editor, prints pro "Big Football" letters to the editor but takes no position. One letter, noting the professionally produced handouts and posters, raises the question of where the money for the current campaign is coming from. The next issue prints a letter answering that question by claiming that a group of Charlemaign's graduates in the local Charlemaign Alumni Club is directing and financing the pro "Big Football" effort.

Marilyn, being the target of this unexpected attack, is understandably anxious to respond. When she reads the second letter to the editor alleging that members of the Alumni Club are responsible, she sees an opening to fight back. Joan

Fitzhugh, the president of the local Charlemaign Alumni Club, is a close friend. Immediately, Marilyn calls Joan to find out what is going on. Joan says the club has taken no action, and, if some members are managing the "Big Football" program, she knows nothing about it.

"Marilyn," says Joan, "I have an idea to help clear up this matter. Tomorrow noon is our regular monthly Alumni Club luncheon. If you will come to talk with us I'll save ten minutes between the lunch and the scheduled program for you to say whatever you wish."

Marilyn is apprehensive because of the short time to prepare her talk. But she immediately accepts Joan's invitation and thanks her for her excellent suggestion.

Preliminary Preparation

Marilyn remembers an organizational pattern suited to limited preparation time, impromptu 1, from a course in presentational speaking she took the previous semester. She reviews her notes and rereads the section in the course text. She finds that the pattern is appropriate when the presenter wishes to limit the options to one. This helps her decide to advocate a definite proposition.

It seems wise to make a positive recommendation on the current situation and argue for it. As the elected head of the student body she has prestige, and as a senior she will soon be eligible for membership in the Alumni Club. This common ground should enable her to establish a relationship with members of the audience and help assure a fair hearing for her recommendation.

But what will the proposition be? She asks herself, what is the best possible resolution to the present predicament? The best thing that could happen, she decides, is to secure agreement for an orderly debate of the "Big Football" issue throughout the first semester, with a scheduled vote to register opinion near the beginning of the second semester. A heavier burden of proof is probably too much to attempt, under present circumstances.

For her talk to the Alumni Club, Marilyn's proposition becomes: "The Charlemaign Alumni Club requests that students and faculty of Charlemaign College debate expanding intercollegiate athletics throughout fall semester and vote on the issue early spring semester." She will urge adoption of the resolution by the members present, immediately.

Marilyn lists the restrictions within which she must operate. There is no opportunity to use visual aids, and the ten minutes allotted is too short to permit verbal interaction with the audience. Therefore, any joint venture she generates will be nonverbal, accomplished by dynamic, friendly, well-projected delivery, and the use of rhetorical questions.

Detailed Planning

Marilyn resists the temptation to plan the opening example and the concluding "twist" before supporting contentions are worded in final form. An exciting opening and close might not fit an argument prepared *post hoc.*

She limits herself to three points, as many as she feels can be dealt with in ten minutes. Deciding on the three best reasons to support her proposition turns out to be a difficult task. After about two hours of juggling possible wordings, she feels she has acceptable contentions. It is dinner time, so she pushes tomorrow's presentation out of her mind, goes to dinner with friends, attends an hour-long choir rehearsal, and returns to her room.

The three contentions still look good. All support the central proposition—Marilyn uses the "because" test to be sure that each one does, directly. She feels sure she can supply facts and reasoning to support all of them. Her long experience with the controversy provides abundant material for the talk. Gathering more information is therefore unnecessary.

Marilyn then writes a first draft of her outline, which will also serve as speaker's notes.

Outline (Also Speaker's Notes)

1.0 Opening incident.
2.0 Proposition.
3.0 Overview of three points (4.0, 5.0, and 6.0).
4.0 A decision made now would prevent adequate examination of a very complex issue.
    4.1 Emotion might prevail over reason.
    4.2 A wealth of variables is involved, many not yet considered.
    4.3 Consequences to college and community are not yet explored.
5.0 Debating the athletics scholarship conflict throughout the fall semester offers many advantages.
    5.1 A cooling off period.
    5.2 Time to study what has happened in institutions similar to Charlemaign College.
    5.3 Time to be sure all interested members of the community, administrators, faculty, and students are thoroughly informed.
        5.31 Any recommendation is necessarily advisory.
        5.32 Formal decision is made by President and Regents.
6.0 Your Alumni Club can make the difference between a hasty, possibly unwise, decision and a carefully reasoned, thoroughly researched outcome.
    6.1 Right now, confusion reigns.
    6.2 A voice of reason from a respected organization is needed.
    6.3 This club can serve its alma mater by recommending a sensible and orderly procedure.
        6.31 This club has great influence.
        6.32 The recommendation is logical and scholarly.
        6.33 Members of this club can contribute significantly to a semester-long discussion.
7.0 Recap and twist.

Opening Incident and Twist

With the body of her presentation, Marilyn is ready to plan the opening example and the twist that will conclude her talk. Since both are brief narrative prose, she decides to write them out as they might be spoken. She will not memorize either, but writing them down will fix them in her mind and give her a chance to look at them objectively.

Opening Incident.   "All of you remember *The Clarion,* our college newspaper. I believe some of you still subscribe to it. So you may know that it has a new editor, Brent Hazeltine, who took office this fall. Brent phoned me Monday. He said he wasn't well informed on the athletic-scholarly emphasis issue and in fact, had no opinion. He said that 'Big Football' advocates had been bombarding him with daily messages, but as yet he hadn't heard from the other side. Brent said he didn't want to knuckle under to one-sided pressure. What did I think he should do?

"I reminded him I was biased, but added that I appreciated the opportunity to make a recommendation. I asked him to hold off committing *The Clarion* to an editorial position for a couple of days, and I would get back to him. Brent said, 'OK.' Now I'm working on my response."

Twist.   "Remember at the beginning of my talk I told you about *The Clarion* editor's call, and his request for advice on how to treat the athletic emphasis or deemphasis issue? I now know the response I would like to make. I'd like to tell Brent Hazeltine to talk with your president Joan Fitzhugh and other Alumni Club members, publish an article or two on what you are thinking, and relying on his good editorial judgment, take it from there."

Details of Implementation

Opportunity to prepare the audience for both Marilyn and her message is limited. There is a forty-five minute social hour before the luncheon. Marilyn called Joan to request that she be invited to take part in the socializing, and Joan offered to introduce her to the members as an honored guest, the president of the Charlemaign student body.

Marilyn manages friendly conversation with most of the twenty-three alumni who attend the luncheon. She does not attempt to develop support for her presentation proposition; rather, she encourages them to talk about the college. By being very interested in the club members and their thoughts, she predisposes them to reciprocate by giving her talk fair and favorable attention. Perhaps more important, she hears comments and opinions and senses attitudes that can be mentioned in her speech.

Watching a clock on the wall enables her to move through the subdivisions of her talk on schedule. Marilyn finishes her "twist" precisely on time. Joan asks if the club wishes to take action. A member moves adoption of Marilyn's resolution. It is approved by a vote of nineteen in favor, none opposed, and four abstentions.

sary
ments
could be

Office i.....the strategy of impromptu 1, Marilyn does *not* mention her topic belt use are plentifu, diê cider*. This increases audience attention, as curiosity is and some results of mandate.y leg..
have been published. John phones th-ntioning the opening narrative, she says ..terms statistics on consequences and to lear.l.ation, which is . . . ," and she re_ranses to enforcement of seat belt legislation.

The most helpful new finding arguing that now is th.......each is seat belt legislation is a trend in public opinion polls. Across the United Stae.speople are increasingly favoring legislative action on seat belts. A Florida poll is typical. Seventy-three percent favor a mandatory law, up 8 percent from the previous poll

CASE STUDY 3
PSYCHOLOGICAL PROGRESSION

Context

The Traffic Safety Coalition, a statewide organization dedicated to making travel by motor vehicle less hazardous, at its annual convention decides that increasing the use of seat belts is its top priority. Many studies over a period of years furnish conclusive proof that persons wearing seat belts survive accidents better and suffer serious injuries less frequently than do drivers and passengers who are not wearing seat belts. But in spite of persuasion, education, and many efforts to frighten people into putting on their seat belts, the percentage of voluntary belt wearers has not increased.

Automatic seat belts that attach themselves to occupants when they enter a vehicle have not been successful. Air bags that inflate themselves in an accident and protect passengers have proved to be impractical and prohibitively expensive. Since seat belts are now standard automotive equipment and since their use provides much protection, it seems that the effort to put this available equipment to use is potentially more productive than other courses of action.

Situation

The Executive Committee of the Traffic Safety Coalition decides that the best approach to increase the wearing of seat belts is to make it compulsory. The previous state legislature voted against a mandatory seat belt law, but by a narrow margin. Reconsideration as well as aggressive lobbying might get the measure passed in the coming legislative session.

The Executive Committee polls the membership to assess the support the organization would give to a campaign to secure passage of a mandatory seat belt law. Ninety-three percent of the members respond, and of those, 99 percent endorse the proposal.

It is now August and the legislature convenes in February. An interim committee is meeting through August and September to review topics for the legislative agenda. Its recommendations carry considerable weight. If the interim committee unanimously gives a problem top priority, it is almost certain to receive early legislative attention.

Since the interim committee is besieged by petitioners, the first thing for the Executive Committee to do is schedule time for a presentation. The Traffic Safety Coalition has a fine reputation, a lot of public approval, and, consequently, considerable clout. The interim committee schedules them for a half hour of committee ti 10:30–11:00 A.M., on a day two weeks away.

Executive Committee Action

 the case with any presentation, the fir

 n. Two issues puzzle the commi

 nd front seat pass

to driver and all passengers in a vehicle and that a standard fine for noncompliance (they suggest $20.00) should be imposed. Individuals, including children, could be fined. The driver would not be held responsible for passengers wearing belts but would be responsible for the availability and operability of seat belts in the vehicle. If a lap belt is fastened, the requirement is met. Shoulder belts are optional.

The Executive Committee agrees to recommend to the interim committee that they request the legislature to pass a mandatory seat belt law. Specifically, driver and all passengers in a motor vehicle must wear seat belts whenever the vehicle is in motion. Failure to do so will be punished with a $20.00 fine. Motorcycles, tractors, and off-the-highway vehicles are not covered.

Although the eight Executive Committee members plan to be present at the scheduled interim committee session, one member, the most experienced public speaker, John McLaughlin, will make the presentation and moderate subsequent discussion. In the allotted half hour, the formal presentation will take fifteen minutes followed by fifteen minutes of interaction with the interim committee.

At this point, the Executive Committee turns over to John McLaughlin the preparation of the presentation. They offer their personal help and the files and staff of the state office. John is to feel free to consult with any of them at any time and to request their aid in collecting information or supplying examples, human interest incidents, and personal experiences.

The Presenter's Preparation

Because the topic is "old stuff" to the interim committee, John must emphasize new information and resist the temptation to rely on the usual horror stories and gruesome accident pictures. His job, however, is to somehow arouse the committee and to produce dissatisfaction with the status quo that might give fresh impetus to action. The obvious choice for a pattern of organization is "psychological progression." His strategy then, is to arouse, dissatisfy, gratify, picture, and move interim committee personnel in the direction of implementing the Traffic Safety Coalition recommendation.

But before planning the psychological sequence, John needs to assemble the logical core of facts and reasons on which final acceptance will depend. Arousing, dissatisfying, and gratifying are best accomplished by sound evidence and clear thinking. John decides to gather possibly useful material in a Unit Plan, so he can see how it supports the proposal. He can use only highly selected information, and, by using a large sheet of paper, he can record much more than he needs and compare possibilities conveniently. In the Unit Plan, he can note and "tighten up" "Neces-
Explanation." Under "Exceptions" he can anticipate bothersome obstacles that
raised by the interim committee.

files and staff simplify the construction of the Unit Plan. Studies of seat
different forms of mandatory seat belt legislation are reported,
legislation in sixteen states where it has been adopted
the states with these laws in order to update
what he can about public res

the year before. John can assert that people are now ready for the law, which was not the case even a year or two ago.

With the Unit Plan completed, John is ready to outline the five steps in the psychological-progression pattern. His task is to add dramatic appeal to a soundly reasoned and well-supported argument using material from the Unit Plan. He needs visual aids, but projection devices could not be managed in the committee room in the brief available time. John decides that all his visuals will be on a preprepared flip chart, easy to carry and set up.

Outline and Speaker's Notes

Arouse

1.0 Record of "The Convincer," a device that simulates a 7 mph collision, *with seat belts.*
    1.1 People who ride "The Convincer" are convinced.
    1.2 General Motors $10,000 life insurance if a person wearing a seat belt is killed.

Dissatisfy

2.0 New data on seat belts saving lives and preventing injuries (prepared flip chart).
3.0 Failure of automatic restraints.
    3.1 Automatic seat and shoulder belts do not work (flip chart).
    3.2 Air bags have proven costly and impractical (air bag record on flip chart).
4.0 Current accident record in our state.
    4.1 Figures from past year (flip chart).
    4.2 Estimated lives saved and injuries avoided if seat belts had been required, assuming what happened in states with mandatory laws would happen here (flip chart).

Gratify

5.0 People are ready for mandatory seat belt law.
    5.1 They were not ready even a year ago.
    5.2 The typical poll results in Florida.
        5.21 Seventy-three percent favor mandatory law (flip chart).
        5.22 Up 8 percent from last year.
    5.3 When people accept a law, behavior will change. They will conform.
    5.4 Vehicles have seat belts ready for use.
6.0 Record of sixteen states where mandatory seat belt laws are working (flip chart).
7.0 Opportunity to improve on legislation in other states.
    7.1 Only driver and front seat passengers are protected in other states.
    7.2 Many of these laws lack teeth.
        7.21 Some rely on reprimand (flip chart).
        7.22 Some enforce law sporadically (flip chart).
8.0 The Traffic Safety Coalition recommends:
    A seat belt law that requires driver and all passengers in a moving motor vehicle to wear seat belts. Penalty for violation, a $20.00 fine. Motorcycles, tractors,

and all off-the-road vehicles are exempted. (Recommendation is on flip chart, left there during remainder of presentation.)

Picture

9.0 People will accept the law. Polls show they want it, now.
10.0 Enforcement will be concentrated in first six months.
 10.1 Graphic portrayal in dramatic terms of initial strong enforcement by state patrol indicating that the state means business.
 10.2 Graphic portrayal in dramatic terms of examples of citizens for which "seat belt habit" has become universal.
 10.3 Little enforcement will be needed after the six-month "get acquainted" period.
11.0 Graphic portrayals of citizens using seat belts and the saving of lives and the avoidance of injuries. Over 20 percent reduction in traffic fatalities is certain.

Move

12.0 The Traffic Safety Coalition requests the interim committee to recommend that the coming legislature give top priority to consideration of a mandatory seat belt law.
13.0 The Coalition requests that the committee report its specific recommendation of what that law should be to the legislature.
14.0 The Coalition recommends that "The Convincer" be made available to the legislature, so that they can experience effects of using seat belts.

Other Preparation

John McLaughlin knows the importance of as much persuasion as possible before the presentation. He has a special newsletter prepared to send immediately to all members of the Coalition. The newsletter gives details from the plans for presenting its proposal to the interim committee, the specific recommendation, and the names of members of the interim committee. Any Coalition member who is acquainted with an interim committee member is asked to talk with that person about mandatory seat belt legislation. After talking with the interim committee member, the Coalition person will write to John McLaughlin or call him on the phone immediately. This audience persuasion and analysis, although done remotely, is extremely important if John is to anticipate committee responses.

John has the office staff prepare a two-page summary of the presentation, including selected statistical support, to be passed out to members of the interim committee *at the conclusion of his presentation.* He knows that distributing the folder before the talk would result in their reading it instead of listening to his speech. He plans to send the folder to all members of the legislature with a cover letter explaining the presentation to the interim committee.

John's plan for the second fifteen minutes of the half hour with the interim committee is to "wing it." He wants to be completely free to interact informally with committee members and to draw on resources of the Coalition Executive Committee members who will be present. The interim committee's possible reservations cannot be accurately predicted, and he wants to be free to adapt to them directly.

The Psychological Progression Presentation

The committee meeting runs late and John does not get the opportunity to give his presentation until 11:30 A.M., thirty minutes after it is scheduled, the coalition members have done their work and a majority of the committee members are present. Although the hour is getting late, John is able to arouse the attention of the members with the striking opening sections of his presentation. Once he has their attention he holds it with the psychologically compelling materials he orders around the basic steps of the pattern.

The fifteen minute audience participation session is livelier than one might expect given the length of the meeting and fact that lunch time is approaching. On balance, the responses are supportive of John. The lobbying efforts of the coalition continue and later when the full legislature has assembled the membership of the Traffic Safety Coalition is gratified when the interim committee recommends that the legislature give top priority to the consideration of a mandatory seat belt law.

Comment

John McLaughlin's thirty minute presentation before the interim committee is, in many respects, the symbolic tip of the iceberg. He portrays the concern of the Coalition in a dynamic and effective fashion. A brief excerpt from his presentation is shown on many of the TV newscasts in the state. It serves as the capstone for the other efforts of Coalition members to get the legislature to reconsider their decision on the mandatory seat belt bill.

CASE STUDY 4
INDUCTIVE EXPLORATION OF POSSIBILITIES
Context

For three years a dedicated group of eleven married couples has labored to realize a dream, to bring a vision to reality. All live in single-family houses in the same residential urban community. All have children of college age or older, and all have experienced their fill of householding. Leaky roofs, plumbing problems, lawn care, attempts to garden, snow shoveling, and on ad infinitum have caused them to explore options other than the status quo.

Three years ago at one of their monthly get-togethers (they go from home to home for this regular late afternoon party for eleven months and omit December in deference to Christmas), the usual grumbling about pitfalls of house maintenance, energized by a member whose furnace has "rusted out," cause a woman who has been listening to quietly ask, "Why don't we do something about it?"

The vision begins to crystallize. Why don't we rent or buy condominiums? Our children are away from home or soon will be. But living in an apartment house is like being institutionalized. And you are at the mercy of the landlord. And you have no control, you live by rules given to you. If you do find a place you like, the location is unsatisfactory.

Let's build our own! We will first find an ideal location that we all like and lease or buy it. Then we'll build a special, high-quality arrangement of well-designed apartments with exercise facilities, workshops, pool, tennis courts, library, a deli, whatever we want. And a really fine dining room, serving dinner weekdays and brunch on Sunday. And it will be a nonprofit cooperative, so occupants cannot be victimized by a landlord and the entire operation can be run democratically.

By now the vision has "taken off into the wild blue yonder." But it has a common-sense core. Somehow, the dreams must be given substance. Facts must be confronted. The twenty-two people in the group are an unwieldy number, and most of them do not wish to spend substantial amounts of time on the project. The woman who started the discussion says, "Maybe we need a subcommittee."

This comment is a conversation-stopper. The gap between wishful speculation —daydreaming—and assembling and interpreting data is wide. There is quick agreement that four or five committed persons should agree to devote their spare time for a year or two developing possibilities. Surprisingly, three women and two men volunteer to constitute such a subcommittee. They obviously find the project an intriguing challenge. The subcommittee promises to organize itself, do what seems important to get underway on the "Co-op House" venture, and report back to next month's meeting of the group.

Early research by the subcommittee builds some guidelines. Available locations seem to be surrounded by high-rise buildings or opportunities for such to be built. The subcommittee rules out a high-rise structure or a location in a cluster of tall buildings. The fine dining room is a high priority, and operating one requires that the Co-op House be larger than originally intended. A minimum of 225 living units, comprising one-, two-, and three-bedroom apartments, is required to support a successful in-house dining facility. Because winters are severe in their climate, underground parking must be supplied to residents. This is expensive, estimated to cost $8,500 per parking space.

Understandably, architects who are consulted become very interested and helpful. They contradict each others' advice, but the one who seems to best understand the needs that motivate this project says that to avoid an institutional atmosphere the building should be no taller than six stories. Ideally, part should be two stories, part four stories, and the largest unit six. The building should "wander around," avoiding any appearance of being a large rectangular box. For insulation qualities, low maintenance, and soundproofing, the construction should be of masonry, that is, brick, steel, and concrete rather than wood.

The large group of eleven couples examines these guidelines with hearty approval and a vote of appreciation to the subcommittee for its excellent work. Spontaneously, the key issue arises, where should the Co-op House be built? One of the subcommittee members quotes a construction executive as saying that the competitive desirability of an apartment complex is determined by considering three factors: location, location, location. The group agrees that moving ahead on their project is totally dependent on acquiring real estate where all of them would like to live. The subcommittee is requested to concentrate on location, take whatever time is needed, and report back when it is ready to recommend a specific place.

After two and a half months of frustrating search, a subcommittee member hears a rumor that an old respected agency for the care and rehabilitation of handicapped persons will close. This institution occupies one of the choice pieces of real estate within the city limits. The property consists of ten and a half acres of oak forest, surrounded by private residences, on a park boulevard overlooking a lake. It is fifteen minutes from the airport and twenty minutes from downtown, and is served by several lines of public transportation.

The subcommittee decides that dynamic action is indicated and that informing the parent group of the possibility would be dangerous, for the news of this choice real estate becoming available would be sure to be "leaked." They interview the director of the agency who refers them to the foundation owning the land. They approach the foundation with their proposal, using the guidelines for their project to convince foundation representatives that the Co-op House would fit into the community and would be as desirable an occupant for the land as could be found. The foundation is happy to keep the conversations with the Co-op House people secret since it has no desire to be overwhelmed with aggressive would-be purchasers. Well-camouflaged but persistent lobbying culminates in a meeting of the foundation's Board of Directors. At the meeting, conditions on use of the land are signed by the subcommittee, a price is agreed on, an "earnest money" down payment is specified, and the foundation agrees not to sell to another buyer unless the transaction fails to be completed within a calendar year, or specified conditions are violated.

The subcommittee now has a *fait accompli* to report to the sponsoring group. The monthly gathering is scheduled as a picnic in the lakeside park across the boulevard from the rehabilitation agency. The sympathetic architect prepares a ground plan sketch of a possible structure and attends the meeting. The subcommittee tells the story of their search, negotiations with the foundation, and commitments made. They also answer questions from the others. The subcommittee suggests a thirty-minute break to walk the grounds, to talk with each other and with the architect. Afterwards, the group reconvenes, and the subcommittee poses the key question, "Shall we go ahead with this?" The group unanimously votes "Yes," and the way is clear to deal with an almost infinite number of details to be managed.

At this point the subcommittee says, "Until today we have made all the decisions. Now it is time for you to get into the act. Between now and our next meeting we will get the information on financing, collect information from other similar projects, get estimates from architects and builders, and whatever else we think will be useful. But now it is your turn to contribute ideas, suggestions, recommendations, and, yes, reservations. We will have an 'inductive exploration of possibilities' involving everybody. We now become a real co-op, with each of us having a voice in determining where we go from here." The group somewhat reluctantly concedes that it must accept more responsibility and agrees to be ready to explore possibilities next time.

Situation

The job to be done in the inductive exploration of possibilities presentation is twofold: (1) to make sure that all twenty-two members of the group are informed of pertinent facts and their significance, and (2) to use group resources to interpret data and decide on directions for future activity.

The subcommittee recognizes that the success of the attempts to involve all members of the group rests on the subcommittee supplying basic information and answering reasonable questions of fact. The subcommittee knows a lot about a number of things, but items of information are randomly distributed among subcommittee members. Imposing system on disorder can be accomplished by a capable leader, reasons the subcommittee. They therefore turn to member Judy Martin, who is more experienced than the others in leading group discussion and moderating panels, and ask her to take over. They tell Judy that it makes sense at this stage for a single person to plan how to prepare and lead the exploration of complicated circumstances. This avoids bickering over minor matters. Individual subcommittee members must "follow the leader," but since Judy is one of the more sensible and best informed of the subcommittee personnel, risk in giving her greater authority is minimal.

Judy suggests that to prepare for the presentation, dividing the problem area into four topics and making each of the subcommittee members responsible for one of them is an efficient way to be sure that no major matters are overlooked. The subcommittee agrees on four divisions that seem to cover urgent issues:

1. Land acquisition and use. Community and city relations, and building codes, inspections, water, sewage, garbage disposal, taxes, electricity, telephone, bus service, etc.
2. Structural basics. Preparation of one-, two-, and three-bedroom units, recommendations of two or three architects for building design, builder's details, and cost estimates. Major options from which a few will be selected.
3. Quality of life in Co-op House. Security, parking, pets, dining room, sauna, workshops, deli, beauty and barber shop, party room, putting green, shuffleboard courts, TV cable and satellite disc, etc.
4. Finance. Possible sources and rates of interest. Role of Housing and Urban Development Agency (HUD). Pros and cons of turning over the entire financing and building of the Co-op House to a nonprofit agency that has completed similar projects (example, the Lutheran Home Society).

Judy tentatively assigns one of the four topics to each of the subcommittee members. Two accept her assignment happily, and the other two aren't sure. They caucus briefly and report back that, if they trade topics, it will be more satisfactory. The rest of the subcommittee and Judy accept the switch. For the remainder of the subcommittee meeting time, the members help each other, sharing information to give each specialist the best possible command of her or his area.

Late in the subcommittee session, one of the members does a double take and exclaims, "We forgot a vital topic. What about advertising and marketing? We'll have a couple of hundred living units to fill!"

It is understandable that marketing would not be an immediate imperative when the characteristics of the structure are not yet decided. But all agree this is an excellent point. What will or will not sell affects items in all four assigned topics. Judy offers to collect information on advertising and marketing. She says that her role as manager was attractive but that she is really more comfortable as a contributor-moderator.

Each subcommittee member agrees to prepare either flip chart sheets or overhead transparencies for items of central importance that might be difficult to remember. The plan is for the subcommittee to play a major role in introducing and defining the problem and gradually withdraw during the explanation phase.

Sequence of Events at the Presentation

Judy opens the meeting by explaining that she will moderate, and that the purpose is to explore possibilities and consider future directions. She lists the five steps on the flip chart, and notes that Steps 1 and 2 will be dominated by subcommittee reports, though questions and comments are always welcome. In Step 3, the group begins to take over and have its say, and in Steps 4 and 5 the group is in charge, the subcommittee reverting to its group member status. Then Judy tears off the sheet with the five steps and tapes it on the wall with masking tape, so everyone can see where the discussion is at any time.

1. Introduction.

   Judy quickly summarizes the subcommittee's actions and explains the division into five topics. Each subcommittee member tells the topic to be reported on in one or two sentences.

2. Definition of the problem.

   Each of the five reporters has five minutes to present the essence of his or her topic. Here the overhead transparencies and flip charts are used. One of the subcommittee members has a home computer with the software to create professional graphs, pie charts, and tables, and these are used with the overhead projector. Each presenter invites questions and comments. In this step, Judy's role is primarily that of a presenting subcommittee member.

3. Explanation of the problem.

   Judy opens this phase with an open question, "What needs to be discussed?" Items of concern emerge, and opinions are expressed. Judy is careful to postpone final decisions. This phase is intended to increase understanding of the variables important to Co-op House development. People question the subcommittee reporters and add information. The subcommittee people function as both reporters and group members.

4. What directions can we identify in what we have done so far?

   Judy reads this question from the flip sheet on the wall and waits. There is thoughtful silence. Then someone says, "I think we are moving in the direction of too many gimmicky extras." This comment is followed by a discussion of specifics and then another comment, "I think we are getting committed to one architect too soon. I mean the one who would like to sprawl Co-op House all over the ten and one half acres." This is the beginning of a completely spontaneous discussion interpreting the implications of the work up to the present time.

5. From this point on, how should we proceed?

   When it seems that the point of diminishing returns has been reached in Step 4, Judy reads Step 5 from the wall flip sheet. The group disagrees on some issues but comes together on these directions.

   (a) Improve design by getting the two preferred architects to work together on a detailed building plan.

   (b) Secure complete information on Lutheran Home Society financing and how it might relate to the financing of Co-op House.

   (c) Give land acquisition and use top priority. All plans assume availability of this real estate.

   (d) Secure hard data on the advertising and marketing needed for Co-op House to be successful.

Comments

The agreement on four ways to proceed establishes priorities that lead to details of implementation. Following the pattern of "inductive exploration of possibilities" contributes order and system to the development of the Co-op House project. The members of the parent group are briefed on factual details and can explore options in a way that can lead to final solutions.

CASE STUDY 5
CEASE-AND-DESIST PATTERN

Context

Productive Leadership, Inc., is a private business that furnishes intensive experiential training to persons who would like to improve their abilities to work with others. It treats leadership and followership as reciprocal activities. A basic premise that sets Productive Leadership apart from other managerial training is: To become an effective leader you must be a competent follower.

Productive Leadership, Inc., evolved from a university classroom. Two professors in the communication department were challenged by the task of teaching students to pool their resources effectively, as is necessary in all group and organizational endeavors. Their courses in interpersonal communication and group dynamics seemed to produce the learning of concepts but few changes in behavior. They agreed to attempt experimenting with intensive experience-based laboratory sessions.

Their change from current practice was based on the conviction that present methods followed popular theories of reinforcement. An individual was rewarded when the approved behavior occurred. These "pats on the head" were pleasant to receive and caused modified behavior in the classroom. But when the situation changed, as, for example, when the person returned to an off-campus job, the newly learned patterns faded and old habits took over. The experimenting professors agreed that reinforcement was not sufficiently powerful and that a more potent psychological process was needed.

The theoretical base for developing new methods was twofold: (1) eliminate reinforcement and (2) learn by experiencing unpleasant consequences. The following techniques were used to achieve these objectives: (1) rule out all reinforcement, that is, no one in a work group is ever told of personal success, (2) create laboratory groups that can make progress only when members play both leadership and followership roles, (3) place persons with strangers in situations where they must decide what to do and how to do it, (4) never allow the staff to help with problems but ask it only to make indirect comments about what is going on, and (5) encourage individuals to evaluate their own contributions to the group by observing results.

Implementing these methods in a university classroom required some adjustment of conventional procedures. Permission was secured for an experimental experiential laboratory course, grading was "pass" or "fail" (to relieve participants of extraneous competition for grades), and the class was scheduled for a two-hour period, twice a week for a semester.

The new experience "caught on." After four years of development, the class title became "Productive Leadership and Followership." Optimum enrollment was found to be forty-eight students, and the group experiences were in three forms: small groups, intergroups, and large groups. Behavioral consequences were found to be significant, with 80 percent of the course graduates reporting increased effectiveness, greater comfort, and quite different personal behavior in their group work off-campus.

As a result of community demand, the course was offered to the public as a university extension course. This in turn led to the formation of a private company, Productive Leadership, Inc., headed by the two professors. Seminars were offered for a fee. People from religious organizations, education, government, a variety of business enterprises, and the military enrolled. After three years of public-subscribed seminars, it was decided that the optimum enrollment was a group of forty-eight strangers from a variety of occupations. They lived in a remote location (preferably a resort) for five days, working a schedule of small-group, intergroup, and large-group sessions throughout each day and into the evening.

The Situation

It is now five years later. Productive Leadership, Inc., has expanded and, in addition to the home office, has branches in nine urban localities. Each branch is headed by a director who has had at least two years of training at the base installation. The seminars have closely followed the original model, but the branch offices have encountered pressures either (1) to shorten the original training, or (2) to do the entire training in-house (usually for a corporation or a military unit), or (3) to do the training in a centrally located place for commuters, persons who come in the morning and leave in late afternoon. Other requests peculiar to particular places have been made, but the three listed above are common everywhere in the organization.

The two former professors who jointly manage Productive Leadership, Inc., decide that the time has come to deal with pressures, various opinions, and plans for the future of the business. After many phone calls to the branches, a date a month away is selected for a two-day meeting at the home office. Each branch is to be represented by its director and assistant director. All directors are informed that day one will be devoted to the state of the organization and possible options for change, and day two is to focus on hammering out plans for the future.

The two partners review the pressures that they have felt and have been reported to them. They consider shortening the training an undesirable change because long experience with this model has demonstrated that it takes four days for the typical trainee to become comfortable with unscripted interaction—the holistic processing of stressful situations—and another day to practice the newly acquired skills. They are confident that the directors will support them in opposing any shorter program. Running the seminar from nine to five for commuters reduces exercise time but, more important, makes it impossible for trainees to compare experiences. Much of the learning, they believe, takes place in informal interchanges after scheduled events.

The demand for in-house training is of major concern to the partners. Several directors have recommended in-house programs for approval. These are attractive because the organization buying the program furnishes the enrollees, training rooms, and audiovisual equipment, and is willing to pay a premium price. There is no expense for advertising and marketing, and the purchaser attends to details of processing registrants, booking facilities, and handling money.

The trouble with in-house Productive Leadership training is that the model doesn't work in that context. People in an in-house seminar know each other. They work together and have formed relationships that distort their behavior in the seminar. The consequences of what they do and say in the experiential sessions follow them home. Only strangers are free to be impulsive in stressful group work and are able to benefit from being truly experimental. The managing partners have tried in-house seminars on two occasions, with unsatisfactory results. They are convinced that effective Productive Leadership training requires most of the trainees to be unacquainted with one another.

The partners decide that the best outcome in the coming two-day conference is agreement that *no* in-house seminars will be scheduled by Productive Leadership, Inc. They plan a team presentation based on the cease-and-desist pattern of organization, scheduled when it seems most appropriate during the afternoon of day two. During day one and the forenoon of day two, the presenters will have ample opportunity to find out what has been done about in-house seminars in the various branches and how the directors feel about them. The presenters can also discuss in-houses informally with attending personnel. They will announce that a presentation on the afternoon of day two will oppose in-houses. They will ask the directors and assistant directors to give it some thought and be ready to contribute to the presentation.

Sequence of Events

The forenoon of day one is devoted to reports of activities at the branches by the directors. Each gives a ten-minute summary of the past year's activities. Some have prepared overhead transparencies, some use the flip chart to record key items, others have slides for projection, and several have videotapes showing highlights of the year as well as graphics. Discussion highlights key issues that the partners note on a separate flip chart.

The afternoon of day one is devoted to particular problems of the branches. The discussion leader's flip chart guarantees that no major difficulties are overlooked. Innovations and proposals for new directions are postponed to the forenoon of day two. At the request of the partners, discussion of in-houses is postponed to day two in the afternoon.

Discussion of new markets, advertising possibilities, opening new branches, and some possible new programs, particularly an advanced seminar for graduates of Productive Leadership, takes up the forenoon of day two and is allowed to run over for one hour of the afternoon. At 2:30 P.M. on day two, the discussion of innovations is terminated as agreed, although much remains to be said, and after a coffee break the group returns for the partners' team presentation.

The Cease-and-Desist Presentation

The partners choose to alternate presenting steps of the cease-and-desist pattern.

1. Introduction (first partner).
   Mention of two major accomplishments of Productive Leadership, Inc., in the past year. Appreciation and praise for directors and their staffs.
2. Quick enumeration of present procedures (second partner).
   An extremely brief summary of activities underway, including in-houses.

3. Selection of one procedure as least productive (first partner).
   In-house seminars are less satisfactory than other projects. A survey of past seminar responses shows substantial dissatisfaction registered by participants (flip chart summary comparing in-house and public-subscribed post-seminar reactions).
4. Reasons and evidence showing this option lacks potential (second partner).
   Model doesn't work in-house. Strangers are essential. In-house usually forces a nine to five schedule with commuters and omits out-of-schedule-events learning. While it is easy and at first profitable, less favorable responses will do damage. Staff finds in-house more difficult, less rewarding. (Second partner records these items on flip chart en route and invites others to add to the list.)
5. Advantages of diverting resources elsewhere (first partner).
   "Turning off" in-houses eliminates a major distraction. Stressing the basic model where it works best pays off, over time. Time and effort are available to develop innovations important to the future of Productive Leadership, Inc. (Mentions two or three exciting innovations from morning discussion.)
6. The cease-and-desist recommendation (second partner).
   "I recommend that we decide here and now, to stop offering the basic Productive Leadership seminar in-house."

Comments

This example of the cease-and-desist pattern illustrates a predominantly ritualistic but essential presentation. It was a ritual of confirmation. Most of the content had been talked about. The CEO team could have accomplished the cease-and-desist proposition by edict. The presentation was an orderly summation of the situation, evidence, and reasons for change, and the final recommendation put the action on record, unambiguously, in front of everybody. Everyone had the opportunity to dissent, and because no one did, the presumption is that the cease-and-desist resolution will be implemented.

This ritual has many obvious advantages over sending out an order from the front office, by memo.

CASE STUDY 6
CREATIVE PROGRAM DEVELOPMENT

Context

On the western, Gulf of Mexico side of Florida, in an area called "The Heart of the Suncoast," is a settlement we will call Egleton. It is in sharp contrast to communities to the south and to the north. It is much older than many other clusters of population.

In the late 1800s, a wave of immigrants came to this area with a commercial motivation: to plant groves of lemon trees to produce lemons used to prevent scurvy in sailors. Commercial fishing was centered here, and the combination of the market for lemons and excellent growing conditions for lemon trees made the project attractive.

The groves were planted, trees matured and produced their fruit, and for some years all went well. Then in 1894 and again in 1895 disaster struck. Strong freezes occurred in the area in both years, killing all the lemon trees and the hope of raising lemons successfully. But the land had been planted in a way that would prevent later crowding. City lots consisted of one acre for a home and ten acres for a "grove."

The residents stayed and turned to lumbering as their next venture. This industry flourished from 1900 to 1923. But there was no program of reforestation, and when the trees were gone, another venture had run its course.

Hunting and fishing enabled the residents to remain in this ideal climate and enjoy the relaxed style of living that characterized Egleton. Others were attracted by superior living conditions. A "low-key" rural village emerged, sustained by the businesses that supply goods and services in a small town and the main industry, fishing, which continues to thrive even today.

The major north-south highways bend inland and pass this quiet community several miles away. When the tourist boom reached this region and neighboring towns up and down the coast rushed into "development," less pressure was placed on Egleton because of its location off the main traffic routes. As "development" produced a profusion of tightly packed condominiums, motels, restaurants, and bars, and ultimately, high-rise apartment buildings, the contrast between Egleton and tourist centers became more striking. Residents of Egleton came home from visiting their commercially flourishing neighbors with new appreciation of their quiet, relaxed rural village environment.

Early measures to safeguard Egleton's lifestyle were uncoordinated and sporadic. The community's chief measure was to avoid publicity. About the only rule Egleton made official was the limitation of all structures to a maximum of three stories. This restriction was effective for a few years, for aggressive developers saw it as a barrier to rapid growth and quick profits. Egleton remained unincorporated by choice. Longtime residents, a substantial majority, informally blocked outsiders' attempts to purchase large tracts of land. Because there was no city government to deal with, would-be developers could only approach individual, small-scale resident owners.

But the power of profits and the attractiveness of the location sabotaged the residents' efforts to make time stand still. Compromises admitted new year-round owners and renters, and a few modest motels, apartments, and trailer parks welcomed persons wishing to escape the rigors of northern winters for days, weeks, or a few months. Perceptive tourists compared Egleton's simple, comfortable lifestyle to relatively hectic, commercialized, crowded resort living, and many found it preferable.

Egleton's resident population is now 20,000 and swells to 32,000 in the winter season. Although still unincorporated, a city government of sorts has emerged. Management is centered in the City Council, a twelve-person elected body. The Council collects and spends all funds required to operate Egleton. It provides a city budget, which is approved annually by referendum. All municipal services are under Council supervision. Informally, ideas and advice are supplied by the Chamber of Commerce, the Resort Owners Association, the League of Women Voters, church groups, and individual citizens with vested interests. The weekly newspaper, the

Egleton Herald, serves as a valuable communication link, facilitating the interaction of city agencies and the local citizenry.

The Situation

A crisis now forces the City Council to abandon its contingency policy, that of handling each emergency as it arises. Within a period of five months, three developers have sued the city of Egleton over policies that restrict their projects. Attorneys for the plantiffs and for the defense have revealed to the public the patchwork of Egleton's rules and regulations. The *Herald* observes in an editorial, somewhat reluctantly, that Egleton has "grown like Topsy." The developers contend that expecting them to conform to a random accumulation of often inconsistent policies is unreasonable.

In an emergency session, the City Council recognizes that the moment of truth, the time for comprehensive action that they have been postponing, has come. Egleton needs a constitution, but no constitutional committee can do the job. Somehow, all the varied interests in the city must be given the opportunity to contribute to a more systematic, consistent code for government.

Betty Whitecastle, the Council Chairperson, says, "Let's use the town meeting model." For the next hour the Council hammers out a plan. The following steps emerge:

1. Use the *Herald* to inform everyone that a new city charter is to be created.
2. Request all residents to send to Chairperson Whitecastle their ideas of essential items that *must* be in the charter.
3. One month after the *Herald* announcement, hold a public "Town Meeting" to discuss problems facing the city and identify as many options as possible.
4. After the Town Meeting, ask the Council to devise a method of utilizing community resources to integrate, prioritize, and, where indicated, implement the options.

The Presentation

During the month-long interval separating the announcement of the city charter campaign and the Town Meeting, the flow of letters to Betty Whitecastle, meager at first, increases to dozens each day. Council members "talk up" the campaign, and the Chamber of Commerce, the Resort Owners Association, and the League of Women Voters assume active roles. Two days before the Town Meeting, the Council meets to survey the mailed-in suggestions. These are grouped under issues or topics. A rank-order listing by frequency of mention is a rough measure of relative concern felt by the citizens who write in. Specific action recommendations are compiled in another list, with no attempt made to prioritize these items.

The Town Meeting is held in the community room of the modest municipal building at 7:00 P.M. on a Wednesday. Notice of the meeting is communicated by posters in most places of business and by a paragraph in the *Herald*'s Coming Events column a week before and on the day of the event. All interested citizens are invited to attend and participate. As is usually the case in such situations, the number attending is difficult to predict. The weather is pleasant, no major athletic contests are scheduled, and the Council is pleasantly surprised when, in addition to Council members, eighty persons appear. Most attendees are, in effect, delegates from the Chamber of Commerce, the Resort Owners Association, and the League of Women Voters. Perhaps a dozen individuals come for purely personal selfish or altruistic reasons. Evidently, the motivation to give an evening of private time to civic problems is not widely shared.

Betty opens the Town Meeting by giving her definition of the problem (Step 1 of the creative program development approach) before the house: "To preserve our Egleton way of life by creating a systematic and orderly city government." This, she admits, is a long-range objective, months or years away. All of the subproblems must be examined in relation to other subproblems, and it must always be remembered that the ultimate outcome is to be a comprehensive sensible program for Egleton's future. She asks the group for their opinion on the nature of the overall, basic problem, and there is general agreement on her wording.

To begin Step 2, "explore the problem area," Cliff Gooden, a Council member, reports the issues and topics developed from the pre-meeting responses. He projects this list on a corner screen with an overhead projector. He talks through the list briefly, answers questions, and receives comments. Leaving the projected list on the screen, he goes to a flip chart and asks, "What else must we worry about?" Group members supply seven topics that are different from any on the projected list, and these are written on the flip chart. The sheet is torn from the chart and taped to the wall near the screen.

Betty returns to the role of moderator, to lead Step 3, "identify possible directions." She says to the audience, "Look at the screen and the flip chart sheet. Very generally, how ought we to go about tackling one of these problem areas?" The problem with this stage is to avoid getting bogged down with specific solutions. When one person makes a definite recommendation, she tells her and the group, "Let's hold specifics until later. Now we're looking for directions, not actions." She moves briskly through the listed items, allowing perhaps five minutes to talk about directions.

The stage is set for Step 4, "apply brainstorming techniques." Eileen Cashman, the most experienced and dynamic group leader on the Council, takes over. She says, "Now we have problems and some directions, and we are ready to build as long a list of possibilities as we can. The more options we have to choose among, the better our decisions will be. So, we will brainstorm what we could possibly do to make progress on any of these problems."

Eileen explains the four brainstorming rules and says she will enforce them. Any idea, direction, or proposal related to any topic listed or talked about is welcome; no criticism is permitted; wild and far-out ideas are appropriate; and hitchhiking (modification) of contributed ideas is encouraged. Quantity is the goal.

Two Council members who write rapidly and legibly station themselves at two flip charts. They record alternate items. Eileen keeps the pace rapid, stops attempts at criticism, and makes sure all items contributed are recorded. As is usually the case with brainstorming, the audience finds the process exciting and exhilarating.

Eileen stops the brainstorm session at thirty minutes and returns the moderator role to Betty.

Betty explains that the first phase of creative program development is over and that consolidation, Step 5, comes next. The report of this Town Meeting, including the listing of problems, the directions suggested, and all the brainstormed topics, will be duplicated and sent to all who attended the Town Meeting. Also in the distributed report will be the action recommendations that come in by mail.

"Finally," Betty adds, "We must have an opportunity for afterthoughts. Who has one, or more?" There are a few. Betty says that these will also be included in the minutes of the meeting.

What now? Betty explains that the Council will now prepare action proposals to be considered at the next Town Meeting. She thanks the attendees for their help and adjourns the meeting.

Comments

An oversimplification that persistently arose during the Town Meeting was, "Do we want Egleton to be a place to live, or a place to make a living?" Obviously, both are important, so what might appear to be an either-or situation is really a weak alternation with two emphases coexisting. An advantage of the creative program development pattern is to expose such false dichotomies. Everyone at the meeting favoring one or the other of these choices came to appreciate the necessity of safeguarding the opportunity of both living well and making a good living.

Index